# TRIALS OF CHARACTER

# TRIALS OF CHARACTER

## THE ELOQUENCE OF CICERONIAN ETHOS

BY JAMES M. MAY · THE UNIVERSITY OF

NORTH CAROLINA PRESS *Chapel Hill and London*

©1988 The University of North Carolina Press
All rights reserved
Manufactured in the United States of America

The paper in this book meets the guidelines for permanence and durability of the Committee on Production Guidelines for Book Longevity of the Council on Library Resources

92 91 90 89 88   5 4 3 2 1

Library of Congress Cataloging-in-Publication Data
May, James M.
Trials of character.
Bibliography: p.
Includes index.
1. Cicero, Marcus Tullius. Orationes. 2. Cicero,
Marcus Tullius—Style. 3. Oratory, Ancient.
4. Characters and characteristics in literature.
5. Ethics in literature. I. Title.
PA6320.M39   1988     808.5′1     87-13884
ISBN 0-8078-1759-7 (alk. paper)

# CONTENTS

# PREFACE

Ethos, asserts George Kennedy, "is much richer in Roman than in Attic oratory and would repay more study than it has received."* This book is intended to meet the need for a closer examination of ethos ("character") as it was used by Roman orators, in particular by Cicero. I have drawn, with gratitude, upon the work of many distinguished predecessors who have touched on this topic; to the synthesis of their ideas I have added my own thoughts and observations about Cicero's manipulation of ethos in his orations.

The book begins with a discussion of the importance of ethos, not just in ancient rhetorical theory but also in the social, political, and judicial milieu of Republican Rome. There follows an analysis, in chronological order, of individual speeches from each of four periods of Cicero's life and career, tracing the changes in the way he depicts character, both his own and others', as a source of persuasion—changes intimately connected with the vicissitudes of his career and personal life. It is my hope that this detailed survey of Cicero's "trials of character" will reveal to students of rhetoric just how vital a role ethos played in the art of the Roman orator.

Not wishing to exclude from my audience those who are interested in ancient oratory but have not acquired the ability to read Cicero in his own tongue, I have quoted all passages in English. The translations are those found in the Cicero volumes of the Loeb Classical Library; I have altered their substance very seldom, but have taken the liberty of making minor changes of capitalization and punctuation in the interest of consistency of presentation. I have not supplied Latin for brief phrases mentioned in

*"The Rhetoric of Advocacy in Greece and Rome," *American Journal of Philology* 89 (1968):436.

passing, but Latin texts that bear directly upon the interpretation of Ciceronian speeches are supplied in the notes.

I owe debts of gratitude to many people and institutions: to the National Endowment for the Humanities for the generous support I received as the recipient of a Fellowship for College Teachers; to St. Olaf College for providing me a sabbatical leave that enabled me to complete this project and for offering a subvention grant to help with the costs of publication; to my colleagues at St. Olaf College, Anne H. Groton and Lloyd L. Gunderson, who spent hours reading the manuscript and making valuable suggestions; to Louis Janus for helping to edit the text on the computer; to the publishers who granted me permission to reproduce here brief passages that have appreared previously in *The Classical Journal* 74 (1979), *Maia*, September–December 1980, and *The American Journal of Philology* 102 (1981); to the distinguished readers for the University of North Carolina Press, W. R. Johnson and D. R. Shackleton Bailey, who offered many perceptive criticisms and mercifully rescued me from numerous potentially embarrassing errors; to the staff of the University of North Carolina Press and especially to Laura S. Oaks, Ron Maner, and Iris Tillman Hill, Editor-in-Chief, whose efficiency, kindness, and consideration have been nothing short of remarkable; and most of all, to George A. Kennedy, without whose guidance and assistance this book could not have been written. For his generosity, support, and words of encouragement, which have sustained me throughout my career, he can never be properly thanked or adequately repaid.

Finally, I would like to acknowledge my wife, Donna, for her selflessness, her unflagging devotion, and her willingness to support wholeheartedly every project I have chosen to undertake during our union of nearly twelve years. In many respects this book is as much hers as mine, and it is to her that I dedicate it, with love.

One of Martial's epigrams accurately describes the contents of most books:

> Sunt bona, sunt quaedam mediocria, sunt mala plura
>   quae legis hic: aliter non fit, Avite, liber.

If there are *bona* in this *liber*, much of the credit for them must go to the people mentioned above; for the *mediocria et mala* I alone, of course, assume responsibility.

St. Olaf College
1 May 1986

# I

# ETHOS AND CICERONIAN ORATORY

On the contrary, moral character, so to speak, constitutes the most effective source of persuasion. (Aristotle *Rhetoric* 1.2.1356a13)

Ethos (defined broadly as "character") is an abiding and essential element in the art of verbal persuasion. Indeed, every verbal undertaking aimed at producing conviction involves, implicitly or explicitly, the presentation of character, an advancement of a persona capable of influencing an audience to no small degree. Even in "pre-conceptualized" or "traditional" oratory, the ethos of the speaker is an important source of persuasion and plays its role accordingly.[1] Persuasive techniques based on such presentation of character are found in Greek literature as early as Homer[2] and figure prominently in subsequent oratorical and rhetorical writings.[3] Nonetheless, it appears that no scientific or analytical examination of ethos and its role in the oratorical art was undertaken until Aristotle produced his *Rhetoric* in the late fourth century B.C.

It was Plato, to be sure, who had laid the foundation upon which his student could construct a system of ethos. Plato had argued that the man who aspires to be a worthy orator must not only possess a good character, but also be informed and alert, able to adapt his argument to his audience, and eager to secure their goodwill.[4] The good speaker, moreover, must embrace the study of philosophy; since the function of a speech is to lead souls (*psychagōgia*), the true rhetor, according to Plato, must examine the nature of the soul and come to know its various forms and characters.[5]

This philosophical and psychological outline of a "true rhetoric" was given detail, color, and depth by Aristotle, who refused to relegate the "psychological" or "psychagogical" elements of persuasion to particular parts of the speech as his predecessors had done.[6] Instead he constructed a rhetorical system based on three *pisteis*, sources of rhetorical demonstration and persuasion. The first, *ēthos*, depends "upon the moral character of the speaker"; the second, *pathos*, "upon putting the hearer into a certain frame of mind"; and the third, *logos*, "upon the speech itself."[7] These sources of persuasion, which Aristotle calls "entechnic" or "artistic" (*Rhet.* 1.2.1355b35) because the speaker himself invents them, are derived from the three components of the speech act: the speaker, the audience, and the speech.[8] Ethos is founded on the moral character of the speaker as presented in the speech; pathos is produced when the orator places his listeners in a particular state of mind and makes them feel emotion; logos, or *pragma*, the logical explanation or rational presentation of the case, is directed toward the intellect of the auditor.[9] As source material for rhetorical demonstration that will induce belief in an audience, all three *pisteis* are essential elements throughout the speech. Thus Aristotle grants ethos a status equal with that of pathos and logos.

A close reading of the *Rhetoric* reveals three kinds of ethos.[10] The first and most important is the moral character of the speaker, the *ēthos tou legontos*, which persuades when his speech is delivered in a manner rendering him worthy of belief (*Rhet.* 1.2.1356a4–13). In Aristotle's view this confidence in the speaker should be established in and by the speech itself and not through any previous notion the audience may have of the speaker; otherwise this type of ethos could not be considered "entechnic." To win trust, confidence, and conviction, the speaker must exhibit *phronēsis* (intelligence, good sense), *aretē* (virtue), and *eunoia* (goodwill). Lacking one or more of these qualities will cause him to err or prove ineffectual (2.1.1377b20–24, 1378a6–15). The orator demonstrates his *phronēsis*, *aretē*, and *eunoia* in the way he exercises his moral choice, or *proairesis* (1.8.1366a8–16; cf. 2.21.1395b13–17; *Poet.* 6. 1450b8–10). Since the invention, arrangement, style, and delivery of his speech all reflect his *proairesis*,[11] it is important for the speaker to choose a design that will help to establish his ethos as sensible, virtuous, and trustworthy. Only then will he be able to realize the potential of his ethos to be "the most effective source of persuasion" (*Rhet.* 1.2.1356a13).

The second type of ethos that Aristotle treats is the character of the audience to which the orator must suit his speech. As it is essential to impress the audience favorably with his own character, so it is important for him to adapt his tone, sentiments, and language to the tastes of his hearers. To do this well, he must have a thorough knowledge of various governments, periods of life, and degrees of society (1.8.1365b21–28, 2.12.1388b31–1389a2).

The third type of ethos outlined by Aristotle can be called dramatic; being closely related to style, it is discussed only in Book 3 of the *Rhetoric* (7.1408a25–36, 16.1417a16–36). This kind of ethos is character-drawing, or *ethopoeia*, most likely modeled on the techniques of the poets. Under the Athenian judicial system, which customarily expected a litigant to plead his own case, it was essential for the logographer to portray the character of the speaker with accuracy, consistency, and credibility. In the speech's narrative sections, too, it was often the task of the speaker or speechwriter to portray the ethos of a third party (cf., e.g., 3.16.1417a16– 36). The focus on the individual distinguishes this type of ethos from the second type, which characterizes whole classes.

This creative, philosophical, and, by most accounts, extraordinary system of ethos, and of rhetoric in general, stands as a tribute to Aristotle's genius. For all of its brilliance and originality,[12] however, the Aristotelian system of *pisteis* appears to have lain neglected, or to have remained largely unknown to subsequent technicians whose rhetorical systems were generally based on the *partes orationis* or a conflation of that method with the Peripatetic five-part system of *inventio, dispositio, elocutio, actio,* and *memoria*.[13] As Aristotle's tripartite theory of *pisteis* lost currency, ethos (along with pathos) as an efficacious tool of persuasion was either omitted from the discussion or, at best, relegated to a less prominent position. Thus, in the two early works of Roman rhetoric that sprang from Hellenistic sources, the *Rhetorica ad Herennium* and Cicero's *De Inventione*, the role of ethos was subsumed under the *partes orationis*.[14] It was not until Cicero's mature works, and specifically the *De Oratore*, that ethos (and pathos with it) would be restored on a par with logos.[15]

Cicero himself asserts that he has written *De Oratore* "in Aristotelian fashion."[16] An important passage in which Antonius, as interlocutor, outlines the chief tasks of the orator (*De Or.* 2.115) demonstrates that the treatise resembles the *ratio Aristotelia* in more ways than in Cicero's repeated demand for a "philosophical" orator:

Thus for purposes of persuasion the art of speaking relies wholly upon three things: the proof of our allegations (*ut probemus . . . quae defendimus*), the winning of our hearers' favor (*ut conciliemus . . . qui audiunt*), and the rousing of their feelings to whatever impulse our case may require (*ut animos . . . ad quemcumque causa postulabit motum, vocemus*).

Here one finds, recast in Latin terminology, the triadic foundation of *pisteis* upon which Aristotle based his work on oratory: *ēthos* = "the winning of our hearer's favor"; *pathos* = "the rousing of their feelings"; and *logos* = "the proof of our allegations." The three tasks required of the orator, *probare/docere, conciliare/delectare*, and *movere*, are mentioned repeatedly by Cicero (e.g., *De Or.* 2.128, 310, 3.104; *Orat.* 69; *Brut.* 185, 276; *Opt. Gen.* 3) and might almost be regarded as the informing principle of his rhetorical system.

Cicero's approach further resembles Aristotle's in that the elements of ethos (as well as pathos), i.e., the *affectus*, are not subsumed under the *partes orationis*, but dealt with separately and given special emphasis.[17] Cicero's concurrence with Aristotle in this matter demonstrates his belief in a rhetoric based broadly on the three major sources of demonstration and persuasion (logos, ethos, and pathos) and on his conviction that such foundations of proof cannot rightly be subordinated to any one structural element of the speech but must permeate the whole, as blood does the body.[18]

Despite these and other important general similarities, Cicero's analysis of ethos is not, in its details, particularly Aristotelian. At *De Oratore* 2.182–184, for example, Cicero has Antonius speak about the position of character as a source of proof equal to logos and pathos:

A potent factor in success, then, is for the characters, principles, deeds, and course of life, both of those who are to plead cases and of their clients, to be approved, and conversely those of their opponents condemned; and for the feelings of the judges to be won over, as far as possible, to goodwill towards the advocate and the advocate's client as well. Now feelings are won over by a man's dignity, achievements, and reputation, qualifications easier to embellish, if only they are real, than to fabricate where nonexistent. But attributes useful in an advocate are a mild tone, a countenance expressive of modesty, gentle language, and the faculty of seeming to be dealing reluctantly and under compulsion with something you are really anxious to prove. It is very useful to display the tokens of good nature, kindness, calmness, loyalty, and a disposition that is pleasing and not grasping or covetous; and all the qualities belonging to men who are upright, unassuming, and not given to haste, stubbornness, strife, or harshness are powerful in winning goodwill, while the want of them estranges it [goodwill] from such as do not possess them; accordingly the very opposites of these qualities must be ascribed to our opponents.[19]

It is worthy of note that both here and in other Latin rhetorical treatises we find no single Latin word directly corresponding to the Aristotelian source of persuasion, *ēthos*. In fact Quintilian, who uses the Greek word itself in his discussion, tells his readers that it has no Latin equivalent (6.2.8). Both he and Cicero before him (cf. *Orator* 128) connect the word with Latin *mores* and *natura*,[20] but Quintilian is quick to point out, perhaps referring to Cicero's *modus operandi*, that "more cautious writers have preferred to render the sense of the word rather than to translate it into Latin" (6.2.9). In his rhetorical works Cicero most commonly uses the words *conciliare* and *delectare*, as noted above, in connection with his discussion of the "three duties (*officia*) of the orator" to convey the concept of rhetorical ethos, its role in the speech, and the orator's duty to employ it. In choosing this terminology, however, the *egestas linguae Latinae* was no less a problem for Cicero than it was for his contemporary Lucretius (*De Rerum Natura* 1.136–139). By using the word *conciliare*, Cicero has changed the focus from representation, i.e., a description of the speaker's character and attitude, to an action of the speaker: "The Ciceronian emphasis on the act of *conciliare*, of winning benevolence, has converted the unstressed motive of Aristotle's proof into its actual method."[21] Furthermore, the conception of ethos presented here in the *De Oratore* and elsewhere in Cicero's *rhetorica* is broader and more inclusive than Aristotle's; it is an ethos concerned primarily with judicial, not deliberative oratory; it is an ethos that deals with the emotions (*affectus*), closely related to pathos but involving the milder feelings (cf. *De Or.* 2.183–185, 212; *Orat.* 128; Quintilian 6.2.9); it is an ethos attentive to and more intricately associated with style.[22]

Perhaps because of the strain exerted on the word *conciliare* by the above applications, in his later works Cicero appears to prefer to render the idea of *ēthos* with the word *delectare* or other periphrases like *fidem facere, animos a severitate traducere, animos devincere voluptate*.[23] Whatever terminology is used, however, it is clear that Cicero did in fact connect his second *officium* with Aristotle's *pistis* ethos.[24] But the rhetorical ethos that we see Cicero describing here and elsewhere and employing throughout his orations is an ethos, as we might expect, radically influenced and conditioned by the idiosyncrasies of the sociopolitical environment of Republican Rome as well as by the demands of the Roman judicial system.

Character was an extraordinarily important element in the social and political milieu of Republican Rome[25] and exerted a considerable amount of influence on native Roman oratory. The Romans believed that character remains essentially constant in man and therefore demands or determines his actions. Since character does not evolve or develop, but rather is bestowed or inherited by nature,[26] an individual cannot suddenly, or at will, change or disguise for any lengthy period his ethos or his way of life; nor is it wise to attempt such alteration.[27] The Romans further believed that in most cases character remains constant from generation to generation of the same family. According to Cato the Elder, for example, wicked actions and even bad fortune are alien to those who are "good men, born of good stock, cognizant of the good" (*ORF* no. 8, frag. 58).[28] He therefore in his speech *De Sumptu Suo* found it natural to defend himself not only by the narration of his own actions but also by the recitation of his ancestors' deeds: "The benefactions of my ancestors were read out; then the things which I had done on behalf of the Republic were read" (*ORF* 8.173). The charges made against him must be false, Cato implies, because they are inconsistent with the criterion of both his individual ethos and the collective character of his *gens*.[29] From this, it is easy to understand how the number of waxen images that decorated the atrium of a Roman's house and determined his degree of nobility could also measure, to some extent, the value of his character and the moral worth of his family. The greater the number of images, the more likely was he, in Roman eyes, to perpetuate the character traits of those whom the images commemorated.

Just as the Romans' veneration of the *mos maiorum* and of their ancestors nourished their belief in the constancy of ethos, so did their respect, indeed, reverence for authority. This attitude, so characteristic of the Romans, was rooted in their admiration of a person who exhibited wisdom gained through practical experience, expert knowledge, and a sense of responsibility in both private and public life.[30] The Greeks too, of course, felt the power of authority, whether it was wielded by the gods, by ancestors, or by men of accomplishment such as Pericles.[31] But it is highly doubtful that the typical Athenian at the height of the radical democracy, who might himself have been called upon by lot to serve the state as prytanis,[32] could have been constrained by respect for authority in the same way or to the same degree as a Roman, whose life from early childhood was shaped by the customary practice of deferring to the judgment of a higher *auctor*, be it his *pater familias*, his patron, a magistrate, or the Senate.[33]

To acquire *auctoritas*, as well as *gratia*, *gloria*, *existimatio*, and *dignitas*,[34] a Roman had to prove, by means of his own actions or his ancestors', that his ethos deserved to be respected. Under such circumstances the attainment of political office was vital; no Roman could hope to be admitted to the ranks of the nobility without the prestige of being a descendant of a consul, or of serving as consul himself. The *novus homo* had slim chance, therefore, of breaking into the privileged circle of the *nobiles*.[35] No matter how much *ratio* might argue for his acceptance, lack of *auctoritas* could be an insurmountable barrier. Conversely, a Roman who possessed great *auctoritas* could achieve more than *ratio* might deem possible. Aemilius Paullus, Scipio Africanus, and Fabius Maximus, for example, are praised by Cicero in his *De Senectute* (61) as Romans "whose authority resided not merely in their opinion but even in their nod." In another context, speaking about the Roman jurisconsults in contrast to their Greek counterparts, Cicero describes the power of their *auctoritas*: "After winning dignity on the strength of their talent, [they] brought it about that, in advising on law, their strength lay less in their unaided talent than in their authority" (*De Or.* 1.198). Perhaps the most poignant and certainly the most poetic statement of the power of a man in possession of *auctoritas* is given us by Virgil in his famous simile:

> As when in some great crowd sedition flares up
> And the ignoble mob rages in spirit;
> Now firebrands and stones fly, fury ministers to arms;
> Then, if by chance they catch sight of some man,
> Influential in piety and deeds, the people stop,
> Struck with silence
> And stand at attention with ears erect;
> And that man rules their high spirits with words
> And calms their hearts.
>
> (*Aen.* 1.148–153)

The dramatic effect of Virgil's imaginary speaker on the crowd suggests that in the hands of real Roman orators *auctoritas* could be a powerful, sometimes frightening, occasionally even subversive oratorical weapon. Ancient testimony confirms that Virgil's poetic picture is true to life. Cicero, for example, tells a story (*Brut.* 56) very reminiscent of this simile: Marcus Popilius, consul and flamen Carmentalis, was able, "both by the authority of his presence and by his words," to quell a riot between the plebeians and patricians. A similar account is given of Marcus Octavius, whose authority and speaking ability caused the people's assembly to abrogate Gracchus' grain law (*Brut.* 222).[36] The *auctoritas* of Marcus Scaurus was legendary: "In the oratory of Scaurus, a wise and upright man, there was great gravity and a certain innate authority, so that when he spoke for a client you had the feeling of one giving testimony, not of one pleading a case" (*Brut.* 111).[37] Quintilian relates (5.12.10) that this same Scaurus, when called to trial on a charge of treason, defended himself by merely denying the charge. Perhaps most shocking of all is the use of *auctoritas* by Scipio Africanus when charged by the tribune M. Naevius with having accepted money from King Antiochus of Asia:

> "I recall, Citizens," he said, "that today is the anniversary of the day on which I, in a great battle in the land of Africa, defeated Hannibal the Carthaginian, the greatest enemy of our empire, and obtained for you peace and a magnificent victory. Let us not, therefore, seem ungrateful toward the gods, but rather let us abandon this fellow on the spot and make way to the Temple of Jupiter Optimus Maximus in order to give thanks." (Aul. Gell. *NA* 4.18.3–5)[38]

The entire assembly that had convened to pass judgment upon Scipio at that point left the tribune standing alone, case in hand, and proceeded to accompany Scipio, "with joy and gratitude," to the Capitol.

Although the Romans recognized the subversive effect that *auctoritas* combined with oratorical ability could have on justice, they seemed in most instances to accept it as a condition of their society. A story told by Cicero (*Pro Mur.* 58), however, shows what might happen in an extreme case: L. Aurelius Cotta, accused by Scipio Africanus Minor, was acquitted by a jury that refused to allow anyone to be assailed by a prosecutor endowed with such eloquence, integrity, and *auctoritas*. Ironically, this rejection of *auctoritas* accounted for, rather than prevented, a miscarriage of justice: Cotta, who was undoubtedly guilty of the charge, won an undeserved reprieve. Perhaps there is some validity in Cicero's assertion that the Roman people, who in deference to *auctoritas* had readily ignored the charge laid against the elder Scipio, were hesitant to arm the younger Scipio, in the role of prosecutor, with the same weapon.[39]

The importance of character in Roman society was responsible in large part for the unusual emphasis upon character portrayal in Roman oratory.[40] Because of the effectiveness of character as a source of proof, Roman orators, from early on, tended to list the facts of the case as reflections of the litigants' characters rather than as a basis for logical argument. Thus biographical description, an "ethical narrative" of sorts, often functioned as the speech's proof—whose efficacy, in turn, relied on the impact that this characterization made upon Roman presuppositions. "This basically unargumented means of proof from character is fundamental to Latin oratorical tradition."[41] Cato, as we have seen, relied on the persuasiveness of his own ethos in his speech *De Sumptu Suo* (*ORF* 8.173). Similar tactics are evident in his defense of his consulship (8.21, 22, 28, 35, 40, 51–54) and his attack on M. Caelius (8.111, 115). C. Gracchus, speaking upon his return from Sardinia (*ORF* 48.23–28), defended his actions with an argument based on his ethos, and Scipio Africanus the Younger attacked the character of his adversaries (*ORF* 21.17, 30). The numerous instances of character-based proof in the orations of Cicero are considered in subsequent chapters of this book.

The ethos defined by Aristotle as an entechnic source of proof demands explication only within the context of the speech; it is neither the speaker's authority nor his previous reputation, but the impression he makes during his speech, that inspires trust in his listeners. Such restrictions upon ethos would have been incomprehensible to a Roman steeped in the tradition of the *mos maiorum*, surrounded by a nobility of rank, and influenced by the culture's general assumptions concerning human nature and character. The Roman view is succinctly, if somewhat obliquely expressed by Cicero in *De Oratore*: "Feelings are won over by a man's dignity (*dignitas*), achievements (*res gestae*), and reputation (*existimatio*)" (2.182). Aristotle's conception of an ethos portrayed only through the medium of a speech was, for the Roman orator, neither acceptable nor adequate.[42]

Sociopolitical circumstances in Rome were not the only influences on the Roman and Ciceronian conception of ethos: it was affected also by the judicial system of the Roman Republic. In an Athenian court of law it was common practice for each litigant (plaintiff or defendant) to speak on his own behalf. Often the litigant resorted to hiring a professional speechwriter, a logographer, whose challenges included composing a speech that would prove not only persuasive in its argument but also appropriate and consistent with the litigant's character. In a Roman law court, on the other hand, advocacy was the custom.[43] A litigant could, and on occasion did, represent himself in court, but a more common practice was to enlist one or several *patroni* to plead the case.[44] Cicero acknowledges the rhetoric of advocacy in his account of conciliation in *De Oratore*:

> A potent factor in success, then, is for the characters, principles, deeds and course of life, both of those who are to plead cases and of their clients, to be approved, and conversely those of their opponents condemned; and for the feelings of the judges to be won over, as far as possible, to goodwill towards the advocate and the advocate's client as well. (2. 182)[45]

Although this passage does not examine in detail the artistic implications and methods for practical application of ethos, the extension of the sphere of ethos is nonetheless striking. The character of the litigant has become but a part of the realm of ethos, which now embraces the characters of the *patronus*, the client, the adversary, his *patronus*, and the judges as well. Actors and opportunities for artistic variation have multiplied.

Conditioned by both the sociopolitical and the judicial climate in Rome, ethos in Roman oratory can only be expected to have taken on a greater significance, played a larger role, and admitted more artistic applications than its counterpart in Greek oratory.[46] We have already taken notice of the power, based on Roman notions of character and respect for *auctoritas*, that a man in possession of *nobilitas* and a sterling *existimatio* could wield in terms of influence and persuasion. By Cicero's day, the speaker's ethos had become an important source of proof in the courtroom; it is common, for example, to find him successfully attempting to "convince the audience that something should be believed because he says so."[47]

The rhetoric of advocacy added an entirely new artistic dimension to ethos. Skillful character portrayal of all the protagonists and antagonists of the case was now crucial. Armed with his *auctoritas*, the orator could identify himself with his client to lend weight to his arguments or, on another occasion, could separate himself from the litigant and speak his own mind, granting a license tó his words that under different circumstances could not be uttered.[48] Add to these observations the point that ethos was considered by the Romans to consist of the same stuff and substance as that most persuasive of rhetorical tools, pathos—only in a milder form (the *leniores affectus*)[49]—and it is easy to understand why ethos was so essential to Roman and Ciceronian oratory, often providing the chief source of proof in the speech.

These same circumstances, which created such an important role for ethos in Roman oratory, could at times present serious problems for the orator. The man whose character was sullied, whose dignity had been diminished, who possessed no influence, who exerted little authority, whose reputation was held of no account, was placed in grave jeopardy when pitted against an orator endowed with authority, "influential in piety and deeds." In his early pre-consular speeches, the young Cicero repeatedly faced the obstacle of *auctoritas*, which at times posed as great a rhetorical challenge as that of devising a convincing presentation of the facts of the case.

The rhetoric of advocacy, despite its artistic advantages, brought with it a comparable liability. Gone, for the most part, was the opportunity for that simple, charming, but lively and persuasive first-person narrative that had proved so effective in Lysias' speeches. The vividness and directness of a speech delivered in first person gave way, under the compulsion of the rhetoric of advocacy, to the indirectness and inherent suspicion of a story related secondhand. No longer could the orator make a strong claim to the veracity of his account, for in most cases he had not been present at the events. Calculated narrative thus replaced spontaneous, immediate experience.[50]

The study of ethos in Ciceronian oratory is necessarily an account of the artistic ways and means by which Cicero grappled with the rhetorical challenges placed upon him by each case and by the idiosyncrasies of the Roman social, political, and judicial systems. Oratory, more than any other literary genre of antiquity, deals with constantly changing circumstances and events. Its art and originality lie largely in the responses it makes to these ever-changing circumstances, to each rhetorical challenge it meets.[51] In the fifty-odd speeches of Cicero that have come down to us, whose dates span nearly forty years of Roman history, the single factor that remains ever constant is the ethos of Cicero; all else is altered with each new case. The story of Cicero's oratorical and public career is, at the risk of oversimplification, a chronicle of his struggle to establish, maintain, reestablish, and wield that very important oratorical and political weapon, an ethos in possession of *dignitas, existimatio,* and *auctoritas.* In the chapters that follow, I trace the course of Cicero's struggle as reflected in speeches from four periods of his life and investigate his artistic manipulation of ethos in response to the demands of the rhetoric of advocacy. I hope thus to demonstrate that for Cicero, as well as for his Roman predecessors, ethos was indeed "a most effective source of persuasion."

# II

# THE PRE-CONSULAR SPEECHES

*The Search for a Persona and the*

*Struggle for* Auctoritas

---

But I have not the same privileges as men of noble birth, who while sleeping still see the honors of the Roman people laid at their feet; in this state I must live under far different conditions and according to a very different law. (*In Verrem* 2.5.180)

Cicero, a young, talented, and ambitious *novus homo* from Arpinum, struggled to gain importance in the Roman state under a set of laws and conditions certainly different from those under which the majority of his rivals operated.[1] With no ancestral deeds to commend his character or waxen images to decorate his halls, the *virtus* and *industria* of the fledgling orator were made to bear the responsibility for establishing a reputation in the eyes of the Roman people that would merit election to offices. This attainment of rank, bolstered by his oratorical skills, could in turn impart a substantial measure of *auctoritas* and *gratia* to his character. Cicero's first speeches display a persona quite unlike the boasting consular ethos of later orations. Here is an ethos struggling against the weight of influence and authority, a challenge that Cicero's later opponents must have faced. Confident enough in his talent and training, Cicero seems at times to have made it his primary concern and chief rhetorical aim to disarm his adversary's authoritative character and deflect the inherent *invidia* that the *nobiles* felt toward an ambitious parvenu commended only by his own deeds. The thin, rhetorical veneer with which Cicero sometimes attempts to mask his feelings is easily stripped away, or at least rubbed to a transparency that exposes to us a revealing and sometimes poignant picture of a man who never ceased to fret over his own ethos and the *dignitas* and *auctoritas* it possessed and projected.[2]

Nevertheless his *tirocinium fori* ("apprenticeship in the Forum," i.e., the lawcourts) and his familiarity with Roman tradition and the exigencies of the Roman social and judicial system provided the young Cicero with a knowledge of the potentialities of rhetorical ethos far beyond those found in his Hellenistic textbooks. The Roman penchant for character-based proof and judgment offered ample room for persuasion supplied from character, and the rhetoric of advocacy, even in his earliest speeches, betrays an uncanny sophistication in its method. The pre-consular speeches show a Cicero who, if not at the height of his powers, nonetheless displays an acute knowledge of the rules of rhetoric and enough common sense, originality, and genius to transcend them when necessary. These speeches are a chronicle of Cicero's struggle with the Roman conception of character and its place in a speech aimed at persuasion. They show us the efforts of an orator, lacking an ethos of *auctoritas* and *gratia*, to mold a persona as persuasive as possible.

## PRO P. QUINCTIO

The first sentence of Cicero's earliest extant oration, the *Pro Quinctio*, establishes a major, if not the primary, theme of the speech. By its very prominence it underscores the importance that Cicero and the Romans laid upon the power of individual character and influence in a court case: "Two things which have most power in the state—namely great influence and eloquence—are both working against us today."[3] The unsuspecting reader, perhaps surprised with this gambit in a relatively complicated case involving a dispute over property possession,[4] will soon realize that Cicero's line of defense revolves chiefly around effective character portrayal of protagonist and antagonist in the hope of reducing the issue of the case to a simple conflict between two antipathetic ways of life. The one *modus vivendi*, supported by overwhelming eloquence and influence and marked by avarice, audacity, and wickedness, has unjustly assailed the other, characterized by modesty, helplessness, and a rustic and simple frugality and supported only—but most importantly—by the truth (cf., e.g., 79, 84, 92).[5]

Character sketches of the dramatis personae, which will continue to be developed throughout the speech, are drawn briefly in the opening sections of the *exordium* (1–10): Naevius, the powerful and unscrupulous adversary; his patron, the eloquent and established orator Hortensius; Quinctius, the poor, abandoned, almost desperate defendant; and Cicero, his patron, whose talent and experience pale in the sight of his adversary (2).

The conventions of the rhetoric of advocacy are, of course, in operation. Cicero as *patronus* fears not only the influence of Naevius and his friends, but especially the power and eloquence of his advocate, Hortensius (1–2, 8). Magnifying his predicament is the fact that he has been called upon to substitute for Marcus Junius, who, having begun the preparation of the defense, was called away by duties of state. As a result Cicero has had little time to make ready his case (3–4), and his *diligentia*, which in previous cases has compensated for his lack of *ingenium*, has not even been granted full rein. Finally, because of the influence and power of Naevius' friends, the court procedure has been unjustly changed, forcing the accused to plead his case before the speech of the accuser has been heard (9). In the face of such obstacles the defense must rest on the simple truth and on faith in the justice and disinterestedness of the judge, C. Aquilius—whom Cicero ingratiatingly imbues with an ethos full of firmness, integrity, and impartiality (4–5, 10). Thus by the end of the *exordium* Cicero has introduced the characters of the litigants, their advocates, and his audience, specifically the chief assessor, Aquilius.

These sketches are given color and dimension in the succeeding narration, which deals first with character (primarily Naevius') in order that the assessors might judge Cicero's presentation of the facts in light of their own expectations and preconceptions, which have been grounded, in true Roman fashion, upon their first impressions of the litigants of the case.[6] Cicero endeavors to portray characters whose actions, which he will subsequently outline, are consistent with, indeed determined by, their ethos. Thus this Naevius, an "excellent man" (ironic, of course), has never been thought to lack talent: he has always proved a witty buffoon (*facetus scurra*) and a humane auctioneer (*inhumanus praeco*) (11), and his move from the Licinian auction halls across the Alps did little to change that character (12)![7] The description of Naevius as a *praeco* (and a *scurra*) will become one of the resonant themes of the speech (cf. 55, 62), calculated to arouse, at least psychologically, a negative reaction in the hearts of the judges with each occurrence.[8] Antithetical portraits of Quinctius and Naevius thus emerge, highlighted not only by Cicero's direct descriptions (e.g., "this veteran gladiator," 29; "a most violent fellow, who had taken possession of the property, had driven Quinctius out, and robbed him of it," 30) but also by more subtle stratagems like the inclusion of a "conversation" between the adversaries (19). The use of such a dialogue, to which Cicero will have recourse again, enables the third-person narrator, the *patronus*, to capture some of the vividness of first-person pleading lost to the conventions of the rhetoric of advocacy; it also enables the audience, by showing the choices made by the speakers (*proairesis*), to form its own impression of them. In this passage a polite and proper Quinctius is made to reply to the rude and arrogant Naevius.

These efforts at characterization, more than mere artistic conventions of protraiture, are calculated to provide a basis, or premise, upon which to build a defense that equity is with Quinctius and his cause. Given the Roman belief in the importance and near immutability of character, Cicero aims at creating a scenario in which, notwithstanding the facts of the incident, Quinctius, a poor, nearly destitute, but innocent and upright victim, is assailed by the scurrilous, conniving, rapacious *praeco* Naevius and his powerful supporters. Once having accepted this interpretation of character, it becomes difficult to see the facts in any other light but that in which Cicero has cast them. Thus proof, finding its source in character, has been inserted in the statement of the facts, and Cicero in practice anticipates by three decades his prescription, given in *De Oratore* (2.310), of suffusing ethos throughout the speech like blood in a body.

In the formal *probatio* (37–85) Cicero tries to neutralize the difficulties of his defense: Quinctius appeared to have deserted a *vadimonium*, and after his property had been possessed *ex edicto* for thirty days, he was said to have been branded *infamis*.[9] Arguments denying that any debt was owed to Naevius, that Naevius had any grounds for application to the praetor, or that Quinctius did in fact desert the *vadimonium* (37–59)[10] are drawn largely from probable assumptions that Cicero bases upon previous and continuing character portrayals of Quinctius and Naevius. His address to Naevius, which does much to corroborate his portraits of the adversaries, displays his method:

> At that time I suppose you did not want to be troublesome to the man whom now you do not allow to breathe freely; at that time you were too modest to call upon the man whom now you criminally wish to murder. I suppose so: you were unwilling or afraid to call upon a man who was your relative, who had a great respect for you, a good man, modest, and older than yourself. More than once (as often happens) after you had bolstered your courage and determined to mention the

money, when you approached him, having carefully prepared and meditated on what you might say, suddenly you, the timid man of virgin modesty, drew back; suddenly words failed you; when you desired to call upon him for the money, you did not dare to do so, fearing that he might feel hurt to hear you. No doubt this was the explanation. (39)[11]

This bitterly sarcastic picture of Naevius, "a timid man of virgin modesty," holding his tongue in deference to his elder, upright, modest kinsman, Quinctius (an action, Cicero implies, that would have been appropriate in such circumstances), must have raised the hackles of Aquilius and the fellows of his *consilium*. Naevius, at least according to Cicero's picture, was incapable of displaying modesty, exhibiting restraint, or disregarding money. His character was inconsistent with such traits, and character is the premise upon which actions are based. Ethos dictates deeds: "The only alternative is that extraordinary negligence or unparalleled generosity stopped you [Naevius] from demanding the money. If you plead negligence, we shall be astonished; if you plead kindness, we shall laugh" (41).[12]

Characterization through direct quotation, dialogue, and conversation remains an important element in this part of the speech (cf. 43, 45–47, 53, 55–56). As noted above, ethos revealed through speech (even if the speech is imagined) tends to establish greater faith in a character sketch than does simple description or labeling.

"P. Quinctius must be driven from all his possessions; I must summon to my aid all men of influence, eloquence, and rank; violence must be applied against truth, threats flung about, perils thrown in his way, terrors brought before him, so that at last, thoroughly terrified by these methods of attack, he may surrender of his own accord." (47)[13]

These words, put into the mouth of Naevius, work to remove some of the doubt that would reside inherently in a third-person account of the story. Here Naevius "admits" Cicero's charges of avariciousness; he professes his opposition to the truth; he boasts of the resources of influence and authority that he has marshaled against the underdog Quinctius. This Naevius, in short, has emphasized all the major themes of Cicero's defense. Cicero soon (55) goes a step further and confirms, by imagining Naevius' own words, the impressions of Naevius' ethos that he has endeavored to fix in the hearts and minds of his audience:

"What have I to do with such severe morality and caution?" says he; "let men of honor worry about such obligations; but as for me, let them consider, not what I possess, but how I have acquired it, the circumstances of my birth, and the manner in which I was brought up. I remember that there is an old saying: it is much easier for a buffoon (*scurra*) to become rich than a good *pater familias*."[14]

It is not surprising that Cicero, who has argued so convincingly, if rather deviously, on the basis of ethos, completes this portion of the speech with a summation of Quinctius' upright character, tinged with irony and sarcasm. Certainly it is to be expected that a rude and boorish man, steeped in the old ways of respect for friends, property, and the principles of duty, a stranger to the Forum, the Campus, and rowdy banquets, should be terrified by his opponent's influence, treated with inequality, and stripped of his possessions, fame, and fortune—a victim of the greed and cruelty of Sextus Naevius (59). Here vigorously expressed ethos approaches pathos, and conciliation transforms itself into animation.

Cicero undergirds his *probatio* by the supports of character portraits upon which he will continue to base assumptions. In his effort to show that Naevius could not have taken possession of Quinctius' goods according to the edict and in his denial that Naevius did take possession of them (60–85), thematic portraiture continues to depict Naevius as a *scurra* (62) and a gladiator (69). Narrative accounts of the actions of Naevius and Alfenus, Quinctius' agent, offer further depth to their characters; a fine comparison (70) of Naevius, his ethos, and his actions with those of Alfenus emphasizes the influential conniving and wicked force behind the personality of Naevius.

The most powerful and effective use of ethos in this part of the speech is again accomplished through an imaginary dialogue (71–72). The subject is by now familiar: the unfairness of the circumstances for Cicero and his client and the overwhelming obstacles that they face under such conditions. Quinctius makes reasonable, modest demands concerning the procedure of the case; Naevius is made to answer abruptly, authoritatively, and unrelentingly, ever refusing to give ground, stealing every advantage from the defenseless Quinctius. The conversation at length reverts to the central theme of Cicero's defense, as Naevius boasts of his eloquent, powerful supporters:

"L. Philippus will fight for me, a man of the greatest eminence in the state for his eloquence, dignity, and position;

Hortensius will speak for me, a man distinguished for his ability, nobility, and reputation; further, men of the highest birth and the greatest power will support me, men whose numbers and presence would make not only Quinctius tremble, who is fighting for his political rights, but even anyone who is outside the risk of such danger." (72)[15]

From the first sentence of the speech, Cicero's chief concern has been the influence, authority, and eloquence of his adversaries. This motif of the unfair struggle of *gratia* and *eloquentia* against the guileless honesty of Quinctius surfaces several times during the speech and tends to delimit groups of arguments (cf., e.g., 47, 53, 59, 71–73, 77, 84–87).[16] In a remarkable outburst to Aquilius (77) Cicero uses his position as *patronus* to speak in his own person and on his own behalf, admitting the fear and apprehension he felt in facing Hortensius. One need not adapt an ironic reading of this passage,[17] or interpret it as excessive diffidence on Cicero's part.[18] Certainly the young orator experienced feelings of nervousness and insecurity against such powerful *patroni*; likewise he must have had enough confidence in his own abilities and in this case to take on such a defense at short notice. However, it is inconceivable that Cicero did not feel the pressure of the influence, authority, and power of Naevius, Hortensius, and Philippus, and commensurately the conspicuous absence of such forces from his client's case and his own ethos.

It becomes senseless, for one lacking equal armaments, to attempt a fight on equal ground. Thus Cicero endeavors throughout the speech to undercut, to neutralize in some way, the *gratia* of his adversaries. By pointing to this situation repeatedly, he has established his client and his case as an unfavored, unsupported cause, playing on the human predilection to favor the hopeless, the disadvantaged. Here he confesses his concern and both underscores and undercuts the influence of the prosecutors by introducing his own *auctor*, Roscius, the kinsman of Quinctius and the greatest actor of the Roman stage.

The implication that a stage actor's influence and advice, albeit that of the great Roscius, might offset the influence of *nobiles* like Philippus and Hortensius only emphasizes the power that Cicero wishes to impart to Roscius' words. The actor assures the young patron that success hinges simply on proving the impossibility of a man's traveling seven hundred miles in three days, the interval between Naevius' application for possession and Quinctius' eviction from his pastures.[19] Indeed, even overwhelming *auctoritas* and eloquence must bow to the most resourceless when his *auctor* is *veritas*: "There is a certain kind of truth so evident that nothing can invalidate it" (80).[20] Thus armed with the authority of truth, Cicero and Quinctius can withstand the assault of Hortensius' *eloquentia*, Philippus' *gratia*, and Naevius' *improbitas*: "All these facts, C. Aquilius, are of such a kind that anyone can clearly see that in this case wickedness and influence are contending against helplessness and truth" (84).[21]

The importance of ethos as a source of persuasion in this speech is made evident again in the peroration. After recapitulating his arguments, Cicero states openly what his method has implied throughout the speech. In the final analysis the issue of the case really revolves around two different sets of *mores*, two antithetical ways of life:

> For the question to be decided is whether the rustic and simple frugality of my client's life is able to defend itself against luxury and licentiousness, or whether, disgraced and despoiled of all that made it honorable, it is to be handed over naked to greed and impudence. P. Quinctius does not compare his influence to yours, Naevius, he does not vie with you in wealth and resources; he concedes to you all the talents that made you great; he admits that he can neither speak elegantly nor accommodate his language to the will of another; that he cannot abandon a friend in affliction and fly into the arms of another who is the favorite of fortune; that he does not live in the midst of profusion and extravagance; that he does not prepare splendid and magnificent banquets; that he does not own a house that is closed to modesty and good living but open, no, freely accessible to passion and debauchery. On the other hand he declares that he has always cherished duty, good faith, industry, and a life that has been altogether rough and ill-provided. He is aware that the opposite mode of living is more highly esteemed and has very great influence in these degenerate days. (92–93)[22]

Overall the oration displays a remarkable use of rhetorical ethos. Taking on a case that presented difficult problems, at short notice, in the face of persons of great influence and authority, Cicero relies on portrayal of the characters of the litigants as premises upon which to build his arguments. Although rational argumentative procedure plays an important and intricately manipulated role in the speech,[23] Cicero treats the modes of life and the characters of Naevius and Quinctius as the dictators of their ac-

New 007 **Daniel Craig** takes a run on the beach yesterday at the Bahamas set of the upcoming Bond flick, "Casino Royale."

# day in the

# Oscar no

…t becomes an Oscar-nominated …nwriter most? Says **Noah** …**bach**, up for "The Squid and …hale," it's New York:

…n and raised in Brooklyn, and …only a little bit of a move. I now …nhattan. I basically try to write …; about New York and try to …und New York. I get anxieties …ut of my comfort zone.

…he New York sensibility. I get …h or whenever I get up, and al-…ve with my wife, I go out for my …coffee. I like those mom-and-…coffee shops. I like the portable … cups with the plastic tops. I …ey feel. I like to carry the thing …ere's no analysis for why, but …s the promise of more, I keep it …it's finished.

… go to my old apart-… West Village, which … office. There I steal …t connection from my … who know I'm doing …for it myself, I'd use it …vaste time more be-…Google people more. … at the desk, working. … every day it's gran-…stes like sawdust.

charge inv… Daly's cou… Whitewate… Dr. **Tom H**… don't like t…

THE Ame… 10 rules… list: D… Never say … truth. Do n… porters; th… not you. Jo… yers, they … fax. Lose … English to … *not* micron… rial approv… Ain't going…

tions, as the ultimate touchstones of the case and the decision. As advocate, the young Cicero has only his own *ingenium, industria*, and *diligentia* to offer, finding himself at a considerable disadvantage to his authoritative opponents. The degree to which this concerns him, and the zeal of his efforts to neutralize the situation, indicate the influence such factors exercised in a Roman court of law. Unable to grapple eye to eye with his adversary, Cicero adopts a strategy of lament, openly and repeatedly complaining about his disadvantage, a method that accounts for a major motif of the speech and the defense. Cast in the role of the defender of the disadvantaged and the advocate of equity and truth, Cicero can appeal to the hearts of the judges and the human predilection to support the honest, innocent, but downtrodden victim in the face of influential, unscrupulous, and dastardly oppressors. In the midst of rational argumentation or pathetic appeal, the characters of the *praeco* Naevius and the *rusticus* Quinctius are ever close at hand.

## PRO SEXTO ROSCIO AMERINO

Cicero's first *causa publica*, his defense of Sextus Roscius of Ameria in 80 against a charge of parricide, displays an extensive and extraordinary use of ethos as a source of persuasion.[24] Faced with the rhetorical challenge of defending a rather humble, helpless man against the onslaught of the wealth, power, and influence enjoyed by satellites of the *regnum Sullanum*, he exhausts all the advantages and manipulates even the liabilities of the rhetoric of advocacy to work for the benefit of his cause.

From the first words of the speech, he begins to draw his own character and fashion his own persona. As a pleader who is virtually unknown, "who neither in age nor ability, nor authority, can be compared with those present," meaning his audience of "so many eminent orators and illustrious citizens," (1), he finds himself again in the predicament of possessing less *auctoritas, gratia*, and *existimatio* than his case demands. Here, however, he ingeniously converts his position to advantage by claiming that his acceptance of the case has been due not to his courage or to his ability or to his eagerness for praise, but actually to the very youth and obscurity that enable him, because of his position (or rather lack of it), to speak freely and with less danger (5) than those in whom highest authority and dignity reside (2). By emphasizing the very weaknesses that beset his ethos, Cicero converts his disadvantageous position to the benefit of his defense, invests his persona with a measure of courage by the denial of its possession, and creates an expectation in the minds of his audience for subsequent frank discussion of delicate facts and dangerous personalities.

Through the introduction of the characters of Chrysogonus and his friends in the *exordium* (6–13), Cicero's line of defense becomes quickly apparent. Greed is the motive of the prosecution, ruthlessness its method. Ironic and sarcastic references to Chrysogonus (6–8) and his desires establish a character-based foundation upon which Cicero will construct his case. Chrysogonus' demand that Roscius be condemned in order that he, freed from anxiety and torment, can squander his victim's fortune is countered by Cicero, who more reasonably requests that Chrysogonus be satisfied with only property and money, and give up seeking his client's life (7). Cicero is at pains to establish certain suppositions about the actors involved in the case by using such methods of characterization early in the speech, so that the Roman belief in character as the determiner of actions will do much (as it did in the *Pro Quinctio*) to corroborate a scenario of unprovoked attack by the evil, powerful, and greedy upon the helpless and innocent.

Chrysogonus and his followers, "assassins (*sicarii*) and gladiators" (a characterization that will resonate throughout the oration),[25] are challenged only by the weak, resourceless Sextus, who is supported only by Cicero, an advocate whose fitness is hindered by his lack of *ingenium*, his impressiveness by his youth, his freedom of speech by the times and circumstances of the trial (9). Cicero could not have expressed more forcefully the diametric opposition of the two parties involved than he does in concluding his *exordium*:

> They are the accusers, who have laid hands upon the property of my client, he is the defendant, to whom they have left nothing but ruin; they are the accusers, who profited by the murder of Roscius' father, he is the defendant, to whom his father's death brought not only sorrow but also poverty; they are the accusers, who passionately desired to murder my client, he is the defendant, who comes even before this court with a bodyguard, for fear he may be killed in this very place before your eyes; lastly, they are the accusers, whose trial the people demands, he is the defendant, who is the sole survivor of their nefarious massacre. (13)[26]

Thus, as in the *Pro Quinctio*, Cicero attempts to portray, at least in broad strokes, the characters of the case as early as possible in the speech. By doing so he establishes certain premises about the characters in the minds of his audience, upon which he can build a defense. If the judges can be led to trust in Cicero's portraits of the dramatis personae, his attempt at persuasion becomes easier as he constantly refers the listener to the touchstone of character, implying or explicitly arguing an action's probability or improbability as demanded by its author's ethos.[27]

As Cicero narrates his version of the facts (15–34), the characters of the case are further defined in terms of their actions, which are described in such ways as to corroborate Cicero's early sketches. The father of Roscius is honest, responsible, respected by men of influence and nobility, a partaker of their *hospitium* (15–16). His enemies, the villains Capito and Magnus, are then introduced:

> The first [Capito] is reputed to be an experienced and famous gladiator, who has won many victories; the second [Magnus] has recently appointed himself trainer to the other, and although, as far as I know, before this last fight he was only a novice, he now easily surpasses the master himself in villainy and audacity. (17)[28]

The description of Roscius' adversaries as gladiators, used first in the *exordium* (7), becomes a motif, like the use of *praeco* and *scurra* in reference to Naevius in the *Pro Quinctio*, that will resonate at various times throughout the speech, calculated to recall the audience to a realization of the ruthless nature of the prosecution. Here Cicero uses it to contrast the character of the villains with that of his client, a devoted son and hard-working farmer, as well as to prepare the way for the near-explicit assertion that Magnus murdered the elder Roscius (18). The power broker Chrysogonus is pictured behind the scene, greedily manipulating his pawns, Capito and Magnus, toward the destruction of Sextus (18–21)— unknown, of course, to Sulla (21–22).

Cicero's own ethos, which had momentarily retired from the narrative, emerges again in section 30 in an effort to reemphasize the dangers of the case and his own courage in undertaking it. The prosecutors were certain that no one would dare to defend Roscius; although the youthful Cicero may have acted rashly in accepting such a case, he intends, despite the threats and dangers, to carry on:

> I have deliberately made up my mind, not only to say all that I consider has to do with the case, but also to say it as I please, boldly, and freely; no consideration shall arise of such

importance, gentlemen, as to make it possible for fear to exert greater influence over me than honor. (31)[29]

This "fine bit of amplification"[30] presents an instructive example of the close affinity between ethos and pathos in Roman oratory and illustrates how easily the milder emotions of ethos are transformed into the vehement and vigorous emotions of pathos. With the rhetorical question "Who is so indifferent that he is able to keep silence and overlook such atrocities?"[31] Cicero heightens the tone to introduce an extraordinarily emotional passage:

> "You murdered my father, although he was not proscribed; after he had been killed, you entered his name in the proscription list; you drove me by force out of my home; you now possess my patrimony. What more do you want?" (32)[32]

The rhetoric of advocacy, whose conventions required a patron to speak on behalf of a client, had removed, at least theoretically, the possibility of such intensely personal, moving appeals of the first person. Here Cicero, defying the conventions, moves from his character to a total identification with his client and speaks in the first person. In the *Pro Quinctio* direct quotations and conversations placed in the mouths of the characters achieved similar goals. Here, even more effectively, the sudden, impassioned outburst in first person causes the audience to forget momentarily that Roscius is not telling his own story and stirs feelings in them as no third-person narrative of the same account could.

In the *partitio* (35–36) to the formal proof Cicero outlines three obstacles that face Roscius: the charge of the formal prosecutor, Erucius, the audacity of the villainous Roscii, and the power of Chrysogonus. He articulates the crucial importance of character as a source of proof, especially in a charge of parricide, at the outset of the *probatio*, where he criticizes Erucius' failure to attack Roscius' character, if only because convention demanded it.[33]

> What arguments do you, as prosecutor, think you ought to employ, Erucius? Shouldn't you show the audacity of the man who is accused of such a crime, his savage character and brutal nature, a life dedicated to every kind of vice and infamy, in short, a character depraved, abandoned, and utterly ruined? You have mentioned none of these things in regard to Sex. Roscius, not even for the sake of throwing them in his teeth. (38)[34]

The implication, of course, is that Roscius' character is so spotless, so upright, that Erucius had no choice but to pass over it in silence. Cicero expends a sizable portion of his speech (38–45) making that assumption explicit.

Cicero likewise brings Erucius' character (46–47) and his role as prosecutor (55–62, 89) into focus. He charges that Erucius assumed the prosecution only for money and with Chrysogonus' assurance that no one would undertake the defense of Roscius under such circumstances. The finest piece of ethical narrative in the speech (59–61)[35] describes Erucius' confident, nonchalant, and arrogant manner of conducting his case, certain that the benches were empty of men of ability and experience:

> He began to show such indifference that, when it came into his mind, he sat down, then he walked about, sometimes called for his slave (to order supper, I suppose); in fact, he treated you who sit in judgment and the general public with no more respect than if he had been absolutely alone. (59)[36]

When Erucius had finished his oration and saw Cicero rising to respond, he breathed a sigh of relief, began to joke, and paid no attention. Then Cicero mentioned Chrysogonus:

> As soon as I referred to him the man immediately jumped up; he seemed to be astonished. I understood what had stung him. I mentioned Chrysogonus a second and a third time. After that, men never ceased running hastily back and forth, I suppose to inform Chrysogonus that there was someone in Rome who was bold enough to speak out contrary to his will. (60)[37]

This vignette, drawn so skillfully, casts a convincing light upon Cicero's version of the facts, corroborates his portrayal of Erucius and the powerful man behind the scene, and underscores his own dauntless courage.[38]

He continues with an excursus on the atrocity of the crime of parricide (60–73) and again links it with character.[39] Unless a man's life has proved disgraceful from youth, polluted by wicked and shameless acts, marked by an audacity and rashness bordering on insanity, the commission of such a crime is incredible (68). Certainly Sextus Roscius' life is inconsistent with such a description:

> A rustic character, frugal living, and a rough and uncultured life are not generally the birthplace of such crimes. As you could not find every kind of crop or tree in every field, so every kind of evil deed is not born in every life. The city creates luxury, from which avarice inevitably springs, while from avarice audacity breaks forth, and from audacity all

crimes and misdeeds are generated. On the other hand, this country life, which you call boorish, is the teacher of thrift, diligence, and justice. (75)[40]

Cicero is, of course, appealing to the Roman sense of character, the assumption that character was for the most part permanent and unchanging and that it was very difficult, if not impossible, for a man to perform actions inconsistent with or outside his previously manifested ethos. Following this line of thinking, it is inconceivable that a man "of rustic manners" would even contemplate a crime of the magnitude and atrocity of parricide; the word would not exist in his vocabulary, the thought could not be conceived by his intellect.

Cicero's chain of crime, from *luxuria* to *avaritia* to *audacia* to *omnia scelera ac maleficia* (75, cf. 118), however, is perfectly consistent with the characters of the Roscii and Chrysogonus, at least as he has portrayed them. Throughout this part of the speech Cicero uses the words *avaritia* and *audacia* to describe the motivation of the Roscii, Magnus and Capito (cf. e.g. 87, 88, 96, 101, 104, 118). The character themes of "assassin" (*sicarius*, e.g., 81, 87, 94; also 151, 152) and "gladiator" (118, 119) likewise reemerge and are joined by "agent of confiscated goods, proscription-monger" (*sector*, which can also mean "cutthroat," 80, 88, 93, 94; also 149, 151, 152), to label the villains responsible for the elder Roscius' murder and his son's demise. Thus presenting two antithetical characters and two diametrically opposed ways of life, Cicero argues from probability for the innocence of Sextus Roscius and the guilt of Magnus (88).

In section 94, for example, he casts the argument in the form of a dialogue between the two, effectively revealing the ethos of both; and through *oratio recta* and the use of first-person speech, he assumes the role and the character of his client:

> You will say, "If I was constantly in Rome, what follows from that?"
> I shall reply, "I was never there at all."
> "I confess that I am an agent of proscribed goods, but so are many others."
> "But I, as you yourself reproach me with being, am a farmer and a rustic."
> "If I have associated myself with a crowd of assassins, it does not follow at once that I am an assassin."
> "But most certainly I, who do not even know an assassin, am far beyond the reach of such an accusation."[41]

As noted earlier, the advocate's escape from the third-person mode of narration allows him to capture some of the simple directness, persuasiveness, and pathos of a person telling his own story.

When Cicero turns to the third part of his argument, dealing with the influence (*gratia*) and power (*potentia*) of Chrysogonus (122–132), he enters upon the part of his defense most dangerous to himself, his client, and his case. Unable to match influence and power with his adversary, he must resort to other methods. In various sections of the speech he has endeavored to mold for himself the persona of a young, somewhat inexperienced advocate, who perhaps with some youthful bravado, but certainly with a large measure of concern and courage, has alone stepped forward to rescue Roscius. That he has done this in the face of Chrysogonus, a powerful henchman of Sulla, in such troubled times and circumstances—of which situation he continually and designedly reminds us—only amplifies this persona and emphasizes his bravery. To be sure, he is careful to separate Sulla from Chrysogonus and his actions (cf. 22, 127, 131, 138–142) and, while assailing Chrysogonus, to protect his client.

This protection is afforded chiefly through the use of a technique offered by the circumstances of advocacy. We have noted just above how Cicero's identification with Roscius, which momentarily violated the conventions of advocacy, would have effectively portrayed character and stirred pathos in the hearts of the audience. Now, however, he exploits to equal advantage the strict conventions of advocacy and separates himself from his client; this stance grants him license to say things that his client, Roscius, could not:

> I beg, gentlemen, that you will listen to the few things I have yet to say with the feeling that I am speaking partly for myself, partly for Sextus Roscius. Things which seem to me scandalous and intolerable, and which, in my opinion, may affect us all, unless we take precautions, these I proclaim on my own account and from a feeling of grief in my mind; things which concern the crisis of my client's life and its legal aspect, what he wishes to be said on his behalf, what conditions will satisfy him, you will hear presently, gentlemen, at the end of my speech. (129)[42]

Cicero here broadens the significance of his case, a technique that will become commonplace in his speeches,[43] as he points to Roscius' dangers as only part of the larger threat to Cicero and the Roman state. By leaving Roscius out of the question (cf. 130) and by separating his sentiments from his client's, Cicero is able to attack Chrysogonus in his own person and portray Roscius as only an unwilling bystander to the assault:

> As I said before, all that I have just said has been said in my own name; it is the condition of the Republic, my grief, and the injustice of those men that have forced me to speak as I have done. Sextus Roscius feels no indignation at any of these acts of injustice, he accuses no one, he makes no complaint about the loss of his patrimony. This farmer and rustic, inexperienced in the ways of the world, believes that all those things which you assert were done through the agency of Sulla, were done in accordance with law, custom, and the law of nations; he desires to leave this tribunal free from all blame and acquitted of this nefarious accusation; if he is delivered from this unworthy suspicion, he declares that he is resigned to the loss of all his property. (143)[44]

Unfortunately, most of Cicero's response to the *gratia* and *potentia* of Chrysogonus has been lost, leaving a considerable lacuna in our text. The speech resumes in the midst of an invective against Chrysogonus (133–142), an attack on his personal life and character that, although related to Cicero's third point of the *probatio*, must technically be classified a movement *extra causam*, a digression calculated to amplify his case and stir indignation in the hearts of the jury. Such a digression, occurring immediately before the peroration of the speech and taking ethos as its primary source for material, will become a regular element in Cicero's judicial orations.[45]

This *ethica digressio* actually possesses a rich heritage in rhetorical theory. An ethical and digressive element is discernible in Theodorus' *epipistōsis* ("supplementary proof") and *epexelenchos* ("supplementary refutation"), in Licymnius' *apoplanēsis* ("wandering," "digression"), and even in Aristotle's rather ambivalent treatment of the *epilogos* in the *Rhetoric*.[46] By Hermagoras' time, the digression is listed as one of the *partes orationis*. Cicero tells us that Hermagoras advised placing a *digressio* (*parekbasis*) after the refutation, but before the conclusion, of the oration. This digression "ought to be unconnected with the case and actual point to be decided; it might contain praise of oneself or abuse of one's opponent, or lead to some other case which may supply confirmation or refutation, not by argument but by adding emphasis by means of some amplification" (*De Inv.* 1.97; cf. *De Or.* 2.80, 311–312).

The "ethical digression" displays a richer tradition in oratorical practice, appearing in an oration as early as Antiphon's *On the Murder of Herodes* (74–84). Palamedes, in the speech by Gorgias so named, after refuting the formal charge, drew on ethos as a source of persuasion and demonstrated his character's incompatibility with the accusation (28–32). Even Socrates, in Plato's *Apology* (28a–34b), included a long digression immediately preceding the epilogue, dilating upon his character and his divine mission in life. Lysias, Aeschines, Demosthenes, and Lycurgus continued to employ the device and develop it concurrently with the evolution of the large-scale judicial oration that was intended for delivery by professionals in important political cases.[47] Given the importance of character in Roman society and the Roman penchant for employing ethos as a source of persuasion, it is not surprising to find that Cicero accepted the Greek tradition of an ethically based digression and adapted it to his own oratory.

Here he begins with a vivid description of the *luxuria* that characterizes Chrysogonus' life (133). Recall that according to Cicero, *luxuria* was the initial step of the downward ladder that leads, via *avaritia* and *audacia*, to *omnia maleficia* (75). Expensive, extravagant, and exotic possessions, art works, marble, and slaves certainly betray the *avaritia* of Chrysogonus, the second step toward crime—a desire for possessions, beyond mere extravagance.

In section 135, Cicero turns to a description of Chrysogonus, including his personal appearance:

> And look at the man himself, gentlemen; you see how, with hair carefully arranged and reeking with perfume, he flits about the Forum accompanied by a great throng of toga-wearers; you see how he despises everyone, how he considers no one a human being compared with himself, and believes that he alone is happy and powerful.[48]

The description of the *audax* is unmistakable. Despising all others and preening himself, Chrysogonus has descended to the lowest step on the ladder, *audacia*, below which lies *omnia maleficia*.

In the second part of the digression (135–138), Cicero turns from deprecation of his opponent to praise and support of himself. The foregoing invective might have been construed as an assault upon Sulla and his fellow *nobiles*, and Cicero had trodden dangerously close to insulting the Sullan regime. Here he is quick to point out his loyalty to the *causa nobilitatis* and to assert that the real aim of the nobility in taking up arms was to recreate and restore the Roman people, not strip it of its wealth and possessions (137).

Finally (138–142), he distinguishes Chrysogonus and his like from the true nobility, who must show themselves vigilant, kindly, brave, and merciful (139); they must welcome a man who has spoken with truth and frankness (140) and resist scoundrels like Chrysogonus, the charlatans of true *nobilitas*. The distinction drawn between Chrysogonus and the *causa nobilitatis* serves Cicero's defense well. It enables the jury to separate the character of Chrysogonus from that of Sulla, to condemn the former's deeds without offending the latter, and to accept Cicero's speech and the scenario he has created.

The placement of an ethically based digression before the peroration is particularly effective, especially when one recalls the Roman belief in the affinity of ethos and pathos. As Cicero inveighs against Chrysogonus near the end of the digression (141), the tenor of his speech rises to fever pitch, transforming the mild emotions of ethos into more vehement feelings of pathos, which he further stokes in the peroration. In this way the *ethica digressio* provides an effective method for heightening the intensity of the speech—a progression that Cicero himself cautions should be gradual.[49]

Following his statement that what he has just said are his own, not Roscius' sentiments (143–144), Cicero once again breaks with the convention of advocacy and speaks as if Roscius were defending himself:

> "You possess my farms; I am living on the charity of others; I yield because I am resigned and it is necessary. My house is open to you, closed to me; I bear it. You have at your disposal my numerous household; I have no slave; I suffer it and think that it must be endured. What more do you want? Why do you pursue me? Why do you attack me?" (145)[50]

The first-person outburst conveys character effectively and stirs emotions befitting the peroration. As the speech comes to its close, the wickedness of Chrysogonus and his helpers and the character themes of *sector* (149, 150, 151) and *sicarius* (151, 152) reappear, drawing for the last time the crucial distinction between characters that argues so convincingly for the innocence of Roscius:

> Is there any doubt who is responsible for the crime, when you see on the one side a proscription-monger, an enemy, an assassin, and at the same time our accuser, on the other, reduced to poverty, a son esteemed by his friends and relatives, to whom not only no culpabil'ty, but not even a shadow of suspicion, can be attached? (152)[51]

Cicero's defense of Sextus Roscius reveals a more sophisticated and artistic use of rhetorical ethos than is evident in any Greek oration or, as far as our scanty knowledge allows us to conclude, in any earlier Roman oratory.[52] As in the *Pro Quinctio*, the ethos of all the dramatis personae provides the ever-present backdrop before which and in relation to which Cicero articulates all action and argument. He repeatedly and consistently portrays Sextus as a simple, frugal farmer whose character could never entertain the thought of a crime as atrocious as parricide. His adversaries, on the other hand, corrupted by *luxuria*, prodded by *avaritia*, and unable to control their *audacia*, are capable of committing any outrage.

As for himself, the young, unknown orator who was speaking his first public case molded an effective persona by cleverly turning his opponents' advantages—great power and influence—to work for himself. Despite his own lack of experience and relative anonymity, he alone stepped forward, courageous enough to face the *gratia* and *potentia* of Chrysogonus and his satellites, to defend the downtrodden and the cause of the true nobility. Brushing close to the sensitivities of the *regnum Sullanum*, Cicero acknowledged his danger but also recognized his opportunity. Masterfully dealing with the demands of the rhetoric of advocacy, exploiting its strengths and neutralizing its shortcomings, he managed to make his gamble pay off. Roscius was acquitted.

## DIVINATIO IN Q. CAECILIUM

Much transpired during the ten years that intervened between Cicero's defense of Sextus Roscius of Ameria and his prosecution of the notoriously corrupt governor of Sicily, Gaius Verres, on a charge of extortion. Cicero had increased in age, wisdom, experience, and reputation; by dint of *labor* and *industria*, the effective harnessing of his *ingenium*, and the promotion of his *virtus*, he had secured the quaestorship for Sicily in 75 and would serve as aedile in 69. Thanks to the admirable discharge of his office in Sicily, he was now, in 70, standing at a significant crossroad of his career and his *cursus* toward *honores, dignitas, gratia*, and *existimatio*. Cast in that role so familiar in Republican political history, the aspirant Cicero approached the prosecution of the powerful Verres, who was supported by Hortensius and the *nobilitas*.[53] No longer plagued with relative anonymity or a neophyte's respect, bordering on reverence, for his formidable adversary,[54] he was nevertheless still haunted by the ghost of his equestrian past, an obstacle that assumed considerable dimensions in a case that involved not only *nobiles* as adversaries but, given the political milieu of the times and the struggle for control of the courts, the collective power of the *nobilitas* as well. He again chose to use ethos, and the opportunities it provided a pleader through skillful rhetorical manipulation, to counterbalance these forces and provide material for the proof of his case.

His first task in pursuing the prosecution of Verres was to secure the right of prosecution against a counterclaim by Caecilius through *divinatio*. Because this procedure was meant to establish which of the rival claimants was better qualified to carry on the prosecution, their characters, at least their professional characters, played a large role in the proceedings.[55] Furthermore, Cicero, who until this time had always stood on the side of the defense, here had to project a persona that did not appear too eager to assume the task of prosecution but at the same time was entirely qualified to handle it.

He addresses this dilemma squarely in the *exordium* (1–9), which becomes a kind of narrative justification for his exchange of the role of defender for that of prosecutor. We catch glimpses of the dutiful quaestor, the harrassed and despoiled Sicilians, and the cruel and greedy governor (2–3) as Cicero describes his uncomfortable position of either disappointing those who had begged his aid or turning prosecutor. He suggests that the Sicilians enlist Caecilius and then represents them as reacting negatively to the suggestion (4). This masterful stroke, presented in a mere two sentences and in an entirely understated manner, summarizes his hesitancy in assuming this hostile role, the necessity of his doing so, and Caecilius' clear unsuitability for the task. At length, overwhelmed by his sense of duty, his honor, his feelings of pity, the example of other good men, and the *mos maiorum*, Cicero is forced to shoulder the responsibility (5). In fact, he goes on to claim that accusation in such a case must actually be considered a defense of the people and province of Sicily (5). Finally, a brief sketch of the monster Verres (6) and descriptions of the despoiled state of the provinces (9) and the shabby state of the law courts (8) enable him, by acceding to the request that he prosecute in order to fight this state of affairs, to assume the persona of the duty-bound, self-sacrificing savior of the downtrodden allies and of the entire Republic (9).

Having in this way dismissed the suspicion and prejudice that he fears he has aroused for taking up the task of prosecution,

Cicero is now free to deal directly with his qualifications and those of Caecilius. Although he and Caecilius are the chief actors of the proceedings and effective presentation of ethos provides the major argument for the selection of one of them as prosecutor, the characters of Verres the culprit, his *patronus*, Hortensius, and the plaintiff, Sicily herself, are ever present in Cicero's demonstration that Sicily desires him to prosecute but Verres prefers Caecilius (11–27). He skillfully handles the awkward task of representing the collective ethos of the Sicilians by having "Sicily" speak:

> "The gold, the silver, all the beautiful things that were once in my cities, houses, temples; all the various privileges which, by the favor of the Roman Senate and People, I once possessed; all these things you, Verres, have plundered and stolen from me. On this account I sue you in accordance with the law for a hundred million sesterces." (19)[56]

We have noted previously the use of direct quotation for establishing conviction through effective character portrayal. Here the innocent victim charges her assailant, and, because she cannot with one voice make such a charge, she enlists (as would an individual in a civil or criminal case) Cicero as *patronus* (19). As Sicily chooses Cicero, so the Sicilians are made to reject Caecilius and, through that rebuff, to confirm the impudence of Caecilius as well as the ability and character of Cicero:

> In such a situation, what man will prove so impudent as to dare to undertake or hope to undertake the cause of other people, when those others, those whose interests are concerned, will not have him? Suppose the Sicilians were saying to you, Caecilius, "We are not acquainted with you, we do not know who you are, we have never seen you before; allow us to defend our fortunes by means of a man whose good faith we have come to trust." (20)[57]

Cicero's then asserts that Verres wants Caecilius as prosecutor and that this fact alone should merit his disqualification (22–27). The character of Hortensius, counsel for the defense, emerges more and more in this part of the speech, perhaps most effectively in section 23 where Hortensius, again in *oratio recta*, is made to ask the court to give preference to Caecilius:

> "I am not asking," he says, "for what I usually obtain if I exert myself more than usual to obtain it. I am not asking that the accused should be acquitted; I am simply asking that the ac-

cused be prosecuted by this man rather than that man. Grant me this request; make me a simple and justifiable concession which nobody will blame you for making; and by so doing you will at the same time be allowing me, without any risk or discredit to yourself, to secure the acquittal of the man in whose behalf I am working."[58]

Hortensius' entreaty reveals indirectly, but most effectively, important aspects of his ethos—at least as Cicero presents it. There is, of course, the implied collusion of Caecilius with Verres and Hortensius. More striking, however, is the picture of a veteran pleader, somewhat complacent, perhaps somewhat apprehensive, looking for a more convenient, less demanding path to victory.[59] By creating the fiction of a plea to the judges in which Hortensius' ethos is revealed by "his own" words, Cicero has provided an opportunity to react to Hortensius' "speech," to make more explicit, while appearing less arrogant, the weakness in Hortensius' character and in his approach to this case:

> He is not so very deeply concerned on Verres' account; it is rather that he dislikes the whole turn of affairs. Before this time, some of the prosecutors have been noble boys whom he has been able to outwit. Others have been profit-hunters: and these, with good reason, he has always despised and neglected. He now sees that courageous men, persons of some reputation, are willing to prosecute and he is aware, that if this change takes place, his own domination of the courts will be at an end. (24)[60]

If Cicero is chosen to conduct this case, Hortensius must change his methods. He must follow the example of Crassus and Antonius and rely on his honesty and talent (25), for Cicero has, in taking up the cause of the Sicilians, actually taken up the cause of the Roman people; in attempting to crush the wickedness of one man, he will attempt to extirpate all wickedness of every kind (26).

Cicero next turns to Caecilius and, in a long passage (27–47) extraordinary for its reliance on and clever manipulation of the techniques of ethical persuasion, outlines the qualifications necessary for a prosecutor. Caecilius and Cicero are the chief actors involved in this *contentio*, although the ethos of Hortensius appears as a foil that underscores and emphasizes the inexperience and unsuitability of Caecilius as well as the preparedness and ability of Cicero.

Maintaining the self-assuredness he has just displayed, Cicero adds a new dimension to his persona in this speech, casting himself in the role of teacher and Caecilius in the role of the hapless pupil:

> Learn from me, since this is your first opportunity of gaining such instruction, how many qualifications a prosecutor must possess; if you find that you possess any single one of them, I shall willingly concede to you the task which you are seeking. (27)[61]

The first requirement for a prosecutor is that he possess an upright and spotless character (27). Caecilius is disqualified on this account because of the Sicilians' suspicion of his quaestorship and his collusion with Verres (28). Secondly, a prosecutor must show firmness and honesty (29). Caecilius' position is again vitiated because of his known dealings with Verres as well as his fear of being proved his accomplice (29–35). Finally, to manage a prosecution requires special talents and abilities: "He must have some capacity as a pleader; some little experience as a speaker; some little training either in the principles or in the practice of the Forum, the law courts, and the law" (35).[62] Cicero knows how dangerously close to *arrogantia* he treads, so he will pass over his own intellectual capacity (36)—at least for the time being. He is concerned only about Caecilius, and again he will speak as a friend and advisor (37).[63] Confidence and condescension set the tone (37): "You yourself, examine carefully your own mind. Recollect yourself. Think of who you are, and what you are able to accomplish."[64] A case of this magnitude demands a strong voice, a powerful memory, the ability to organize and arrange arguments, arouse emotions, demonstrate every fact, conciliate an audience (37–39). Even if Caecilius had received the finest education, had he studied Greek literature at Athens instead of Lilybaeum, and Latin at Rome instead of Sicily, this case would still be extraordinarily demanding (39).

More than a decade of study and hard work, of experience in the Forum and the law courts and at the polls, have garnered for Cicero a confidence and a reputation that he does not hesitate to invoke for his benefit:

> Everyone knows that my life has centered around the Forum and the courts; that few men, if any, of my age have defended more cases; that all the time I can spare from the business of my friends I devote to the study and hard work that this pro-

fession demands, to make myself fitter and readier for forensic practice. (41)[65]

Despite the rigors of this curriculum, Cicero still trembles at the thought of appearing in such a trial (42), whereas Caecilius' naive fearlessness and false confidence serve only to emphasize his unsuitability for the prosecution (43).

Nowhere can we better gauge Cicero's growing confidence in his own persona and the awareness of his own maturing powers than in his treatment of Hortensius in this speech.[66] Hortensius is still the measure of eloquence for Cicero, respected but not feared, admired but not idolized: "For myself, I can praise his genius without being terrified by it; I can admire him, yet believe it possible that he will enchant me more easily than entrap me" (44).[67] Thanks to his experience and the familiarity it has fostered (44), Cicero speaks as an insider, privy to the world of the *iudicium*; he is confident enough in his own ability to realize that he presents a threat to Hortensius' dominion of the courts:

> He will never crush me with his cleverness; he will never lead me astray by any display of ingenuity; he will never try, by his great powers, to weaken and dislodge me from my position. I know all the gentleman's methods of attack and all his oratorical devices. . . . However talented he may be, he will feel, when he comes to speak against me, that the trial is among other things a trial of his own ability. (44)[68]

Hortensius also sets the standard by which Caecilius' ability for this prosecution is measured. "With a rather jocular malice,"[69] in a type of ethical narrative, Cicero constructs a scenario, humorous but also telling, of Caecilius' helplessness and ineptitude:

> As for you, Caecilius, I can already see how he will outwit you, and make sport of you in every possible way; how often he will give you the fullest freedom to choose between two alternatives—whether a thing has happened or has not happened, whether a statement is true or false; and how, whichever you choose, your choice will tell against you. Immortal gods! What confusion, what distraction, what befuddlement will assail you, poor innocent! Think of it, when he begins to subdivide your speech for the prosecution and tick off with his fingers the separate sections of your case, when he proceeds to smash them up, clear them away, and polish them off one after the other! Indeed, you yourself will begin to fear

that you may have set out to bring ruin upon an innocent man. (45)[70]

The development of Hortensius' ethos and the establishment of his oratorical ability as the gauge by which the effectiveness of either prosecutor is measured are a masterstroke on Cicero's part. His own experiences and his past association with Hortensius (cf. 44) bring influence and weight to his own ethos and enable him to project a persona in possession of the necessary confidence and skill required to meet such an adversary in such an important case. In sharp contrast, Caecilius' ability, experience, and oratorical know-how are so dwarfed by the ethos and eloquence of Hortensius that the scenario of Caecilius' conducting a prosecution with Hortensius' "aid" becomes pathetically humorous.

Cicero continues for a short time in the same vein (46–47) and then turns to Caecilius' *subscriptores*, whom he dismisses summarily (47–51). After the refutation of two points that Cicero anticipates Caecilius will advance in his own behalf—that Verres had wronged Caecilius (52–65) and that Caecilius is qualified to prosecute because he had served as Verres' quaestor (59–65)—Cicero includes a brief excursus (66–71), ethically based, before concluding his speech.

He begins the digression by supporting the honorable notion of defending the oppressed, an action sanctioned by historical precedent and the *mos maiorum* (66–69). Mention of the names of men who possessed great authority and sterling reputations, M. Cato Sapiens, Cn. Domitius, P. Lentulus, and P. Africanus, contributes to the force and conviction of Cicero's argument. The implied identification of Cicero's character with these great men is made more explicit in sections 70–71, where Cicero endeavors, as he did in the *exordium*, to justify his move from defender to prosecutor. The only remedy for the diseased Republic and corrupt, contaminated courts is the defense of the laws by the most honest, incorruptible, and industrious men (70). Like those great men who preceded him in this task, Cicero is willing, for the sake of his country, to put his reputation on the line: "That is why the most diligent and painstaking prosecutors have always been those who feel that their own reputations are at stake" (71).[71]

The short peroration (71–73) recalls the characters of Caecilius and Cicero and their suitability for the task. Caecilius, considered a "nobody" by Cicero, is dismissed harshly: "He has nothing to lose in failure: he may come out of the business as an infamous scoundrel, and yet not find that he has lost any of his former distinctions" (71).[72] Cicero, however, operates under a different set of laws (72). The Roman people hold many things hostage that Cicero must fight valiantly to secure:

> It holds as hostage the office to which I seek election; the ambition that I cherish in my heart; the reputation which I have gained by much sweat, labor, and vigilance. If I can prove in this case that I have done my duty to the best of my power, I shall, by the favor of the Roman people, be able to keep those precious things unharmed and safe. But I have only to fail, only to take one little false step, and I shall lose in a moment all the good things I have acquired, one by one, through a long period of time. (72)[73]

He concludes his speech by summarily equating the selection of Caecilius with the judges' rejection of an "honorable, strict, and diligent prosecutor" (73).

We remarked earlier that the Verrine affair represented a crucial turning point in Cicero's career, in his *cursus* toward office, dignity, influence, and reputation. That Cicero realized the magnitude of the stakes involved is clear from his concluding remarks. Defeat at Hortensius' hands would deal a blow to his reputation,[74] but its effect would certainly not be commensurate with the glory a victory would impart, a victory that, far from merely maintaining his position, would markedly advance his ethos and its *existimatio*. A risk it certainly was, but one that a *novus homo* of Cicero's ambitions could hardly afford not to take.[75]

## IN C. VERREM, ACTIO PRIMA

The persona Cicero projected in the *divinatio*, that of a vigilant, industrious, hard-working, self-assured pleader, wary of but not frightened by his formidable adversary, continues to play a central role in the first action, where it is set continually in sharp contrast to the depraved character of Verres and the compromised, if not conniving, ethos of Hortensius. From the outset, we notice that the action is not a typical opening speech in an extortion trial,[76] but a clever if rather unorthodox gambit calculated to explain the procedural and political problems of the case, demonstrate Cicero's preparedness and ability, and force the hand of the defense, thereby quelling Verres' chances for bribery and delay.

A statement at section 15 seems to summarize Cicero's method accurately: "Indeed, the great multitude that has assembled to hear this case has done so not, in my opinion, to learn from me the facts of the case, but to join me in reviewing the facts that it knows already."[77] Cicero need not teach, argue, and establish the facts of Verres' outrageous behavior; these are well known. Rather, he will construct a biographical narrative, a review of Verres' character that becomes the proof that Verres is depraved and un-Roman.[78] He begins by casting this trial in a role of broader significance, a god-sent opportunity to mitigate the unpopularity of the senatorial order and restore the Republic (1). Verres appears almost immediately, "a man already condemned, in the world's opinion, by his life and deeds; already acquitted, according to his own confident assertions, by his vast fortune" (2).[79] Throughout the speech Cicero continues to develop to his advantage this two-fold aspect of Verres' ethos: the man is already condemned by his character and deeds, and therefore helpless; but he is also redeemed by his money and power, and therefore threatening. Cicero's own ethos enters immediately: the rigorous *accusator*, backed by the Roman people, identified with the senatorial order, who fears not so much the magnitude and importance of the case as he does the nefarious assault that Verres is planning to launch upon him, upon Manius Glabrio, the praetor of the court, and upon all that is in word or deed truly Roman (2–4).

Cicero contrasts the audacity and folly that mark Verres' character (5, 7) with his own diligence and preparedness in readying the case (6, 7), as the *exordium* moves almost imperceptibly into the narration. In reality, this narration functions as the argument of the speech, whose source of material is ethos, particularly the story of Verres' character.[80]

Cicero begins with Verres' attempt to buy the jury (7–9), which, he claims, proves Verres' contempt for the courts and the senatorial order (cf. 8, 9). By casting Verres in the role of an enemy of the state and a despiser of the senatorial order and "all good men," he is, of course, attempting to alienate his audience and the senatorial jury from one of their own. His fear that, even barring bribery, cronyism might prevail in this case, although not explicitly stated, is clear and becomes more apparent in the course of the oration. He banks on his anti-Roman portrait of Verres, the widespread knowledge of his crimes, and the prospect of losing control of the courts, which was then threatening the senatorial order, to counteract these nepotistic inclinations, naturally strong in a *nobilitas* whose ranks were jealously guarded.

After complimenting the court and its president and expressing his confidence in their incorruptibility (10), Cicero turns to the other aspect of Verres' ethos, his depraved life of crime. With a passing reference to Hortensius' distinction as an advocate, he returns to the theme of the already condemned life of Verres (10), which cannot be defended, even by the most eloquent. The story of Verres' quaestorship, legateship, praetorship, and conduct in Sicily rolls on in a breathtaking narrative (11–15) that Cicero never interrupts to substantiate a charge. What would be the need? "I do not think that a human being exists who has heard the name of Verres and cannot repeat the story of his nefarious deeds" (15).[81]

He then shifts back to the ethos of Verres the manipulator, the bribery agent, the power-monger:

> The knowledge of these things has led this abandoned mad-man to adopt a new method of fighting me. It is not his real purpose to find the eloquence of someone to oppose me. He relies not on the influence, not on the authority, not on the power of anyone. He does indeed pretend that he confides in these things; but I see what he is doing, nor does he do it very secretly. He displays against me a hollow show of noble names, the names of a set of very arrogant persons, who harm my cause by their being noble less than they forward it by their being known: and he pretends to confide in their protection, while all the time he has been engineering a quite different scheme. (15)[82]

Cicero's goal here is, of course, to direct the attention of the judges toward Verres' attempts at bribery and delay, his next topic (16–23). Yet his denial of Verres' reliance upon *eloquentia, gratia, auctoritas*, and *potentia* is rather astonishing in its obvious contradiction of the truth, even according to Cicero's subsequent admissions. Hortensius was, after all, the most eloquent pleader of the day; his election to the consulship as well as the support he enjoyed from other *nobiles* in this case did bring with it a measure of *gratia, auctoritas*, and *potentia* that, particularly before a senatorial jury, presented no imaginary obstacle to Cicero's prosecution. We noted earlier Cicero's fear that blind loyalty and nepotistic favoritism might debilitate his case. Here, by disqualifying these factors from the defense through Verres' own intentions (i.e. *simulat*), perhaps Cicero hopes to disqualify them as factors in the minds of the jury.

At any rate, considered in another light, these comments lend valuable insight into Cicero's own ethos, particularly in his early speeches. There is a personal intensity in these words not often voiced in a public oration. Cicero finds himself in a desirable but still rather awkward position. He had realized early in his career that a man's character and the persona it projected were extraordinarily important elements for success in oratorical and political endeavors. A noble name, a glorious reputation, the dignity and authority of one's character, could persuade people and win votes. But it was rare that a *novus homo* from an equestrian family breached the jealously guarded barrier of the *nobilitas*, and then only after a great struggle fought according to its own rules. That Cicero had the issue in mind in this context is suggested by a passage from the undelivered second action against Verres, which is quite direct.[83]

> I have not the same privileges as men of noble birth, who while sleeping still see the honors of our people laid at their feet; in this state I must live under far different conditions and according to a very different law. . . . We see with what jealousy, with what hatred, the virtue and industry of "new men" are regarded by certain nobles; that we have only to close our eyes for a moment to find ourselves caught in some trap; that if we leave them the smallest opening for any suspicion or charge, we suffer the wound immediately; we see that we must never relax our vigilance, that we must always labor. . . . There is hardly anyone of the nobles who looks kindly on our industry; by no services that we render them can we capture their goodwill; they withhold from us their interest and sympathy as completely as if we and they were different breeds of men. (*In Ver.* 2.5.180–182)[84]

Operating under these circumstances, Cicero, who was certainly endowed with the necessary intellectual gifts, had managed to secure for himself some measure of reputation and esteem as well as election to two public offices by the time he approached the prosecution of Verres. Facing Hortensius in what would prove to be perhaps his most important triumph, Cicero had every right to expect recognition and acceptance from the *nobilitas*. Unqualified acceptance, however, was not forthcoming for the son of a Roman knight; Cicero, as he indicates in another passage from the second action against Verres, realized this fact as well as anyone might:

> There is the fact that your friendship, Hortensius, and the friendship of all men of rank and birth, is more freely avail-

able for this unprincipled rogue [i.e. Verres] than for any of us honest and honorable men. You hate the industry of "new men," you scorn their honesty, you contemn their sense of decency, you seek to thwart and suppress their abilities and their virtues: You love Verres. (*In Ver.* 2.3.7)[85]

These are words of anger, resentment, bitterness, and frustration that betray the lonely feeling of rejection, a feeling that haunted Cicero, at least intermittently, throughout his life.[86] Even at the height of his career, in the glory of his consulship, this greatest parvenu of the Republic was never fully welcomed into the circle of the *nobilitas*. This rejection, always recognized but never accepted by Cicero, certainly provides the psychological motivation for many of his actions[87] and accounts for the poignant, if ultimately futile struggle of a gifted and very patriotic man striving to win a recognition from his peers that, owing to its intrinsic nature, was beyond his grasp even before the struggle had begun.

In the passages cited above, the rhetorical veneer wears quite thin, almost to a transparency, and Cicero's real feelings show through, as if he were speaking to his friend Atticus in a letter, and not to judges in a courtroom or the Roman public in general. Although he has won for himself by his work in the courts a reputation of some renown and has secured a measure of *dignitas* for his ethos, although he has projected the persona of a capable, confident, and well-prepared prosecutor, although Verres' crimes are so well-known that they have condemned him before his trial, the power and influence of his supporters, the *nobiles*, remain a force with which Cicero must reckon and a specter that never removes itself from his sight.

In a narrative (16–23) remarkable for its subtle yet effective methods of revealing the ethos of Verres, Verres' supporters, and himself, Cicero skillfully articulates the threat of the collusion of the *nobilitas* with Verres by means of their influence, protection, bribery, and intrigue. The story of the consular C. Curio's actions on the day Hortensius had been elected consul is aimed at arousing indignation at corruption of the courts and unscrupulous abuse of authority, as well as sympathy for Cicero's position. Direct quotation here and at other key points enlivens the narrative and imparts a sense of realism to the character. " 'I hereby inform you that, by today's elections, you have been acquitted' " (19),[88] Curio says assuredly to Verres. Cicero and other well-intentioned men of state are shocked and outraged:

Why, is the presence at Rome of all Sicily and its inhabitants, of all its businessmen, of all its public and private records—is all this, then, to count for nothing? No, not if the consul-elect will not have it so. What? Will the court have no regard for the charges, the testimony of the witnesses, the reputation of the Roman people? No; everything is to be steered by the hand of one powerful man. (20)[89]

After another comment in *oratio recta* by anonymous concerned citizens (*optimus quisque*) lamenting that Verres will surely be acquitted and that such acquittal means the loss of the law courts, Cicero reveals his own distress (21): "I did my best to pretend that I felt no uneasiness myself; I did my best to cover the anguish in my heart with the expression on my face and to conceal it with silence."[90] This frank confession of his fear and his courageous attempt to conceal it are calculated to evoke sympathy and support from the audience. We are made to feel his distress and empathize with it. In addition, even allowing for rhetorical hyperbole, it is instructive to note the power that the *auctoritas* of a consul might wield in such matters, even to the detriment of the Republic and the miscarriage of justice.

After a short interlude (21–23) describing the activities of Verres' bribery agents, which were aimed specifically at destroying Cicero's chance for office, Cicero returns to the sympathetic portrayal of his own ethos. The young lawyer finds himself in a predicament, torn between obligations that are, in some sense, conflicting.[91] The duty he owes to the Republic, his own canvass, and his own career seems now somehow juxtaposed and contrary to the service he owes to his fellow citizens, his clients the Sicilians, justice, and his own conscience:

Within the same short space of time I had to face more than one pressing anxiety. My election was upon me; and here, as in the trial, a great sum of money was fighting against me. The trial was approaching; and in this matter also those baskets of Sicilian gold were threatening me. I was deterred by concern for my election from giving my mind freely to the business of the trial; the trial prevented me from devoting my whole attention to my candidature; finally, there was no sense in my trying to intimidate the bribery agents, since I could see that they were aware that the conduct of this trial would tie my hands completely. (24)[92]

This is not the picture of a fearless hero who stands undaunted by any threat, but rather the believable portrait of a courageous young statesman, beset by real, human fears and emotions, who nevertheless is unwilling to fold under the pressure exerted by his powerful and unscrupulous enemies.

Once relieved of the anxieties of his canvass, Cicero turned all his attention to the trial, only to discover Verres' plan for delay (26–32). This narrative again provides ample scope for the development of ethos, first that of Verres, who in a long and detailed "speech" in *oratio recta* (29–30) rehearses his agenda for delay, then that of Cicero and Hortensius. Verres' plans for delaying the trial until circumstances would be more favorable to him presented an interesting rhetorical challenge to Cicero, whose objectives in the case seemed to work at cross purposes.[93] Having secured the opportunity to prosecute Verres, Cicero hoped to produce a literary masterpiece that displayed all of his abilities and would establish his reputation as a great artistic orator. Counter to this desire, however, was the necessity of quick, decisive action in order to resolve the case before Verres' plans could take effect. "The situation [was] a significant one for the course of Roman rhetorical history: oratory as a practical device of persuasion [was] in conflict with oratory as an artistic product or as self-expression of the orator."[94] In this instance, the need for persuasion won out, but Cicero cleverly capitalized on this oratorical sacrifice to enhance his own persona:

> If I shall spend upon my speech the full time allotted me by law, I shall reap the fruit of my labor, industry, and diligence; my conduct in this prosecution will show that no man in all history ever came into court more ready, more watchful, more prepared than I come now. But there is the gravest danger that, while I am thus reaping the credit for my industry, the man I am prosecuting will slip through my fingers. . . . The harvest of fame that might have been gathered by making a long continuous oration let me reserve for another occasion, and let me now prosecute the man by means of documents, witnesses, written statements, and official pronouncements both private and public. (32–33)[95]

Cicero has expended much time and effort in this speech to create a persona that appears to be aware and cautious of the dangers that threaten him, yet prepared, vigilant, and able to meet the challenge; to display an ethos possessed of enough experience and courage to deal with Verres and enough talent and confidence to challenge the authority and reputation of Hortensius. In an apostrophe to Hortensius (33–37), an extraordinary outburst that approaches the intense level of pathos, he presents this persona in its full dimensions:

> But now, since all this tyrannical domination of our courts delights you so much, and since there are men who find nothing shameful or disgusting in their own wantonness and vile reputations, but appear to challenge, as though of set purpose, the hatred and anger of the Roman people: I will declare boldly, that the burden I have shouldered may indeed be heavy and dangerous for myself, but is nevertheless such that my industry and my sinews may fitly strain to bear it. Since the whole of our poorer class is being oppressed by the wickedness and audacity of a few, and groaning under the infamy of our courts, I declare myself to these criminals as their enemy and their accuser, as their pertinacious, bitter, and unrelenting adversary. It is this that I choose, this that I claim. (35–36)[96]

This bold declaration of war against wicked, corrupt men like Verres presages the proclamations Cicero will make against the Catilinarians in a few years. The ethos of a Cicero near the height of his oratorical powers and gaining in reputation, influence, and dignity, has taken on flesh. Still at a decided disadvantage in terms of rank (aedile, versus Hortensius the consul) and therefore in terms of influence and power, Cicero, as we have seen him do elsewhere, converts his disadvantageous position to his benefit. By the very stress he places upon his inferior rank in relation to his adversary, he emphasizes his own aedileship and the magnitude of his actions in this case, and minimizes the influence of Hortensius:

> Hortensius will then be consul, endowed with supreme command and power, while I shall be an aedile, nothing much grander than an ordinary citizen: yet the thing that I now promise to do is of such a kind, so welcome and acceptable to the Roman people, that the consul himself must seem even less than a private citizen, if that were possible, when matched against me on this issue. (37)[97]

After the impassioned apostrophe to Hortensius, the emotionalism recedes. Cicero declares his plan of action (37–40), laments the terrible reputation that the extortion court possesses among the allies (40–42), and enlarges upon the theme first introduced in the opening lines of the speech: that Verres' trial is a divinely sent opportunity that will enable the senatorial order, by its conviction of Verres, to reestablish its dignity (42–50). Verres' ethos is still present as well as Cicero's, whose confidence seems to have reached its high-water mark:

> In the next place I declare to you, gentlemen, and to the Roman people, that if other evil-doers exist, I will, so help me God, sooner lose my life than lose the vigor and perseverance that will secure their punishment for their wickedness. (50)[98]

With that same sense of confidence and determination, he concludes his speech, first with a personal exhortation to M'. Glabrio, the praetor (51–52), then with a restatement of his own resolve to prevent delay and an outline of the methods he will employ to that end.

The *Actio Prima* of the *Verrines* is an extremely important speech for the study of ethos in Ciceronian oratory. Faced with the task of prosecution and the unusual threat of delay by Verres and his supporters, Cicero employs a rather atypical opening gambit for an extortion trial: he brings no formal charges, he adduces no real arguments to substantiate Verres' crimes. Rather, ethos provides the chief source of argumentative material, and we find long sections of biographical, that is, ethical narrative, calculated to portray Verres in an immoral and un-Roman light. The theme of Verres' prior condemnation by the court of humanity is important and recurrent (e.g., 2, 10, 15, 50).

The real protagonist of the speech, however, is Cicero, and the most interesting uses of ethos are those that center around his creation of a persona for himself that is important and influential enough to deal with Verres, confident and vigorous enough to challenge Hortensius, and, at the same time, strong and convincing enough to avoid alienating the senatorial jury. Although the speech may be unusual for the *actio prima* of a Roman extortion trial, in many ways it typifies the important role that ethos plays in Roman and Ciceronian oratory. Through the ethical narrative of his criminal actions, we are led, like the rest of the world, to despise and condemn Verres. We are made to realize the power that character endowed with the eloquence, reputation, and influence of an orator and consul like Hortensius could wield in the Roman social and political setting. We catch a glimpse of the bitterness and loneliness of Cicero the *novus homo*, seeking acceptance among the nobles; we can focus upon his dilemma and are made to sympathize with him as he struggles and succeeds to mold a persona that can counteract their inherent prejudices and win for itself a place of dignity, respect, and leverage in Roman society.

From other extant orations of this period many more examples could be cited that would corroborate the thesis that ethos plays an important and central role in Ciceronian oratory: for example, the portrait of the upright, honest, and brave governor Marcus Fonteius, assailed by lying, treacherous, and audacious Gauls;[99] or of the criminal cutthroat Oppianicus and the wanton Sassia, who, marked by an unnatural capacity for wickedness, violated nature's strongest bond, that between mother and child;[100] or the persona of Cicero himself, as he ascends the public dais for the first time, endowed now with a praetor's *auctoritas*, to expand upon the virtuous, authoritative, and felicitous character of Pompey.[101]

The pre-consular speeches that have been considered here display remarkably varied and artistic uses of ethos as a source of persuasion. Given the strong influence of character and heritage on Roman society, the ethos of clients and adversaries often becomes a kind of undergirding structure, a foundation upon which Cicero can build his case, using as bricks and mortar probabilities whose validity is measured by their consistency or inconsistency with the character presented. At other times ethos bolsters a rationally based argument or, crossing into the realm of pathos, sparks an appeal directed toward the emotions.[102]

Ethos is not restricted to one or two parts of the oration, but rather pervades its structure and often supplies the material for an excursus or digression, not strictly relevant to the case but certainly supplemental and supportive of it. The conventions of advocacy in Rome significantly expanded the realm of ethos and of opportunities for its artistic application. The Roman respect for an individual's rank, reputation, dignity, and authority thus became a special weapon for advocates and clients who were in possession of such *desiderata* and a considerable liability for those who lacked them. Cicero's response to this rhetorical challenge is particularly interesting. In the earliest speeches his strategy as a young, inexperienced beginner was to deal with his powerful and important opponents by frankly professing the unfair advantage they possessed, while projecting for himself the persona of an intelligent, capable champion of the downtrodden. Through clever manipulation, he worked to convert his disadvantageous situation to a position of strength.[103] As he grew in experience and reputation and successfully completed the *cursus honorum*, he began to wield with greater and greater force the power, dignity, authority, and reputation that he had earlier decried as unfair advantages in the courtroom. By the time of the consular orations, he could impose the weight of his *auctoritas* against almost all charges, to crush his adversaries.

# III

# THE CONSULAR SPEECHES

## *The Ethos of* Auctoritas *and the*
## *Persona of a Consul*

---

Great is the name, great the splendor, great the dignity, great the majesty of a consul. That greatness your narrow mind cannot comprehend nor your shallow nature recognize; your spiritless heart and feeble understanding cannot grasp it; nor can you, with your inexperience of prosperity, sustain a persona so eminent, so dignified, so august. (*In Pisonem* 24)

The year 63 B.C. marked the high point in Cicero's life and public career. His accession to the consulship, the final and highest step in the *cursus honorum*, and his subsequent disclosure of the Catilinarian conspiracy, which obliged him to exercise his consular *potestas* in an extraordinary and memorable way, would remain for him a source of pride, influence, and renown and provide for his enemies an almost continual source of irritation, annoyance, and grudging envy. Cicero had won, at least temporarily, his struggle for dignity, authority, influence, and reputation, even in the eyes of, or perhaps in the face of the *nobilitas*. He certainly had a right to be proud of his achievement, and he did not hesitate for a moment to assume the consular persona, a mask that, despite its unaccustomedness, seemed to fit quite comfortably.

Cicero's first official act as consul was to speak in opposition to the agrarian law proposed by Rullus. In his oration to the people, the consul projected this new dimension of his ethos and underlined the magnitude and uniqueness of his accomplishments. The comments Cicero makes concerning himself in the opening sections of the speech provide a convenient *principium* for our examination of the consular ethos.

With his election to the consulship—the first "new man" to be so honored in a very long time—the Roman people had broken the barrier of the *nobilitas* and opened the office to virtue (*De Leg. Ag.* 2.3).[1] Even more impressive than the fact of his election was the time at which he had secured it, having been selected at the youngest possible legal age, in "his own year," a feat no "new man" had ever accomplished (2.3). Still more glorious and illustrious than this, however, was the manner of his election, for he had been universally acclaimed by the Roman people (2.4).[2]

The exceptional qualities of Cicero's election to the consulship, rehearsed here at great length, further ennoble his ethos. But exceptions to the rule, although often glorious and remarkable, are not always welcome, especially to those who have established the rules. A consul who has been "created in the Campus, not in the cradle,"[3] must be especially diligent in guarding the Republic:

> Many serious thoughts occupy my mind, citizens, thoughts which leave me no share of rest day or night—above all, as regards maintaining the dignity of the consulship, a great and difficult task for anyone, but above all for myself, since no mistake of mine will meet with indulgence; if I am successful, scanty praise and that forced from the people is in prospect; if I am in doubt, I can see no trustworthy counsel, if I am in difficulty, no loyal support from the nobility. (*De Leg. Ag.* 2.5)[4]

We see here in more than a nascent state the persona that would emerge into full light with the eruption of the Catilinarian conspiracy: that of the proud, patriotic, and capable consul, whose time, talents, and thoughts were entirely consumed by his care for the Republic.

Cicero's accession to the consulship also meant, of course, the acquisition of a new oratorical weapon, consular prestige. By 63 the advocate had already secured for himself, by virtue of his hard work, his willingness to accept and plead many cases, and his important victories in those cases (especially over Hortensius in the Verrine affair), supremacy in the Roman courts. The addition of consular dignity and authority to his character was the crowning jewel of his *industria, virtus,* and reputation. Cicero understood fully the impact that consular prestige was capable of exerting in Roman society, politics, and especially in the courtroom, and he recognized the advantages it bestowed on its possessor— advantages that in his early career he had worked vigorously to neutralize when present in his adversaries. Now in possession of supreme *auctoritas*, Cicero would exploit, almost indiscriminately, those advantages in defense of his client and himself.

The consular speeches,[5] to be sure, are still marked by their reliance upon ethos to provide a source for persuasion, but now the character of the advocate plays an increasingly important role, stepping more and more often onto the stage, at times even completely overshadowing the ethos of his client. The rhetoric of advocacy is approached in new and interesting ways. At times the trial of a client seems to be, at least according to Cicero's perception, a trial of his own authority, dignity, and credibility. We are seldom, if ever, allowed to lose sight of his consular ethos, and often his proof is not based on any methodical presentation of the facts of the case or on effective refutation of the specific evidence against his clients, as much as it is on Cicero's reliance upon the consular persona's power and his insistence that the jury be persuaded by the weight of its influence.[6]

Throughout the years from his consulship to his exile and in the speeches delivered during those years, the armor of consular ethos provided an ever-present bulwark for Cicero and his clients. There was, however, an irreparable chink in that armor, of which Cicero himself was always aware and about which he had expressed his concern in his first consular address to the people: his lack of faithful counsel and loyal support from the nobility (*De Leg. Ag.* 2.5). As this chink widened, Cicero's vulnerability to the dangerous and ever-advancing threat of exile became increasingly more apparent. It is against this backdrop that the drama of the consular speeches unfolds.

## IN CATILINAM ORATIO SECUNDA
## AD POPULUM

Although this study is concerned primarily with the role of ethos in Cicero's judicial speeches, ethos, particularly that of the orator himself, plays an important part in political oratory. The statesman's persona, as well as the audience's perception of his disposition toward them, contributes essentially to the persuasiveness of his speech.[7] Cicero's *Catilinarian Orations* are important, not only for their character portraits of Catiline and his followers (calculated, of course, to arouse fear, hatred, and alienation in the hearts of the Roman people), but also for their portrayal of Cicero, the consul, who skillfully used this opportunity to promote his own ethos and increase his authority, glory, and dignity.

The second oration against Catiline, addressed to the people following the conspirator's flight from the city, is a biting invective in which Cicero aims at demonstrating to the Roman people that Catiline and his followers, by virtue of their debauched and un-Roman characters and their heinous deeds, have forfeited their rights of citizenship and their privilege of being called Roman. Set in contradistinction to their ethos is the character of the consul, who stands for and protects all things Roman.

The initial sections of the speech typify the portraits of the two parties that Cicero attempts to brand into the hearts and minds of the people, Catiline the monster, the fire-and-sword-brandishing pestilence, and Cicero the consul, who has driven him out.

> At long last, citizens, we have expelled Lucius Catilina, or, if you prefer, sent him off, or followed him on his way with our farewells as he left Rome of his own accord, raging with audacity, breathing crime, foully plotting the destruction of the fatherland, and threatening you and this city with fire and the sword. (*In Cat.* 2.1)[8]

Cicero quickly and deliberately characterizes the conspiracy as a war and Catiline as the enemy general (e.g., "this one true leader of this civil war"; "We shall now wage a just war with a public enemy"; "so fatal an enemy," 3; "how formidable an enemy I consider him to be," 4). A complementary portrayal of Cicero will soon emerge.

After explaining his reasons for not arresting Catiline before he had left the city (3–4), Cicero launches a full-scale invective against him and his followers (5–11). The assumption, of course, is that crime and all manner of wicked deeds can issue only from such abominable characters; one's ethos accounts for one's actions.

> What evil deed or crime can be imagined or thought which that man has not already conceived? What poisoner in the whole of Italy, what gladiator, what bandit, what assassin, what parricide, what forger of wills, what cheat, what glutton, what spendthrift, what adulterer, what whore, what corrupter of youth, what rogue, what abandoned character can be found who does not admit to having lived on the most intimate terms with Catiline? (7)[9]

Inserting this invective at this point in the speech provides an argument based on character, marshaled to support Cicero's decision for allowing Catiline to leave the city in the hope that the monster might take with him all the dregs of his conspiracy: "O fortunate Republic to have baled out this bilge-water of the city!"

(7; cf. 10). Cicero crowns the familiar picture of Catiline,[10] able to endure in animal-like fashion cold, hunger, thirst, and lack of sleep (9), with a description of his perversion of the Roman virtues of *industria* and *virtus*: Catiline has harnessed these virtues not for the benefit of the state or his own good reputation, but rather for the exercise of his lust and boldness.

It will continue to be Cicero's objective in this speech to draw a sharp distinction between Catiline and his satellites and the loyal supporters of Rome. This task is, of course, complicated by the fact that despite his treachery Catiline nevertheless possesses Roman citizenship, the rank of a senator, and a noble heritage. Cicero's rhetorical challenge thus lay in convincing the people and Senate of Rome that fellow citizens, many of whom were in possession of considerable *gratia* and *existimatio*, had, owing to their depraved, un-Roman characters and criminal actions, relinquished their claim to *civitas* and had become enemies of the state. As a result, passages based on character, comparing the brave, prudent, and watchful patriots with the depraved and disgusting Catilinarians, perform an important function:

> But who can bear this—that cowards should hatch plots against brave men, fools against the wise, drunks against the sober, sluggards against the wakeful? Reclining at their banquets, embracing their whores, stupefied by wine, stuffed with food, crowned with garlands, reeking with unguents, enfeebled by debauchery, they belch out in their conversation the slaughter of loyal citizens and the burning of the city. (10)[11]

The orator concludes this portion of the speech with an important passage (11) that reiterates that the conspiracy is, in fact, a war (cf. 1) and proclaims boldly that he himself will assume the generalship for this war:

> There is no foreign nation left for us to fear, no king able to make war on the Roman people. Peace reigns abroad by land and sea thanks to the valor of one man. Civil war remains; within are plots, within is danger, within is the enemy. The battles we must fight are against luxury, madness, and crime. I offer myself, citizens, as your leader for this war; I accept the enmity of the wicked; I shall find a way to cure what can be cured; what needs excising, I shall not allow to remain to destroy the state. And so let these men either go forth or keep the peace; if they remain in Rome and in the same mind, let them expect what they deserve. (11)[12]

Particularly interesting here is Cicero's allusion to Pompey, the great general who, by his virtue in war, had established peace abroad. By his subsequent self-declaration as general (*dux*) of this domestic war, Cicero not only sets himself up as the protagonist of the drama and the foil to Catiline but, more importantly, invites comparison with Pompey. These themes become more explicit both in this speech and in others that deal with the conspiracy. The consular persona has begun to assume a new feature.

In the next part of the speech (12–16), Cicero answers the second charge that he suspects might be leveled against him: that he had driven Catiline into exile unjustly. Cicero's refutation is based on the premises that one who has voluntarily gone to war cannot have been driven into exile (cf., e.g., 14) and that one who by his character and deeds has declared himself an enemy (*hostis*) cannot rightly be considered a citizen (cf., e.g., 12). Martial and military language heavily colors this passage (e.g., 13, 14), as Cicero continually reminds the people of the bellicose nature of the conflict.

Cicero's own ethos likewise emerges. He has discovered what all people in positions of responsibility discover, that the role of leader can be a lonely and frustrating part to play: "Oh, wretched the lot of those who administer the state, and even of those who save it!" (14).[13] If Catiline were suddenly and unexpectedly to abandon his plans for this criminal war, Cicero, for taking the necessary steps to save the Republic, would come off looking like a tyrant. Nevertheless, he is willing to sacrifice his own feelings and endure this tempest of hatred for the safety of the Roman people: "Citizens, it is worth my enduring the storm of this undeserved and unfounded hatred, provided only that you are spared the horror and danger of civil war" (15).[14]

The consul next turns from the enemy Catiline to a discussion of all the enemies who have remained behind in the city (17–25). Like the invective that followed Cicero's justification for allowing Catiline to leave the city, this passage, also based primarily on ethos, balances Cicero's refutation of the idea that the conspirator's exile is unjust. He divides the Catilinarians into six groups, draws a short character-sketch of each, and then offers his own analysis and advice. In this way we are able to see not only the ethos of each group but also Cicero's consular ethos; we can contrast its controlled, sane, and salutary advice with the extravagant, deranged, and destructive plans of the enemies of the state. The sixth group, Catiline's very own, last in order as well as in character (22), is drawn most vividly:

These are the men you see with their carefully combed hair, sleek with oil, some unbearded, others with shaggy beards, with tunics down to their ankles and wrists, and wearing frocks not togas. All the industry of their lives and all the labor of their waking hours are devoted to banquets that last till dawn. In this herd are all the gamblers, all the adulterers, all the filthy-minded lechers. These boys, so dainty and effeminate, have learned not only to love and to be loved, not only to dance and sing, but also to brandish daggers and sprinkle poison. (23)[15]

These Catilinarians have denied their *Romanitas* both in appearance (they no longer wear togas),[16] and in their perversion of the Roman virtues of *industria* and *labor*. This accusation is designed to make it easier for the Roman people to disassociate themselves from Catiline and his followers, despite their status as fellow-citizens.

We have seen in other contexts Cicero's attempt to paint the characters of a speech in the sharply contrasting colors of black and white, to reduce a judicial dispute to the simple juxtaposition of two antipathetic characters or ways of life, one honorable, upright, in keeping with the *mos maiorum*, the other its un-Roman antithesis.[17] In this instance Cicero has aimed his entire speech at creating such a gulf between the Roman state and Catiline and his followers; grey hues, so many of which in reality colored the Catilinarian affair, scarcely enter the picture. The contrast is nowhere more forcefully expressed than in the conclusion to this part of the speech:

On our side fights modesty, on theirs shamelessness; on our side morality, on theirs debauchery; on ours good faith, on theirs deceit; on ours respect for right, on theirs crime; on ours steadfastness, on theirs madness; on ours honor, on theirs disgrace; on ours self-control, on theirs a surrender to passion; in short, justice, temperance, fortitude, prudence, all the virtues, contend with injustice, extravagance, cowardice, folly, all the vices. In a word, abundance fights against poverty, incorrupt principles against corrupt, sanity against insanity, well-founded hope against general desperation. (25)[18]

In the peroration to the speech (26–29) Cicero's ethos again emerges, the provident consul, who has taken care for the protection of his fellow citizens and the city (26) and is prepared, if necessary, to die for them (27). The major themes of the speech are likewise repeated. Cicero reminds the people that the Catilinarians, though born citizens, are now enemies (27), that it is a war which is being waged by those enemies against the state, and that he has proclaimed himself general to do battle against them in that war. In this last regard, Cicero's words are extraordinary:

> And all these things will be so done, citizens, that the most important things will be administered with the least disturbance, the greatest perils will be averted without any tumult, and a rebellion and a civil war, the greatest and most cruel within the memory of man, will be suppressed by me alone, a leader and commander dressed in the garb of peace (*togatus dux et imperator*). (28)[19]

Even granting room for rhetorical hyperbole, this statement is remarkable. Cicero, who had seen action in the Social War and witnessed the bloodbath of the Marian and Sullan regimes, certainly could not have seriously maintained that the Catilinarian conspiracy was "the greatest domestic war within the memory of man."[20] What he did recognize, however, was the great opportunity that the conspiracy offered to him for bolstering his ethos and adding a new dimension to his consular persona.

In Republican Rome a man generally won recognition, glory, and a reputation in one of a limited number of ways: he might inherit his reputation through a noble family and enhance it by his personal character and his association with other great men; he might enter upon a military career and distinguish himself as a soldier; or he might, by cultivating his eloquence, build a name for himself in the courts.[21] Though Cicero had chosen the course of eloquence, at which he was indeed very successful, military glory seems to have always attracted him.[22] In this second speech against Catiline, Cicero initiates a theme that will appear in other speeches concerned with the Catilinarian affair, that of the *dux* or *imperator togatus*, "a general dressed in the toga," that is, in the garb of peace.

The mention of *dux* in this passage immediately calls to mind a statement earlier in the speech (11) in which Cicero, for the first time, declared himself to the people as leader (*dux*) in this domestic war, implying a comparison of his role with that of Pompey, who had pacified on land and sea all external enemies. Important in the present passage is the use of the adjective *togatus* with *dux* and *imperator*. Cicero certainly realized the opportunities that a military command offered for amassing glory, fame, and reputation, and he seems to have perceived his lack of a military reputation as a deficiency or liability to his ethos, particularly in comparison with Pompey. By creating the role of a *dux* or *imperator togatus* for himself, a "civilian general," if you will, Cicero can share in the glory of a kind of military command and victory but still maintain the persona of the man of peace who, in favorable contrast to those men of war who resort to violence in order to solve the political problems of Rome, is able to save the state without recourse to arms.[23]

This persona of the *imperator togatus* is certainly prominent in subsequent speeches.[24] Perhaps the most instructive passage concerning this theme is found in the third oration against Catiline, also addressed to the people:

> In return for these great services, citizens, I shall ask from you no reward for my courage, no signal mark of distinction, no monument of praise except the eternal memory of this day. In your hearts I wish all my triumphs, all decorations of honor, the monuments of glory, the insignia of praise to be founded and set up. . . . I know that the same length of days—and may it be eternal—has been destined for the safety of Rome and for the memory of my consulship and that in this Republic there have arisen at one time two men, one of whom has fixed the boundaries of your empire not by the limits of the earth, but by the limits of heaven, and one who has preserved the home and seat of this empire. (26)[25]

The persona of the *imperator* is unmistakable. The triumphs, honor, glory, and praise of a *dux togatus* may be of a different sort, celebrated only in the hearts of the people, but they are triumphs, honor, glory, and praise just the same. Comparison with Pompey, hinted at in the second oration, Cicero here makes explicit and addresses the great general as an equal.[26]

Even more forceful is a statement in the final Catilinarian (4.21) where Cicero identifies his achievement with the feats of other great Roman heroes, all of whom distinguished themselves on the field of battle:

> I acknowledge the renown of that Scipio whose skill and valor compelled Hannibal to leave Italy and return to Africa; the signal fame of that other Africanus who destroyed two cities of our greatest enemies, the cities of Carthage and Numantia;

the distinction of that Paulus whose triumph was adorned by Perses, once the most powerful and noble of kings; the eternal glory of Marius, who twice freed Italy from siege and the fear of enslavement; and greater than all these, Pompey, whose deeds and virtues are limited only by those regions and boundaries that confine the course of the sun. There will certainly be some place for my fame amid the praise of these men, unless perhaps it is a greater thing to open up provinces for ourselves to which we may go forth than to take care that those who have gone out to them have a homeland to which they may return from their victories.[27]

Identification with former great generals imparts weight and authority to Cicero's own ethos and credence to his newly created role as *imperator togatus*. On a deeper level the equation of himself with Pompey is perhaps the manifestation of Cicero's current political philosophy, which called for an alliance between the *imperator militaris* and the *imperator togatus*, the soldier and the statesman, the Scipio and the Laelius.[28]

In pragmatic terms, the ethos of a consul was by its very nature a powerful source for persuasion in Republican Rome. More powerful still was the ethos of a consular *imperator*. Cicero cleverly seized the opportunity presented to him by the Catilinarian conspiracy to add to his role as consul the persona of the *imperator togatus*, whose achievements equaled, and in Cicero's eyes, even surpassed those of the greatest *imperator militaris*, Pompey. That this claim was more than mere Ciceronian rodomontade is perhaps most clearly indicated by Pompey's cool reception of Cicero's accomplishments and self-appointed role as civilian general of the Republic. Cicero, *imperator togatus*, had, at least in this battle, outflanked Pompey, *imperator militaris*.[29]

## PRO L. MURENA

While still embroiled in the Catilinarian affair, Cicero met a rhetorical challenge that forced him to assume a rather different persona: his defense of the consul-elect, L. Murena.[30] Not only did the timing of the trial complicate matters,[31] but the prestigious and powerful characters of the prosecutors, Servius Sulpicius and Marcus Cato, by virtue of their authority and reputations, presented a formidable obstacle to Cicero's defense. Bound to both by the strong bonds of *amicitia*, Cicero somehow had to neutralize their authority without alienating their goodwill toward him. The speech that resulted is almost entirely dependent upon ethos for its source of argumentative material and, for this reason, comes closest of all Ciceronian speeches to the native Latin oratorical tradition that appears to have valued the character of the litigants more highly than the facts in establishing one's case.[32] In addition to relying so heavily on aspects of character, Cicero continually sets them in a typical and traditional Roman context: for example, the importance of political office; traditional Roman methods for obtaining such office; Roman views of *auctoritas*; the responsibilities of clients and patrons. Such treatment lends valuable insight into the Roman conception of ethos and corroborates our thesis concerning the importance and centrality of character in Roman society in general and in Ciceronian oratory in particular.

The *exordium* (1–10) presents the chief characters of the speech—Cicero, Murena, Cato, and Sulpicius—but it stresses Cicero's ethos in relationship to the others involved in the case. Cicero recasts the consul's *rogationis carmen*, pronounced on the day of Murena's election, as a plea for peace, calm, tranquility, and harmony, all of which can be insured through Murena's acquittal (1–2). Of course, the supreme authority of the consulship, by its very presence, imparts great persuasive weight to Murena's defense, and Cicero quickly stresses his role in this regard: a consul now pleads for a consul (3). With this, Cicero introduces an important character-bond between himself and Murena, which will resonate throughout the speech.

A rather lengthy and intricate *apologia pro se* follows, presenting Cicero's justification for defending Murena first to Cato (3–6) and then to Sulpicius (7–10). Cato seems to have realized the advantage that consular prestige might contribute to Murena's defense; but nothing could be more appropriate, Cicero maintains, than for a consul to be defended by a consul (3). Nor does this action compromise Cicero's previous actions against electoral corruption, for in Murena's case there has been no violation of the law (5). Finally, far from revealing any inconsistency or fickleness in his character, Cicero's defense of Murena emphasizes his natural inclination toward *lenitas* and *misericordia*:

I have always willingly played the part of leniency and mercy which Nature herself taught me; I have not been eager to assume the mask of sternness and severity. But when I had it thrust upon me by the Republic, I wore it as the majesty of this office demanded at the time of the citizens' supreme peril. (6)[33]

Cicero's stress on *misericordia* and *humanitas* not only serves to stir goodwill in the minds of the jury, but establishes very early in the speech his own character as a contrasting foil to Cato's ethos, itself marked by an unbending Stoic rigidity that Cicero will later attack.[34]

He next (7–10) turns to Sulpicius' charge that he had, by taking up Murena's defense, violated the bonds of friendship (*amicitia*). Cicero's loyalty and support of Sulpicius during his campaign could not be questioned then, nor should it be doubted at the present. However, a greater *officium*, a higher moral obligation now demands his attention: the defense of another friend *in periculo*.[35] To abandon Murena in such straits *would* be a violation of *amicitia*, and would brand Cicero with the stigma of arrogance and cruelty (8). But Cicero promises Sulpicius that owing to their bond of friendship, he will temper his pleading and treat him as he would his own brother (10).

This rather long and somewhat unorthodox *exordium* has certainly worked to Cicero's advantage. He has managed to show both the political and personal sides of his ethos in a favorable light. The dutiful, concerned consul, who has doffed his persona of severity in favor of one of *humanitas*, bound by high moral obligation but ever so concerned to maintain his *fides* and *constantia*, cannot have failed to stir goodwill in the hearts of his audience, even at the outset of the speech.

A brief *partitio* (11) vividly demonstrates the importance of character for the Romans and the regard that they held for proof based on ethos.[36] The prosecution had divided the case into three parts: (1) criticism of Murena's life (*reprehensio vitae*), (2) discussion of his merits for the consulship (*contentio dignitatis*), and (3) the allegation of bribery (*crimen ambitus*). To a modern audience, the last charge, the allegation of bribery, would seem the only relevant one and should, on that account, receive the central focus of the speech. According to Cicero, however, the first topic ought to be most telling: "Of these three, the first, which should have been most weighty, was so feeble and trivial that a sort of convention rather than any true ground for abuse compelled the prosecution to say something about the life of Lucius Murena" (11).[37] We have seen in another context Cicero's insistence upon character as the chief source of proof in regard to a particular crime.[38] In this speech the sentiment expressed at this point is certainly reflected in his subsequent treatment of the defense.

By emphasizing the prosecution's summary treatment of the *rep-*

*rehensio vitae*, Cicero indicates, of course, that it has no grounds upon which to attack Murena, and this is the stance he firmly assumes in this part of the speech (11–14). In short order he dismisses charges against Murena's behavior in Asia during the Mithridatic War of 83–81, and also Cato's accusation that Murena was a dancer. Cicero treats the latter issue almost contemptuously; the tone is ironic, almost mock-serious.[39] By the prosecution's tacit admission that Murena's character is spotless, the foundations of Cicero's defense have been laid.

> Nothing, then, can be said against the life of Lucius Murena, nothing at all, I say, gentlemen. My defense of the consul-designate is that no deceit, no greed, no treachery, no cruelty, no intemperate language can be alleged against him in his entire life. Excellent! The foundations of his defense have been laid. Not yet our praises, which I shall later employ, but almost the admissions of his prosecutors prove this to be a good and honorable man whom we are defending. (14)[40]

The *contentio dignitatis* (15–31) is noteworthy for its considerable length and its clever manipulation of ethos as a source for argumentation. Sulpicius, boasting his patrician roots and noble status, apparently had alleged that his own defeat and the victory of Murena, a man of lower social standing, over him was in itself grounds for suspicion of *ambitus*.[41] That such an argument could be made in a court of law indicates again the importance that heritage and rank, important elements of one's ethos, exerted in first-century Republican Rome.[42]

Cicero dismisses Sulpicius' distinction between patricians and plebeians as an "anachronistic class-consciousness"[43] but treats his claim to nobility in a more clever manner. Although Sulpicius' nobility is undeniable, it is the sort, because of the antiquity of its source, that is more familiar to historians. Furthermore, because his father was of equestrian rank and because Sulpicius' *virtus* and *industria* have shone so brilliantly during his career, Cicero has always tended to consider Sulpicius a fellow *novus homo*!

> I have for this reason always included you in my own company because, although you were the son of a Roman knight, by your character and industry you made good your claim to the highest distinction. (16)[44]

Through a "perverse kind of rhetoric of advocacy,"[45] Cicero has identified himself with his legal adversary, endowed him with the honorable qualities of a "new man," and thereby reduced him from a high social status and category of *dignitas*, that of a patrician possessing *nobilitas*, to the lower status of an equestrian-born *novus homo*. As A. D. Leeman comments, "the undeserving Sulpicius must have been furious at this stage, and must have wondered if Cicero's 'brotherly treatment' amounted to [this]."[46]

Cicero now turns to a consideration of the careers of Sulpicius and Murena. In playing down Sulpicius' priority of election to the quaestorship (18), Cicero certainly appears to have changed his own tune about such matters,[47] yet his reference to Sulpicius' mention of the *renuntiatio* twice in this *contentio dignitatis* (cf. 35), and his efforts at explaining the situation, reveal how very important such matters really were to the Romans.

Ethos also plays an important role in this portion of the speech, particularly in the ensuing comparison of professions (19–30). Cicero employs the methods of stock character-portrayal in his analysis. By casting him in the mold of the legal-minded, pettifogging jurisconsult, Cicero destroys Sulpicius' case with a brilliant parody of the law and the lawyer. Murena, despite a rather modest military career, is shown favorably as a Roman general and statesman. The vivid and spirited antithesis that highlights the comparison of occupations captures well the tone of this portion of the speech:

> You are awake late at night to give opinions to your clients, he to arrive early with his army to its objective; you are woken by the call of cocks, he by the call of trumpets; you draw up a form of proceedings, he a line of battle; you protect your clients against surprise, he his cities or camps; he understands and knows how to keep off the enemy's forces, you rain water; he has been engaged in extending the boundaries of our empire, you in regulating the fences of your clients. (22)[48]

Continuing in the same vein, Cicero ridicules both the triviality and literalness of the law and its ritualistic formulae (25–27). Veiled references are made to his own character and career in this part of the speech as he establishes oratory as the second best road to the consulship: "It is not surprising that even men who are not nobles have often reached the consulship because they were good orators . . . " (24).[49] Indeed, most jurisconsults had originally aspired to become orators but, unable to achieve this goal, slid down to the study of the law (29). In any case, all civil, peacetime activities, including those of both Sulpicius and Cicero, depend upon the tutelage and protection of military prowess (22).

Again Cicero identifies himself and his lot with Sulpicius and his position. Under such circumstances they must admit Murena's superiority:

> Let the Forum give way to the camp, peace to war, the pen to the sword, shade to the heat of the sun; in short, concede first place in the state to that profession which has made the state first of all states. (30)[50]

Throughout the *contentio dignitatis* Cicero employs a method of ethical argumentation that appears, from all indications, to be uniquely Roman: that of portraying the *accusator* as an *amicus*.[51] We have seen a variation of this tactic in Cicero's treatment of Caecilius in the *Divinatio*, and it occurs in other of his speeches. Despite various circumstances, three elements recur: (1) the *patronus*, Cicero, identifies the *accusator* as a friend or connection; (2) he points out to the prosecutor some action, habit, or circumstance that both men have in common; and finally, (3) he distinguishes between the ways in which he and the *accusator* partake in this similarity, he in a good, beneficial, or adept way, his opponent in a way that is bad, malicious, or inept.[52] Cicero's friendly relationship with Sulpicius has been emphasized throughout the speech (cf., e.g., 7, 10). In the *contentio dignitatis* we have seen Cicero identify himself with Sulpicius as two creatures of the Forum (21, 22). The distinction, however, that works to Cicero's advantage is that his labor in the Forum has been oratory, a legitimate path to the consulship (cf. 30), whereas Sulpicius' work has been the civil law, a vocation whose electoral benefits cannot compare with oratory's, not to mention those of the military. "Consular dignity has never belonged to that profession of yours, which consisted wholly of imaginary and fictitious details, and popular favor even less" (28).[53]

Cicero employs the same tactic in the closing sections of the *contentio dignitatis* (43–53), where he attempts to explain Sulpicius' failure at the polls.[54] The common ground here is, embarrassingly, Sulpicius' campaign for the consulship, which Cicero had supported (43). That Cicero had been a successful candidate for the consulship, and Sulpicius had not, provides the point of distinction between the friends. This difference allows the *patronus* to assume the role of the experienced politician, who can then instruct his friend on the reasons for his failure. Conveniently forgetting his own actions in the Verrine prosecution and the favorable persona that those actions enabled him to project, Cicero attributes his friend's failure to the distraction caused by his prosecution of Murena:

> I repeatedly told you, Servius, that you did not know how to conduct a campaign for the consulship, and I was always telling you that the spirit and energy that you brought to all you said and did made you look to me more like a brave prosecutor than an astute candidate. (43)[55]

The orator has cunningly transformed his embarrasssing situation into a position of strength, underlining the confidence, foresight, and political savvy of his own ethos while emphasizing Sulpicius' "blunder."

The character of Catiline enters to deal the final blow to Sulpicius and his political hopes:

> But still, Servius, what sort of hatchet-blow do you think you struck at your campaign, when you frightened the Roman people so badly that they feared that Catiline would be elected consul while you were preparing for your prosecution but giving up and utterly abandoning your own campaign? (48)[56]

The subsequent characterizations of Catiline (48–53; e.g., "The face of that man full of frenzy, his eyes full of wickedness, his speech full of arrogance," 49) are calculated, of course, to send a shiver down the spines of Cicero's audience, to emphasize his own courageous actions, illustrate Sulpicius' lack of appreciation of the situation, and underscore Murena's readiness to supplant Cicero. The Catilinarian threat, mentioned directly here for the first time, is an important subject to which the orator will return.

The third portion of Cicero's defense, *de ambitus criminibus* (54–77), contains Cicero's answer to Cato, an answer that does its best to avoid the formal charges by dwelling upon Cato's ethos, characterized in terms of its strict adherence to Stoic doctrine. The importance Cicero attaches to Cato's presence is instructive and indicative of the influence and power that an ethos endowed with *auctoritas, dignitas,* and *existimatio* could wield in a Roman court of law. According to Cicero, Cato stands as the foundation of the prosecution, whose authority he fears more than the actual charge (58). He is likened to P. Africanus and to his ancestor, M. Cato, whose opponents, even though guilty of the charges, were spared by the Roman people, who thought it unfair for men to be crushed by the weight of such overwhelming influence, regardless of guilt or innocence (58). It would have been neither practical nor efficacious, of course, for Cicero to plead such a line of defense openly, but by dwelling on the point and illustrating it with stories, he plants the suggestion in the minds of the jury to encourage a similar reaction on their part. Certainly his brief manifesto on principles of advocacy, which seems in fact to describe Cicero's own methods throughout his career, points in that direction:

> I do not believe that a prosecutor should bring to court overweening power, an excessive force, extraordinary authority, or too much influence. Let all these assets be used to deliver the innocent, protect the weak, and help those in trouble; for the trial and destruction of fellow citizens, let them be rejected. (59)[57]

To undermine the ethos and authority of Cato by traditional methods—invective, for example—was, Cicero knew, out of the question. The *virtus* of such a man, his embodiment of principles for which the state and the *mos maiorum* stood, prevented any such attack (cf. 60). But Cicero knew as well as anyone that a man's greatest source of strength can very often also be his greatest source of weakness, and that often only a fine line separates virtue and vice. Cato's philosophical convictions provided Cicero with the perfect arena. As the informing principles of Cato's life, Stoic teachings accounted for his virtuous conduct and revered reputation. When taken out of context, dissected, and exaggerated, Stoic virtues and their chief exponent become caricatures at which, despite all their value, we (and even the Romans) can only chuckle.

Cicero, in contrast, appears as the humane counselor whose *lenitas* and *humanitas* mark a more reasonable, less pedantic approach to life (cf. 60, 63). Cato, he counsels, would do well to consider the teachings of other philosophers (Plato and Aristotle, for example) whose beliefs are a little more moderate, a little more merciful (63–64). Even his famous ancestor would provide an excellent model for imitation in this regard:

> Do you think that anyone was more kind, more sociable, more inclined in every way to accommodate his fellow men than Cato, your great-grandfather? When you spoke with truth and conviction of his noble virtue, you said that you had an example to imitate in your own family. (66)[58]

This ironic characterization of the old Censor must have proved quite novel and very humorous to Cicero's audience as well as embarrassing enough to the inflexible younger Cato to have prompted his famous remark, "Gentlemen, what an amusing consul we have!"[59]

At section 67 Cicero finally turns to a refutation of the specific charges, only to return to Cato and his rigid creed in 74–77. The defensive stance is denial of the fact (*constitutio coniecturalis*), the normal line in a case of *ambitus*.[60] But by suggesting that Murena's friends were practicing acceptable and praiseworthy liberality, not criminal bribery, Cicero slyly introduces a second *status, constitutio definitiva*, which was on rare opportunities admissible in a case of *ambitus*.

In the final part of the speech preceding the peroration (78–85), Cicero employs yet another defensive stance, *constitutio iuridicialis* (*generalis*), arguing that the acquittal of Murena is no longer demanded by virtue of his innocence of the charge of *ambitus*, but rather by the danger of beginning the new year with only one consul to oppose Catiline (80).[61] In certain respects, this portion of the oration can be considered an extension of the *probatio*; however, its position in the disposition of the speech, following the completion of Cicero's announced partition of topics, its "digressive" introduction of a new line of defense, its reliance on ethos, its attempt to expand the case to universal proportions, and its heightened emotional pitch recall the characteristics of the *ethica digressio*.

Turning from the characters and undermined *auctoritas* of Sulpicius and Cato to his own ethos and consular authority, Cicero addresses the jury:

> What I am doing, gentlemen, I am not only doing for the sake of the friendship and dignity of Lucius Murena, but also, as I emphatically declare and call upon you all to bear me witness, for the sake of peace, quiet, unity, liberty, our preservation, in short the very lives of us all. Listen, gentlemen, listen to a consul—I shall not claim too much but this much I shall say—to a consul who spends all his days and nights thinking about the Republic! (78)[62]

The emphatic vocatives, the dramatic repetition of the imperatives, and the appeal to consular authority set a tone more akin to peroration than proof. A broadening of the base of appeal from particular to universal terms, one of Cicero's foremost talents, is evident. The specter of Catiline rears its head, as the theme of internal war, so prevalent in the *Catilinarians*,[63] here graphically returns: "The Trojan Horse is within, within our walls, I say; but never while I am consul will you be surprised in your sleep" (78).[64] The vigilant consul Cicero has checked the monster at every turn. But his office is coming to an end; a consul like Murena is needed to carry on his work (80).

Cicero next shifts back to the ethos of M. Cato (81–83). No longer the stern, severe, narrow-minded Stoic, the butt of Cicero's wit, Cato is here depicted as the dedicated tribune-elect, whose tribunician power stands greatly threatened by the spreading contagion. Cicero has cleverly linked Cato's well-being and effectiveness as tribune with the salvation of the state and made these conditions both contingent upon the possibility of there being two consuls for 62, a possibility made reality by the acquittal of Murena. Thus Cicero makes Cato become Murena's ally in the preservation of the Republic:

In such important and dangerous times as these it is the the duty of a man like you, Marcus Cato, born in my view to serve your fatherland more than yourself, to understand what is going on, to retain as your helper, defender, and ally in the service of the Republic, not a self-seeking consul, but—and this is the present situation's demand—a consul suited by his position to embrace peace, by his professional skill to wage war, by his spirit and experience to perform any task you like. (83)[65]

In the final sections of this excursus (83–85) Cicero again addresses the jury. The ethos of Catiline and his conspiracy looms large. If the villain himself had a vote in this trial, he would cast it in condemnation of Murena. By this statement Cicero poses a dilemma to the judges: a vote for condemnation is a vote in support of Catiline. As he was the consul who thwarted Catiline's first assault, Cicero's ethos and his words in this regard carry great persuasive weight. Added to this is the flame that he must have ignited in the hearts of his audience by his vivid description of the encroaching enemy:

The enemy is not at the Anio—which seemed the most hopeless moment in the Punic War—but in the city, in the Forum—immortal gods! I cannot say it without a groan!—there are even some in that shrine of the Republic, yes, in the very senate-house there are some enemy. (84)[66]

Cicero's eloquence is irrepressible. Just as the word "enemy" (hostis) frames and encompasses the sentence, so does an enemy more frightening than the Carthaginian at the Anio encompass

Rome. The anaphora of "in" emphasizes Catiline's infiltration; with each occurrence, he stalks closer to Rome until he is finally in the "shrine of the state, the very senate-house." Cicero, the *dux togatus* (84), will lay plans to smash this enemy, but Murena will have to carry them out. The emphasis on the ethos of Catiline and his company is somewhat remarkable in that Cicero has here extended the scope of his ethical examination to a character totally unconnected with the actual charge (*ambitus*). Nevertheless, the ethos of Catiline and his band is essential for the effective presentation of the major point of the digression, that the threat posed by such an ethos demands Murena's presence and vigilance, and therefore his acquittal.

Cicero continues the high level of emotionalism begun in the digression into the peroration (86–90), which in essence comprises a *commiseratio* on behalf of Murena. Cicero's consular ethos is present (86, 90), particularly at the conclusion of the speech. In an echo of the beginning of the oration, one consul pleads for another consul, the former wielding his *auctoritas* in defense of the latter's superlative character:

> If my commendation carries any weight or my support any authority, I, a consul, commend him, a consul, to you with the promise and the guarantee that he will be most eager for peace, most zealous in the support of loyal citizens, most active in the suppression of rebellion, most brave in war, most hostile to this conspiracy which is now rocking the foundations of the Republic. (90)[67]

The *Pro Murena* is an extremely important speech for the study of ethos in Ciceronian oratory, both in its method and in its matter. Cicero's method is based almost exclusively on argumentation found in ethos. Murena's own life and career, his *contentio dignitatis* with Sulpicius, the parody of the jurisconsult and his trade, the undermining of Cato's authoritative character, and the portrayal of Cicero, the vigilant consul, and Catiline, the insidious enemy, all find their roots and their source for material in ethos. More interesting and important than the material that provides the building blocks for Cicero's ethical constructs is, perhaps, the valuable information that this speech reveals about the Roman conception of ethos—which in turn corroborates our major theses.

We see, on the grand scale, a speech constructed almost entirely on the basis of ethos. We are told that a *reprehensio vitae* should be the most important element in such a case; we can see in the *contentio dignitatis* just how important to the Romans were the considerations of birth, rank, profession, possession of dignity, and even priority of election. The power of Cato's authority, the respect with which Cicero approached it, and the amount of caution with which he laboriously dealt with it illustrate the great role it and virtues like it—*dignitas, gratia, existimatio*—played, even in Cicero's day. Cicero's consular ethos backing the defense, and the menacing character of Catiline stalking close to the heart of the Capitol, added just enough weight to tip the balance of Justice; Murena served Rome as consul in 62.

## PRO P. SULLA

The glory of his consulship and of the Nones of December was short-lived for the *imperator togatus*. Only a few days after a public thanksgiving had been decreed in his honor and Cato himself had hailed him as *Pater Patriae*, Cicero felt the sting of *invidia* and experienced an attack on his glory and dignity by his enemies. Upon laying down his office on 31 December, he was prevented by the tribune Metellus Nepos from addressing the people in customary fashion. Forced to confine himself to the oath that he had faithfully performed the duties of the consulship, Cicero made the best of the situation, swearing that by his efforts alone the city and the state had been saved. The people thunderously confirmed his oath, and Cicero had, for the time being, dispelled the clouds of disgrace.[68] But these clouds were only a faint warning of the larger storm that lingered on the horizon, from which only exile would ultimately offer shelter.

That Cicero should find in one and the same source both the cause of his dignity, glory, and reputation and cause of the ignominy of exile, the diminishment of his dignity, and the destruction of the persona he had labored so long and hard to fashion must have been psychologically devastating. In the speeches that follow his consular year, we can discern his struggle to grapple with this strange and contradictory set of circumstances. In them Cicero appears almost to be testing the validity of his consular claims and the power of his consular *auctoritas* as he relies increasingly upon his consular prestige to sway the jury, at times almost to the exclusion of the specific evidence against his client.[69] Under these circumstances ethos plays an extraordinary role, and the rhetoric of advocacy assumes a slightly different complexion in that Cicero, who finds it necessary to defend his actions more vigorously as the threat of exile moves closer, often links his own defense with the defense of his client.

The speech on behalf of P. Sulla, who in 62 was accused of complicity in the Catilinarian affair, graphically illustrates several of these points. A brief *exordium* (1–2) introduces the speech and with it three important themes: the mildness and compassion of Cicero's ethos, Cicero's friendship with Torquatus, the prosecutor, and the orator's consular *auctoritas*. The importance of the third is immediately emphasized:

> But he [Torquatus] realized that any damage he inflicted upon my authority would to that extent weaken the defense of my client, and therefore I feel that if I prove to you the reasonableness of my action and my consistency in undertaking this obligation to defend him, I shall also prove the case of Publius Sulla. (2)[70]

Cicero here indicates the link he perceives between the defense of his own actions and the cause of Sulla. This statement also serves as a kind of *propositio* that divides the main body of the speech into two parts: a defense of Cicero the *patronus*, and a defense of Sulla the client.

In his speech for the prosecution Torquatus had apparently attacked Cicero violently for taking part in the defense of Sulla.[71] For this reason and in consideration of other circumstances mentioned above, Cicero felt compelled to devote more than a third of his speech to his own defense. Answering first the charge of inconsistency (3–20), the orator argues that Sulla is also being defended by Hortensius and supported by other distinguished citizens. Indeed, the very act of defending Sulla and no other accused of conspiracy, Cicero claims, indicates that his client, unlike the other conspirators against whom he had so vehemently raged (especially Autronius), is and always was above suspicion. Cicero goes to great lengths in this portion of the speech to portray himself as a man whose ethos is marked by *lenitas* and *misericordia*:

> If this is the character you would impose upon my whole life, Torquatus, on account of what I have done, you are very much mistaken. Nature wished me to be merciful, my country wished me to be firm; neither my country nor my nature wished me to be cruel. Furthermore, my disposition and nature herself have taken from me that stern and harsh mask which the exigencies of time and the Republic forced me to

assume. My country demanded severity for a short time; my nature all through my life has longed for mercy and gentleness. (8)[72]

This passage, which echoes closely a passage in the *Pro Murena* (6), presents a theme that is prominent in Cicero's speeches following his consulship. Eager to justify to himself and to others the execution of the Catilinarians, he claims for himself an ethos mild and merciful by nature. The time and the circumstances of the Republic forced him to assume the persona of sternness and severity against his will. In this way Cicero is able to project the character of a patriot whose natural inclinations toward kindness and mercy were selflessly and resignedly sacrificed for the greater cause of the state. Such a portrait enables him to continue to bask in the glory of his own deeds, and justifiably so, for he had, as a good consul should, submitted his own will to the demands of the Republic. At the same time, he can appear as the mild-mannered, humane advocate whose pity for his fellow man, in this case Sulla, cannot be ignored. Corroboration of this portrait and reiteration of this theme occur throughout this speech, most notably in sections 18–20, 87, 92–93.

The other aspect of Cicero's ethos that becomes critically important for Sulla's defense is that of the consular man whose words and actions concerning the conspiracy, because of his leading role in its suppression, carry great influence and authority. By pretending to depreciate the power of this *auctoritas* in regard to the defense of Sulla, Cicero emphasizes it all the more:

Perhaps great weight should be given to this statement of that man who, as consul, had for the Republic's well-being unearthed the conspiracy by his prudence, disclosed it by his truthfulness, punished it by his resoluteness, when he says that he heard nothing against Publius Sulla, and entertained no suspicion about him. I am not yet, however, using this statement to defend Sulla; I shall use it rather to clear myself. (14)[73]

Well aware of Cicero's unfair position of authority in this case, Torquatus charged him with abusing his personal *auctoritas* by choosing to defend Sulla. Using the same tactic Cicero had employed with such success in the *Pro Murena*, he had apparently attempted in his speech to undermine the consular prestige of the *defensor* by referring to Cicero's consular term as a *regnum*, a word whose associations were traditionally hated by the Romans. Cicero now parries the thrust, however, by stressing that all his actions, far from representing an attempt at tyranny, have been safeguards to freedom (21–29). Most interesting in this connection is Torquatus' charge that Cicero represents the third foreign *rex* at Rome—aimed, of course, at disparaging his provincial birth. That a consular man who had earned the claim of *nobilitas* for his posterity, who had recently been honored with a public thanksgiving, and who had been hailed as "Father of the Fatherland" would be subjected to such an attack, and that he himself should expend considerable effort in rebutting the assault (22–25), provide an important commentary on Republican societal prejudices and the stigma that Cicero, even at this point in his career, struggled continually to erase. At any rate, throughout this portion of the speech, the character of Cicero remains in the foreground, constantly and consistently that of the patriot who unselfishly has offered his services to the state and his fellow man (26), who courageously saved the Republic and its citizens from destruction (cf., e.g., 26, 27), and who alone is still faced with waging a war against the wicked designs of traitors who plot his and the Republic's demise (29).

Cicero concludes his defense of himself, the first half of the *argumentatio*, by launching a counterattack against the prosecutor, his friend Torquatus. After criticizing Torquatus' ridiculous manner of pleading (30–31), faulting him for his lack of oratorical foresight in not recognizing what sort of treatment this case required (31), and censuring his inability to comprehend the interests of the state (32), Cicero recurs to his own consular *auctoritas* by means of an ironic deprecation of it: "Observe, then, Torquatus, how I deprecate the authority of my consulship! At the top of my voice, so that all can hear, I say it now and I shall never stop saying it!" (33).[74] He then continues with an extraordinarily impassioned rhetorical period:

> When an army of abandoned citizens, herded together in a secret plot, had prepared for their country the most cruel and grievous destruction, and when, for the overthrow and destruction of the Republic, Catiline had been placed in command of the camp and Lentulus in command among our temples and homes, I the consul, by my decisions, by my efforts, and at the risk of my life, but without any state of emergency, without a levy, without use of arms, without an army, by the arrest and confession of five men, freed the city from burn-

ing, the citizens from slaughter, Italy from devastation, and the Republic from extinction. By the punishment of five mad, abandoned men, I saved the lives of all the citizens, the peace of the world, this city, the home of us all, the citadel of foreign kings and peoples, the light of nations and the heart of empire. (33)[75]

This manifesto and, at the same time, *apologia* of Cicero's consulship is the most forceful expression of the consular ethos in the speech, calculated to arouse not only goodwill in the hearts of the audience but also the more vehement emotions associated with pathos. Ethos has once again crossed into the realm of high emotion, and conciliation gives way to animation.

Cicero concludes his attack on the prosecutor with a stroke of genius. In a strange (if not perverse) but certainly brilliant use of the rhetoric of advocacy, Cicero identifies Torquatus and his actions with his own (34–35).[76] As close friends, Cicero and Torquatus had both opposed Catiline's designs; now, however, by attacking Sulla, Torquatus might be indicating a change in sentiment. Cicero will save Torquatus' reputation in this regard (and, of course, undermine the credibility of his friend's prosecution in doing so):

And I will add this too, so that no scoundrel may suddenly take a liking to you, Torquatus, or build up his hopes of something from you; and that all these men might hear it, I will say it at the top of my voice. In all the decisions and measures which I took during my consulship for the safety of the Republic, Lucius Torquatus, who had been my comrade in the praetorship as well as in the consulship, came forward in his capacity as the leader, organizer, and standard-bearer of the youth to be my agent, my helper, and my associate. . . . Do you see how I am rescuing you from any sudden popularity with scoundrels and reconciling you with all loyal citizens? They hold you in high esteem and will not now or ever let you go. If by chance you abandon me, they will not allow you on that account to fail them, the Republic, or your own dignity. (34–35)[77]

The second half of the *argumentatio* (36–68) contains Cicero's defense of Sulla and consists primarily of a refutation of the charges and testimony that had been brought against him by Torquatus and his *subscriptor*, C. Cornelius. Even here the consular ethos is irrepressible. We see Cicero cast in the role of the agent of the immortal gods (40, 43);[78] we hear of his providence, vigilance, and scrupulousness in dealing with the conspiracy; we can agree with his common-sense reasoning and, because of his position, trust in his words (45).

Most interesting in terms of the use of ethos, perhaps, is Cicero's second counterattack against Torquatus (46–50). Here the orator returns to the character of Torquatus and the relationship between them. The tone of patronizing condescension is almost painful; it recalls Cicero's treatment of Caecilius in the *Divinatio* and foreshadows his handling of Atratinus in the *Pro Caelio*. The consular orator, veteran of the courtroom, and leading pleader of Rome takes advantage of his position to bully and humiliate Torquatus under the pretext of being merciful to him. Only out of regard for Torquatus' family, his friendship, and his youth has Cicero endured these outrages and tempered his own assault— which, at a moment's notice, could prove devastating to the audacious youth. The mighty lion has played kindly with the cub; but the cub must not dare to become too bold:

> The excuses made for the injury you have inflicted carry conviction with me—your quick temper, your youth, our friendship—and I have decided that you are not yet strong enough to make it right for me to wrestle and do battle with you. But if you were older and more experienced, I would behave as I usually do when provoked; but in this case I will so deal with you that I shall seem to have borne an injustice rather than to have returned a favor. (47)[79]

After systematically refuting a number of charges leveled by the *subscriptor*, Cornelius (51–68), Cicero turns to a full-scale character presentation of Sulla (69–85). In a rare statement of purpose at this point in the speech, he introduces this excursus by apologizing, in a way, for the prominence of his ethos and the corresponding absence of Sulla's in the opening sections of the oration. Because the formal charges have been dealt with, this excursus represents a digression that includes a consideration of the ethos of Sulla, the characters of the Catilinarians, and, of course, their nemesis, Cicero *consularis*.

The basic premise of this *ethica digressio* is that "the character of Publius Sulla does not admit the allegation of such serious and dastardly crimes" (68).[80] At the outset, Cicero makes an important statement about the Roman attitude toward character and the power it should wield in a court case:

In any matter more serious or important than usual, gentlemen, what anyone has wished, thought, or done must be
judged by the character of the accused, not by the accusations
against him. For no one of us can be molded in an instant nor
can a man's life be suddenly changed or his nature altered.
(69)[81]

The Roman belief in the relative immutability of character and in
its role as the dictator of one's intentions, plans, and actions is
strongly in evidence (cf. 79). Cicero employs this belief as the
touchstone against which to measure the Catilinarians and Sulla:
"You will see that every single one of them stood condemned by
his own life before he was condemned by your suspicion" (71).[82]

Sulla, on the other hand, is a man whose character is marked by
dignity, in his service to Roman citizens, in his private life, and in
his devotion to the Republic (72–75). Cicero heightens the tone
and tempo of his oration at this point, as he describes the character of Sulla in exclamatory terms (73):

What need have I to recall the firmness of purpose in the rest
of his life, his dignity, his generosity, his moderation in private life and magnificence in public? . . . What a house he
had, what crowds of visitors every day, what dignity from his
close associates, what a throng from every class in society![83]

These are the marks of a true Roman, a man like Sulla, whose life
and character simply cannot be reconciled with the ethos of the
Catilinarians or with a charge of complicity in their designs: "No, I
say, that sort of suspicion does not square with a character like
his, modesty like his, a life like his, or a man like him" (75).[84]

In sharp contrast is set the ethos of the conspirators, the allies of
Catiline (75–77). Their behavior, like Sulla's, was a manifestation
of their characters; their actions were the logical consequence of
vices accumulated from their youth. The barbarity of their characters and the enormity of their crimes brand them not only un-
Roman, and therefore alien to a good Roman like Sulla, but even
inhuman. By the savagery and cruelty of their heinous attempt,
they have renounced their humanity: "They were wild beasts,
sprung into being from monstrosities, awful and fierce—animals
clothed in human form!" (76).[85] The description continues and
recalls the description of Sulla cited above (73) as it parallels that
passage in rhetorical device, spirit, and exclamatory mode:

Look deep into the minds of Catiline, Autronius, Cethegus, Lentulus, and the others. What passions you will find there, what crimes, what baseness, what boldness, what madness beyond belief, what stains of crime, what proof of parricide, what heaps of evil-doing! (76)[86]

Surely Sulla would never have permitted himself to be aligned or associated in any way with such monsters. Do not cast Sulla, Cicero pleads, "from the flock of most honorable men" into this herd of beasts (77).

Cicero concludes this first part of the digression on character by again stressing its importance in determining the validity of a charge. If anyone (or anything) is to be tortured in order to extract evidence, let it be the life of Sulla that is placed on the rack (78). This is the most truthful, the most convincing witness (78): "Let his life be the most telling witness to condemn or acquit a man; it alone, as you see, because of its own nature, can be most easily examined, but cannot suddenly be changed or feigned" (79).[87]

A return to the topic of consular *auctoritas* marks the second portion of this ethical excursus (80–85):

What then, shall my authority—for I must always speak of it, although I shall do so hesitantly and with moderation—shall my personal authority, I say, have no power whatever to assist Publius Sulla, when I have taken no part in the other cases arising out of the conspiracy but am defending him alone? (80)[88]

This rhetorical question articulates the rationale behind the emphasis Cicero has placed upon his authority here and throughout the speech: as the consul who detected the plot, crushed its efforts, and thus saved the Republic, who is better qualified to speak for Sulla's innocence in regard to the conspiracy and this charge? In an attempt to undermine this *auctoritas*, the prosecutor Torquatus had pointed out that many consulars had come to the assistance of Catiline, the leader and instigator of the plot (81). Cicero thus shifts his emphasis for the moment to the *consulares* in general (81–82). Their aid was given to Catiline before any signs of conspiracy were recognized; their help was only mercy shown to a friend and suppliant; in fact, Torquatus' own father was at one time Catiline's *advocatus* (81). But once the conspiracy had been brought to light, better, braver, more steadfast ex-consuls were never witnessed (82). Contrary to what has been urged by the prosecution, therefore, the men of consular rank, in this crisis as in others, proved to be the bulwark of the state (82).

Cicero at length returns to his personal *auctoritas* (83–85). His argument is one of probability, or rather improbability, as he stresses how unlikely it would be for the consul who had saved the Republic to work for the salvation of one of its destroyers. There is no timidity here (cf. 80), no egregiously feigned attempt to mollify the impact of the authority of the *Pater Patriae*:

> But since the highest office of my career is at stake and the unique glory of my achievements is involved, and since the memory of the salvation won by my efforts is renewed each time a man is convicted in connection with this crime, would I be so insane, would I induce people to think that the things I did to secure the safety of all were the products of chance and luck and not of my courage and statesmanship? (83)[89]

Here is a Roman speaking to Romans. This seemingly candid statement coming from Cicero, a proud, important, and much-honored consular, would have made sense to the jury and thus must have contributed enormously to the defense of Sulla. Cicero has endeavored to make the choice of the jury quite simple: "It seems to be offensive that the man who searched out the conspiracy, who exposed it, who suppressed it, whom the Senate thanked in a decree without precedent, to whom alone, clad in the garb of peace, it decreed a thanksgiving, should say in a trial: 'I would not be defending him if he had been a conspirator' " (85).[90] (That is, don't concern yourselves with the facts; I dislike pointing out the obvious, but if Sulla were guilty I would not be speaking for him here today.)

The peroration to the speech (86–93) includes an invocation to the gods that serves to invest Cicero's consular *auctoritas* with the support of *auctoritas divina* (86–87), a *commiseratio* (88–91), and a final plea for Sulla's acquittal (92–93). Cicero's consular ethos recedes little, if at all, as he concludes the speech by reintroducing a character theme so prominent in its beginning (cf. 1, 8, 18–20), that of the *patronus* who has laid aside the persona of sternness to allow his real ethos of mildness, mercy, and compassion toward his fellow man to shine through.

Cicero's plea was successful; Sulla, a defendant generally believed to have been guilty of the charge,[91] had been acquitted largely by the influence of Cicero's consular *auctoritas*. Considering the speech in its entirety, we can see that its major body (3–68) is divided equally into a defense of Cicero (3–35) and a defense of Sulla (36–68). This structure is in turn complemented chiastically by a digression (69–85) that considers Sulla's ethos (69–79), then the ethos of Cicero *consularis* (80–85). Just as the character of Cicero *consularis* frames the structure of the oration, so does his ethos surround and almost pervade the defense, and by its weight nearly alone secures the acquittal.

Despite the neatness of structure and the ultimate success of the plea, Cicero's speech on behalf of Sulla remains somewhat unsatisfying, at times unconvincing. Possessing neither the intensity and immediacy of the *Catilinarians*, nor the wit and skillful manipulation of character of the *Pro Murena* (excepting Cicero's treatment of Torquatus), the *Pro Sulla* is perhaps too blatant in its appeal to authority for a modern audience; or perhaps one is repelled by the apparent miscarriage of justice. More likely, however, is the detection by the reader of a bit of laziness, a kind of smug complacency on Cicero's part (analogous, perhaps, to the feelings with which Hortensius approached Verres' case); he seems content to thunder the threat of his authority continually and without much variation. Pragmatically, it was certainly effective, but whether it represents the effort of a Cicero who was at the height of his intellectual and political powers is questionable.

Nevertheless, the *Pro Sulla* is important for our understanding of ethos in Ciceronian oratory. The crucial significance of a man's character and life as measures of his guilt or innocence, as touchstones that remain fairly constant and unchanged, is repeatedly stated. The dimension that consular *auctoritas* adds to ethical argumentation is significant and unmistakable. The facts of the case seem to be pushed further and further into the backround, as *auctoritas* high-handedly battles for acquittal. Cicero's real argument for Sulla's innocence resides in the fact that he himself, the enemy of the conspiracy and all conspirators, has chosen to defend Sulla. The inevitable conclusion, of course, is that Sulla must be innocent.

The most interesting and artistic use of ethos in the speech is Cicero's manipulation of the young prosecutor, Torquatus, who is portrayed as Cicero's friend and, through a clever twist and variation of the rhetoric of advocacy, is made to support Cicero's cause. The entire posture of Torquatus' prosecution is likewise illuminating for our study of ethos in Roman and Ciceronian oratory. It is obvious from Cicero's reply that Torquatus had spent much effort and a large part of his speech attempting to undermine or at least disarm Cicero's consular authority. Apparently he realized that his own *auctoritas, gratia,* and *existimatio* were no match for Cicero's and that this disadvantage could prove just as devastating to his case as would a poor presentation of the factual evidence—perhaps more so. He therefore protested Cicero's use of his influence and reputation, charging abuse of his consular *auctoritas* to the point of setting himself in the position of a *rex* (cf. esp. 21–25). Correspondingly, just how important it was for Cicero to exert that authority is evident from the emphasis that he gives to these points in his speech.

Torquatus' complaints against the unfair exercise of personal influence recall vividly the young Cicero's laments about fighting against the same overwhelming obstacles, the *dignitas, auctoritas, gratia,* and *eloquentia* of Naevius, Hortensius, or Philippus in the *Pro Quinctio,* or the judicial *regnum* of Hortensius in the *Verrines.*[92] Thus the speech sheds valuable light both on the condition of possessing an ethos of great personal authority and on the condition of possessing an ethos that lacks it. The oration graphically illustrates the burden that the Roman belief in character and respect for authority placed upon orators and the great difficulties under which a young man labored when he met with the challenge of an ethos of authority. That Cicero, now in a position to do so, exploited this advantage almost ruthlessly, that this speech and the prosecutor's speech were, in large part, concerned with this topic, and that *auctoritas* makes its presence felt in most Ciceronian speeches of this period (and even anecdotally in those speeches),[93] all confirm that a character's personal authority, or lack of it, became in Roman oratory a commonplace of ethical argumentation that seems to have produced more than commonplace persuasion.

## PRO L. FLACCO

Cicero's speech on behalf of L. Flaccus, former governor of Asia who in 59 stood accused of extortion, shows greater balance and more variety than his earlier defense of Sulla. The orator unites elements of humor that recall the *Pro Murena,* with a kindling of Roman prejudice against the provincials (cf. *Pro Fonteio*), and a more subtle use of his consular *auctoritas* to secure once again the acquittal of a client who was probably guilty.[94]

That ethos will provide in this speech a major source for persuasive material is evident from its opening lines. Cicero fashions for himself the familiar portrait of savior of the Republic and endeavors to link Flaccus, a paragon of Roman virtue and nobility and a friend who had aided him in crushing the conspiracy, with this consular ethos. Cicero touches upon the character of Decimus Laelius, the prosecutor, as he expresses his shock and dismay that such a distinguished young man would take on a prosecution that is more befitting the mad hatred of criminals rather than the virtue of his youth (2). The orator likewise secures the attention of his audience by amplifying the importance of this case, making it not merely the trial of one accused of extortion, but rather the trial of the Republic itself (3). In this connection Cicero further broadens the basis of the case, as he had done in the *Pro Sulla*, by interpreting Flaccus' trial as also a trial of himself and his actions.

In the speech on behalf of Sulla, Cicero's apparent need to defend himself had accounted for a kind of dual defense. Here this need for self-justification is much more obvious. During the three years that had intervened between the two speeches, Cicero saw the glory he had won in his consulship slowly wane until his redemption of the Republic—the feat in which he took most pride—became, largely through the machinations of Publius Clodius and the members of the triumvirate, a millstone around his neck that ultimately dragged him down into the disgrace of exile. Now keenly aware of the threats and dangers that surround him, Cicero identifies the attack upon Flaccus with the mounting enmity toward himself and consequently views Flaccus' *causa* with his own:

> Perhaps, gentlemen, you do not see what is being tested in this trial, what is at stake, for whom the foundations of the case are being laid. The man [C. Antonius] has been condemned who destroyed Catiline when he was leading troops against his country; should not then the man [Cicero] who drove Catiline from the city have good cause to be afraid? The man [Flaccus] is being rushed to punishment who secured the evidence of the universal plot; what reassurance can there be for the man [Cicero] who ensured the disclosure and publication of that information? Those who shared his counsels, his agents and comrades, are being harried; what are the authors, the leaders, the principals to expect? (4–5)[95]

Unfortunately a break in the text at this point precludes any further development of this extraordinary variation on the rhetoric of advocacy; the clever juxtaposition of client and *patronus* surfaces later in the speech to contribute to an effective conclusion of the defense.

Despite the fragmented nature of the text here, we can conclude from what survives (fragments and sections 6–8) that the first part of Cicero's speech comprised a rebuttal of an attack made by the prosecutor, Laelius, upon the life and career of Flaccus. Cicero's goal seems to have been to portray Flaccus' ethos in strikingly Roman terms: a skillful and courageous soldier, an honest citizen, a responsible magistrate, a man who, in short, provides a perfect example of that famous, pristine Roman *gravitas*.[96] When joined with the next part of the oration, which is devoted to an arousal of pro-Roman prejudices against the Greek witnesses who had testified on behalf of the prosecution, this first part of the speech (fragments and text through section 26) forms something like a *praemunitio*, a preliminary fortification of Cicero's defense, based on sharply contrasting portraits of the ethos of the parties involved.

The attack upon the Greeks relies on a generalized, stereotyped portrait of the provincials.[97] Comparisons between Roman and Greek witnesses are first developed (8–15). Cicero, himself a confessed philhellene, must tread carefully in this regard, for he is faced with the difficult task of impugning the Greek character while maintaining some sort of consistency in his own ethos.[98] He meets this challenge cleverly by candidly professing his sympathies toward Greeks in interest and disposition, but distinguishing sharply between their literary and intellectual achievements and their reliability as witnesses:

> I grant them literature, the knowledge of many arts; I do not deny the charm of their speech, their keenness of intellect, or richness of expression; finally, if they make other claims I do not deny them: but that nation has never cultivated a scrupulous regard for honesty when giving evidence, and it is quite ignorant of the meaning, the importance or the value of anything to do with it. (9)[99]

Having made this distinction, Cicero proceeds to attack the Greeks on these terms. Even their appearance and demeanor betray their unscrupulousness (10). Unlike a Roman witness, who approaches the witness stand with fear and trembling and respect for his oath (10–11), the Greek's only fear is to be refuted, to be proven wrong, and he will do anything to prevent it (11–12).[100]

After Cicero arouses odium against Laelius, whose thirst for distinction (for himself and the triumvirs) accounts for his prosecution (13–15), Cicero returns to the Greeks and the fickle, irresponsible, and excessively liberal nature of their public assemblies and public decrees (16–24). Again the point of comparison and contrast resides in the Romans, who have traditionally refused to allow power to rest in public meetings (15). The license of public meetings in Greece, on the other hand, was the sole cause for its downfall and destruction (16). When evidence is gathered through such means, it is not evidence at all, but only empty clamor and impulse (23).

To conclude this *praemunitio* Cicero returns to the contrasting character of Flaccus (24–26), who carries on, by the exercise of his own deeds, the splendid ethos of his family, which gave the Republic a consul in its first year and by whose valor the kings were banished and liberty established. This "preliminary fortification," which has been based entirely upon the presentation of the contrasting characters of Flaccus and his adversaries, is important for Cicero's defense. Here, as in other speeches, Cicero attempts to reduce the case from a legal battle involving two litigants to a struggle between two antithetical ways of life or characters. Flaccus is portrayed by Cicero as a good Roman. In this regard, his family's impressive nobility, its magnificent feats, its continuous glory as well as Flaccus' own reaffirmation of his legacy, and the *mos maiorum* are emphasized. At the other end of the spectrum are the Greeks, the antithesis of Romans like Flaccus, whose personal and collective means of rendering evidence and testimony violate all Roman principles. By dealing almost exclusively on the level of ethos in this initial stage of the speech, Cicero has supplied the jury with a rule of character by which it can measure the facts as he subsequently presents them, a touchstone against which it can test the probabilities of the case.

Cicero now turns to the formal proof of the case. Beginning with the common complaint of the Greeks concerning Flaccus' levy of a fleet (27–33), Cicero moves to a rebuttal of the various charges and complaints of the separate Greek states (34–69). The refutation relies primarily on arguments based on probability and the skillful use of his disarming and caustic wit in combination with the defamation of the character of each city's chief witness. Acmona (34–38) is represented by the low-life Asclepiades, "a man without means, scandalous in his way of life, condemned by public opinion, a fellow relying on his nerve and audacity" (35). Some "nobody," an utterly unknown Phrygian, who attacks Flaccus, a most noble citizen (40), speaks for Dorylaeum (39–41). There is Heraclides of Temnus, "a silly chatterbox," the chief instigator of the Greeks, whose character as a scoundrel and a cheat is detailed in an effective ethical narrative (42–50). Witnesses from Temnus (51) and Tralles (52–59) are dismissed in similar terms.

Cicero concludes this portion of the speech with a clever reversal as he draws a different kind of distinction, between Asiatic

Greeks and "true" Greeks (60–66). Men from Athens, "where men think civilization, learning, religion, agriculture, justice, and laws were born and thence spread into every land" (62), and Sparta, "whose well-known and famous virtue is thought to have derived its strength not only from their nature but also from their upbringing" (63), and other "true" Greeks are present to commend Flaccus. "These are the men whom Flaccus has as character-witnesses, and to testify to his innocence—if I may oppose the cupidity of Greeks with the aid of other Greeks" (64).[101] This striking juxtaposition of Greek versus Greek is then underscored by a caustic invective against the Asiatic Greeks (65–66) in which Cicero resorts to an appeal to blatant bigotry, stoked by several racially derogatory "proverbs."

The formal refutation of the charges is completed with Cicero's response to the Asiatic Jews (66–69) and to three Roman citizens, Decianus (70–83), Sextilius Andro (84–89), and Falcidius (90–93). He again uses ethical narrative (e.g. 72–74) to tint the complexion of the charges as he endeavors to show that Flaccus, in all instances, had acted in accordance with Roman law and custom. From this last point of rebuttal, he springs into a digression that reintroduces a theme touched upon briefly in the *exordium*: the amplification of this case from the specific defense of a governor of Asia, charged with extortion, to the defense of himself, of those who worked to save the state, of the Republic itself: "But why do I say so much about the letters of Falcidius, or about Sextilius Andro or Decianus' census returns, while I am silent on the question of the safety of us all, the future of the state, the highest interests of the Republic?" (94).[102]

The gravity of the political situation is stressed by the mention of the condemnation of C. Antonius, the threat posed to Flaccus by this trial, and the danger that surrounds Cicero himself, in a passage (94–97) that recalls vividly sections 4–5 of the *exordium*. The union of the defense of the defendant Flaccus with the defense of the defender Cicero is striking, first in section 96—"We are now named by informers, accusations are being invented against us, trials are being prepared for us"[103]—and then again in 97, where the first-person plural pronoun (*nos*) yields to the first-person singular, and Cicero, not Flaccus, becomes the focal point of the speech:

So if anyone calls me there, I come. I do not refuse to be judged by the Roman people, I even demand it. Let there be no violence, no recourse to swords and stones, let the hired gangs withdraw, let the slaves remain silent. No one who hears me, provided that he is a free man and a citizen, will be so unjust as not to think that I deserve reward rather than punishment.[104]

This identification of client and client's lot with *patronus* and *patronus'* lot enables Cicero to wring from his consular ethos a few last drops of *auctoritas* in defense of his client, and in defense of himself to recall his own service and devotion to the Republic.

Cicero next bemoans the irony of the situation, that he and Flaccus, who braved the sword of the conspirator and the judgment of the mob, should now fear the votes of Rome's leading citizens (97). Historical examples are cited of cases in which the interests and the common safety of the state took precedence over specific charges (98), including the *cause célèbre* of Manius Aquilius, who despite his acknowledged guilt was acquitted of the charge of extortion because of his bravery in the Sicilian Slave War of 101. Three other precedents involve Cicero himself, including his defense as consul of two other consuls, Piso and Murena. The appearance of the word *consul* four times within a very short interval (about three lines of printed text) is no accident.[105] Cicero *consularis* attempts to deepen the significance of his case by identifying it with others he has mentioned. Moreover, he contributes to his defense an authority upon which the jury can rely to cast their vote for Flaccus' acquittal, despite any evidence of his guilt.

A return to the ethos of the adversaries involved in this case marks the next sections of the digression (100–101). As he had done earlier (64), Cicero places, in opposition to the prosecution's witnesses, other witnesses hailing from the same province, "true Greeks" who have come to assist Flaccus: "Against the Greeks of Lydia, Phrygia, and Mysia, there will stand the Greeks of Massilia, Rhodes, Sparta, Athens, all of Achaia, Thessaly, and Boeotia" (100).[106] Once again he upholds the value of a man's character and past life in respect to a criminal charge. In this case, Flaccus' life should offset in the balance an accusation that involves only one year (100). A military record worthy of his ancestors, which includes the offices of tribune, quaestor, and legate to the most famous generals, in the most honored armies, in the most important provinces (101), distinguishes his career. Finally, Cicero deftly reintroduces his own ethos and once again unites Flaccus and his deeds with Cicero, the defender of the Republic: "Let it also be counted in his favor that here before your own eyes amid the perils shared by us all, he has shared my dangers with me" (101).[107]

With his persona as *consularis* and savior of the state again brought onstage in union with the defendant Flaccus, Cicero makes a final appeal to the influence and authority which he had accrued by foiling the Catilinarian conspiracy. Marked by four dramatic and impassioned apostrophes, this passage (102–103) raises the emotional tenor of the speech to a perorational height from which it never recedes.[108] The closeness of the two defendants, Cicero and Flaccus, continues to be emphasized and is indicated even by the artistic arrangement of words.[109]

Cicero's final plea (104–106) provides the jury with a last glimpse at the character of Flaccus:

> And indeed, gentlemen, if a grave injustice should be done to Lucius Flaccus—and may the immortal gods avert the omen— even so he will never regret the foresight he displayed for your salvation and the counsel he took for you, your children, your wives, and your possessions. He will always feel that he owed this decision to the dignity of his family, to his duty to himself and his country. (104)[110]

He then concludes the speech by cleverly reducing the verdict of the jurors and the issue of the trial to a vote in favor of or against a life of devotion to the Republic. Their decision will be a message sent to young citizens, especially to Flaccus' son, who now are looking for a guiding principle to inform their lives and their characters:

> To this poor boy, a suppliant to you and to your children, gentlemen, you will give by your decision a rule of life. If you acquit his father, you will show him what sort of citizen he should himself be; but if you take his father from him, you will show that you have offered no reward for a plan of life that has been upright, steadfast, and honorable. (106)[111]

The final words of the speech are a request to preserve the noble reputation of Flaccus out of regard for his character and heritage: "Whether it be for his family's sake or for his ancient lineage or for the man himself, preserve for the Republic a most illustrious and glorious name" (106).[112]

By the time the tears dried, Flaccus had been acquitted. Once again, in aid of a guilty client, Cicero had successfully marshaled his rhetorical weapons—effective portrayal of ethos, amplification of the significance of his case, and the power of his own consular *auctoritas* stemming from the overthrow of the Catilinarian conspiracy—to overshadow scanty factual evidence and argumentation.

Two strategies, both finding their basis in ethos, seem to characterize the defense. The first is the establishment of antithetical portraits of the parties involved. Early in the speech we see the character of Flaccus emerge, the patriot and noble Roman par excellence; juxtaposed in striking contrast are the Greeks, lying and loquacious. Such characterization is continued throughout the speech, and even the refutation of specific charges is, in most cases, marked by an attempt to undermine damaging testimony through defamation of the witnesses' character.

A second and particularly interesting technique is Cicero's identification of a personal defense with his defense of Flaccus, introduced first in the *exordium* and developed extensively in the emotional ethical digression that introduces the peroration. By identifying the advocate with his client and depicting Flaccus as the consul's right hand in crushing the conspiracy of 63, Cicero enables Flaccus to partake in the prestige, respect, and influence that he himself, the *patronus*, presumably still enjoys as the *consularis* who snatched the Republic from the clutches of Catiline.

Indeed, the prominence of Cicero's own ethos is perhaps the most outstanding feature of the consular orations. In many respects he seems to conduct himself in these speeches according to the rationale of the *defensor* that he had enunciated in his speech on behalf of Murena (59). There, the rights he denies to an *accusator*—overweening power (*potentia*), excessive force (*vis maior aliqua*), overwhelming authority (*auctoritas excellens*), and excessive influence (*nimia gratia*)—he appropriates for use on behalf of those *in periculo*. During his *tirocinium fori*, Cicero had certainly witnessed the force of these weapons, and in his early speeches he labored (as Torquatus had done in the *Pro Sulla*) to overcome their advantageous power. Once in full possession of his own arsenal of such weapons, Cicero does not hesitate to brandish them, relentlessly and even ruthlessly, in defense of his clients and himself.

His continual references to the Nones of December, his consulship, and his own *auctoritas* became, even in Cicero's own time, a source of pain and irritation to his critics. Indeed, Louis F. Lord, in his Loeb edition of the *Pro Flacco*, comments, "It is a pathetic sight, Cicero dragging out once more the spavined stalking horse of the Catilinarian conspiracy."[113] What critics sometimes fail to recognize, however, is that despite its pathetic appearance, the ploy seems to have been effective. "Cicero delivered his orations to audiences intimately concerned with the issues and ramifications of each case, audiences whose attention, credence, and support were essential for his own success as a public figure. And his success was stunning."[114] Thus it was all the more ironic and tragic that in the year following the *Pro Flacco*, the same deeds that had accounted for so much of his personal influence, and that he had called upon so often in defense of others, were not only rendered impotent in defense of himself, but proved ultimately to be the cause of his downfall.

# IV

## THE *POST REDITUM* SPEECHES

*The Search for a New Persona and*

*the Struggle for* Dignitas

So then I saved the Republic by my departure from Rome, gentlemen of the jury; by my own grief and sorrow I kept off from you and your children devastation, fire, and rapine; alone I twice saved the Republic, once with glory, the second time with misery to myself. (*Pro Sestio* 49)

The threats and dangers that had haunted Cicero from the time of the execution of the Catilinarians finally came to a head in 58 B.C., following the election of his archenemy, Publius Clodius, to the tribunate. Three years earlier Cicero had antagonized Clodius by rendering incriminating evidence against him when he was on trial for appearing in women's clothing at the Bona Dea festival; Clodius now used the power of the tribunate to avenge himself. In February 58 Clodius promulgated a bill, *de capite civis Romani*, that outlawed from Rome anyone who had put to death a Roman citizen without a trial. Although worded in general terms, the measure was clearly aimed at Cicero and his handling of the Catilinarian conspirators. Pressed by this move and finding little relief from the triumvirs and outright hostility from the consuls, Gabinius and Piso, Cicero left for Greece in late March without awaiting prosecution. On the same day, Clodius' bill was passed and was followed a few days later by another, *de exsilio Ciceronis* (certainly unconstitutional), that specifically identified Cicero as an outlaw. Friends and supporters back in Rome, however, were not lacking and soon rallied to his cause. On 4 August 57 the Comitia Centuriata, boasting representatives from all Italy, sanctioned his recall, and the orator returned triumphantly to the city the following month.

Just as Cicero's consular year marked the high point of his life and career, so did the year of his exile mark its nadir. Psychologically crushed by the reality that the Nones of December were also the cause of his forced departure from Rome, Cicero, in the depths of despair, even contemplated suicide.[1] Letters to his friend Atticus dating from that year display an unseemly yet understandable mood of depression from which he gradually recovered only upon his recall.[2] For the *novus homo* who had worked so long and so diligently to enhance his own ethos with dignity, authority, influence, and reputation, and to construct a persona of persuasive capabilities, the exile was a devastating setback.[3] His personal *dignitas*, of course, had been seriously undermined and that consular persona of the hero who had saved the state without recourse to arms was gravely damaged, if not altogether destroyed. Cicero was forced once again to scramble with all of his energies and resources to reconstruct and secure for himself an ethos of *auctoritas* and a persona befitting his station in Republican society. The struggle to do so was, for the most part, fraught with frustration, anxiety, and humiliation.

His glorious return from exile, described so vividly in a letter to Atticus,[4] was the foundation upon which Cicero attempted to rebuild his persona. Still the consular senator, the premier orator of Rome, who had now been recalled in triumph, he took advantage of his current position, if not to whitewash the ignominy of his exile, at least to place his actions in a light as favorable as possible. As a result, the speeches from this period, particularly those that deal directly with his exile and return, as well as others whose political ramifications touch upon the events of 58, are often as much *apologiae* on behalf of Cicero as political deliberations or defenses of clients. Marked at times by turgidity and a kind of grating shrillness, the *post reditum* speeches are the chronicle of Cicero's quest to reestablish and regain what Madvig called "that ancient eminence of dignity and authority" which had previously marked his ethos.[5] Armed with a somewhat diminished *existimatio* and faced with doubt and anxiety about his own status in the state, Cicero consciously and very skillfully developed a network of recurring themes calculated to justify his own actions and portray his character in the most favorable terms.

The ethos of Cicero, savior of the Republic, is still in prominence, but tinted now with a slightly different hue. Clients are still defended not merely on the strength of their own characters but also by their association with the great consular orator. The rhetoric of advocacy is still important, but artistic variations make it even more interesting. In short, ethos as a source for persuasive material is as much in evidence as it had been in earlier Ciceronian oratory and, as always in earlier speeches, its use is altered, adjusted, and adapted to meet Cicero's needs, the ever-changing rhetorical challenges of each case, and the requisites demanded for persuasion.

## PRO P. SESTIO

Within a few months following his celebrated recall, Cicero was presented with the opportunity of defending P. Sestius, the former tribune who had championed the cause for his return, who had been indicted for violence (*vis*) at Clodius' instigation. Interpreting the charge as an attack upon himself as well as Sestius, Cicero set forth not only a defense of his friend and an *apologia* for himself and his actions, but also a stunning manifesto of his political philosophy. Given an audience and a stage from which to perform, Cicero seized upon the defense of Sestius as an opportunity to justify his exile and rebuild his persona. The speech that resulted epitomizes in many ways the ethically grounded tactics and the several character themes that generally distinguish the *post reditum* speeches and, for this reason, provides an important source for our study of ethos in Ciceronian oratory.

A brief *exordium* begins the speech (1–5) and explains Cicero's motive for taking up the case of Sestius: to express his gratitude and to restore to life the man who labored to restore him to the Republic. Distinction is immediately drawn between the two parties whose struggle is represented in this trial: those who have come to the aid of an afflicted Republic, and those who seek to violate and overturn all things human and divine (1). This distinction and the parties involved in it become better defined and dimensions are added to their characters as the speech continues. Already there is an indication that the speech will extend beyond the general requirements for an oration of defense, as Cicero begs the indulgence of the court should he plead his case "more passionately" and "with greater freedom" than those who have spoken before him (4). Finally, in a statement that resembles a partition, he indicates the importance of ethos in his defense as he asserts that his speech will deal with the "entire position" of Sestius, including most significantly "his manner of life, his character, his habits, his extraordinary affection for the loyal citizens, and his zeal for the preservation of the general welfare and security" (5).[6]

A long narration follows (6–77) in which Cicero sets out to accomplish much of what he had proposed. Tracing his client's life and career chronologically, he begins with Sestius' birth and heritage and extends the account up to his tribunate in 57 (6–14). Cicero's purpose in this ethical narrative is to show that his client's ethos is thoroughly Roman and in keeping with the *mos maiorum*; in this regard, the biography reads like an extended Republican epitaph, expanding on Sestius' parentage, his filial piety, and his duties to the state.[7]

Sestius' father was "wise, dignified, and stern" and, along with Sestius' first father-in-law, embodied those famous, very dignified, and old-fashioned Roman manners (6). That Sestius endeared himself so to these pillars of the *mos maiorum* implies, of course, his adherence to their principles. The filial *pietas* he displayed toward his father and his fathers-in-law (6–7) only corroborates this portrait.

With a *praeteritio* that emphasizes Sestius' military tribunate, Cicero turns to his client's service to the Republic and specifically to the assistance he rendered Cicero during the latter's bout with Catiline. Although Antonius' quaestor by lot, Sestius proved to be Cicero's faithful supporter in all his plans (8). This link with Cicero, established in these early sections of the speech (8–12), is an important bond that had become a familiar feature of the Ciceronian rhetoric of advocacy. The line of reasoning and argument implied is that Cicero's actions were justified; what Sestius did, in turn, supported Cicero; therefore, Sestius' actions were justified (cf. 14). As the speech continues, the bond between client and *patronus*, and this line of argument, become more important and correspondingly more prominent.

Upon reaching what should prove the focal point of his narrative—Sestius' tribunate—Cicero breaks off the account and shifts from the ethos and career of the defendant to his own character, the characters of his enemies, his exile, and other events of the previous year, in a long passage (15–70) that is striking in its virtual silence about Sestius. He begins by describing what he calls the "complete shipwreck of the Republic in the year before"; it was "to collecting the wreckage and to restoring the public's safety that Sestius' every deed, word, and thought were directed" (15).[8] This portrait of Cicero's client, as restoring the shipwrecked Republic to order, establishes an important theme that will be continued and expanded in subsequent uses of the image.[9]

Cicero then proceeds, without explicitly naming Clodius, to sketch his character and describe his rise to power in the tribunate (15–17). He combines allusions to Clodius' savage madness (*furibundus, iratus*, 15) with stock elements of invective (e.g., "born from the offscourings of every sort of crime," 15) and specific accusations of bestial, uncivilized behavior (dissipation and debauchery, including incest, 16) to paint a portrait of his archenemy that is at once frightening and entirely antithetical to the Roman way of life and to Romans like Cicero and Sestius.

Cicero next turns from Clodius to his collaborators, the consuls Piso and Gabinius (17–25). He draws their characters skillfully and in some detail, though not without recourse to stock motifs and methods of invective. Gabinius' portrait (18) is marked by its affinity to the stock traits of a comic character: "Here is one of them. Dripping with unguents, with curled hair, looking down on the collaborators of his debaucheries and the old abusers of his dainty youth, puffed up with rage against the Puteal and the herd of usurers" (18).[10] Piso is his tragic counterpart: "The other—good gods! See him marching along, how hideous, how fierce, how terrible he was to look at!" (19).[11] The adjectives (*taeter*, *truculentus*, and *terribilis*) are ambivalent enough to describe "either a monster or an ancestral Roman hero,"[12] and Cicero capitalizes on the ambivalence to present a caricature of the debauched consul, an ironic foil to the genuine, old-time Roman represented (cf. 6) by Sestius, his father, and his father-in-law: "You would have sworn that you were gazing upon one of our bearded forefathers, a perfect specimen of the old regime, the image of antiquity, a pillar of the Republic" (19).[13]

As the characterization of the consuls continues, Cicero recurs to the metaphor of the ship of state to lend color and vividness to his portrait of Gabinius:

> Who could imagine that to hold the helm of so great an empire, and guide the rudder of the ship of state, as it sped along amid tempestuous waves, was in the power of a man who had suddenly emerged from a long sojourn in the dark, from haunts of debauchery, a man worn out with drunkenness, gluttony, lewdness, and adultery . . . who in his drunken bouts was not only unable to see a threatening storm, but could not even endure to look at the light, so long a stranger to him. (20)[14]

The implication is obvious: it was under the hand of one possessed of such a character that the Republic had headed for the inevitable shipwreck, from which Sestius had later begun to salvage the pieces.

In contrast to the transparency of Gabinius' character, Piso, at least for a time, fooled people (21–23). His noble birth and familial heritage, his grave look, even his cognomen, Frugi ("temperate," "frugal"), all contributed to the deception. The screen, however, was soon penetrated by discerning eyes, and the true nature of his life and his ethos, informed by the principles of Epicurus (23), was laid bare.

The narrative continues, further characterizing the ethos of the two consuls, their alliance with Clodius, the promulgation of Clodius' two bills that resulted from that alliance, and the subsequent assumption of the garb of mourning by the Senate and Roman people (24–30). The emotional level of the account increases as the threat of exile moves closer to Cicero. At section 31, however, the orator breaks the flow of the story and interjects a short apology for the direction the speech has taken and its preoccupation with events that surround him rather than Sestius:

> But my intention is to show that the whole policy and purpose of Sestius' tribunate was to heal, as much as it could, the wounds of an afflicted and ruined Republic. And if, in laying open these wounds, I seem to say rather much about myself, you must pardon me. For both you and all loyal citizens considered that the disaster that befell me was the greatest possible wound to the Republic, and that Publius Sestius is a defendant not on his own account, but on mine; and since he devoted all the strength of his tribunate to promoting my welfare, my cause in past time must by necessity be linked with the defense of Sestius in the present.[15]

The device of patron–client identification is, as we have seen repeatedly, a tactic commonly employed under the Roman system of advocacy. Here the union is made quite explicit, but the device is marked by an interesting variation: Cicero, the ex-consul who had saved the state, whose exile was mourned universally, who was recalled in triumph, who, in short, represents the force of good working in support of the Republic against the forces of evil working for its overthrow (personified in Piso, Gabinius, and Clodius) employs his own ethos and *auctoritas* in support of his client; but because he views himself as being in some sense on trial, he depicts himself as a "client" and chooses for himself an extraordinarily powerful "patron"—the *res publica*.[16]

Throughout the *post reditum* speeches Cicero exerts a conscious effort at identifying himself, implicitly or explicitly, with the Republic. His wounds are the wounds of the state, his exile her exile, his recall and return her recall and return, his *causa* the *causa rei publicae*. A stirring passage from the *Post Reditum in Senatu* graphically illustrates this point:

> But realizing that my absence from this city would not outlast the absence from it of the Republic itself, I did not think it my duty to remain there after its extinction, and what is more, no sooner was it recalled than it brought me back in its company. With me the laws, with me the courts of justice, with me magisterial jurisdiction, with me the authority of the Senate, with me liberty, with me a plentiful grain supply, with me all reverence and all compunction in matters human and divine were absent. Were these things to be lost to us forever, I should rather bewail your misfortune than regret my own; but I recognized that, should a day come when they should be recalled, it would be my duty to return with them. (34)[17]

The speeches that follow Cicero's recall abound with statements similar to this one.[18] In our passage from the *Pro Sestio*, the link between Sestius and Cicero and Cicero and the Republic is clearly expressed: the wound of exile inflicted upon Cicero was the gravest wound inflicted upon the Republic; furthermore, Sestius is a defendant not on his own account but on Cicero's—his defense is the defense of Cicero. Thus Cicero as *patronus* identifies himself and his *causa* with his client Sestius, but in another sense, as client in his own right, identifies himself and his *causa* with the patron state.

In order to make such identification more explicit, Cicero employs throughout the speech two metaphors: the image of the Republic as a wounded or afflicted body,[19] and the reference to the movement for Cicero's recall as the *causa*, or "court case" of the Republic. He has already described the alliance of Piso and Gabinius with Clodius in terms of the afflicted state: they handed over the Republic to Clodius, prostrate and fettered, and then ratified the pact by the shedding of Cicero's blood (24). The same metaphor is used in a later passage with extraordinary force: "The moment I was struck down they flew to drink my blood, and while the Republic was still breathing to strip it of their spoil" (54).[20] Here, Cicero almost becomes the Republic!

At another point in the speech Cicero refers to his enemies as feeding on the lifeblood of the Republic while he is away (78). Earlier he had called Gabinius a "devourer of his country" (*helluo patriae*, 26), and the mobs that voted for the legislation against

him are eventually characterized as "frenzied furies flocking together, as it were, to the funeral of the Republic" (109).[21] In this
connection, interesting and very artistic ethical portraiture complements the image of the Republic as a wounded or afflicted
body, as Cicero casts the ethos of Clodius (and/or Piso and Gabinius) in the role of the wounder or pestilence that has afflicted
it.[22] This tactic, of course, presents a strong argument, based on
ethos, against Cicero's (and Sestius') enemies and also reinforces
Cicero's identification of himself and his wound with the Republic
and its affliction.[23]

The continual reference to his *causa* (the movement for his recall) as the *causa rei publicae* in later sections of the narrative further
emphasizes the role of the Republic as Cicero's *patronus*. The Senate and people (38), Pompey (41, 67), Milo (87), and Sestius himself (71) all take up the "cause of the Republic" as they work for
Cicero's recall. The implications of the use of the technical term
*causa* in these contexts are obvious: the movement for Cicero's recall, his *causa*, becomes, in the courtroom and under the practices
of the rhetoric of advocacy, the *causa* of Cicero's *patronus*, the Republic. Because the return of Cicero meant the return of the Republic, those who labored for the orator's recall were, in reality,
laboring for the recall of the state. Sestius, by working for Cicero's
cause, was actually working for the *causa rei publicae*.

Through this clever variation on the rhetoric of advocacy Cicero
has cunningly wrought a veritable chain of authority in support of
his client: Sestius is supported by the *patronus* Cicero, who is himself as a client supported by his *patronus*, the Republic. By aligning
Sestius with himself and himself with the state, and juxtaposing
this layered unity against those who have attacked and wounded
the state, him, and therefore Sestius, Cicero once again creates the
familiar antithetical portraits of personified good versus personified evil, ethical portraits that provide the foundation for his
defense.

After his self-intrusion at section 31, Cicero resumes his narrative as he describes the terrible condition of the state, owing
chiefly to the machinations of the mad tribune Clodius and the debauched consuls, Piso and Gabinius (32–35). At length he comes
to the account of his own exile and includes a long apology (36–
54) defending his action of voluntary withdrawal. In a long rhetorical question, marked by great gravity of style and emotion, the
orator introduces yet another character-theme that is important in
the *post reditum* speeches. He portrays himself as a willing sacrifi-

cial victim, who chose to suffer exile in order that the storms of sedition and discord buffeting the ship of state might subside:

> For if it happened to me, gentlemen, when sailing in a ship with my friends, that pirates coming in numbers from many sides threatened to sink that ship with their fleets, unless my friends surrendered me alone to them, if the passengers refused to do so, and preferred death with me to handing me over to the enemy, I would rather have cast myself into the deep to save the others, than I would bring those loving friends, I will not say to certain death, but into great danger of losing their lives. But when this ship of state, after the tiller had been torn from the grip of the Senate, tossing about on the deep and buffeted by blasts of sedition and discord, seemed likely to be attacked by many armed fleets, unless I alone were given up; when proscription, bloodshed, and plunder were threatened; when some were not defending me because they suspected it would be dangerous to themselves, others were roused by their inveterate hatred of loyal citizens; while some envied me, others thought that I was an obstacle to their plans, others wanted to avenge some grievance of their own, others hated the Republic itself and the status and peaceful security of the loyal citizens, and for these reasons demanded that I alone should be sacrificed—was it my duty to fight it out, I will not say to your utter ruin, but certainly with danger to you and your children, rather than alone take upon myself and endure, one on behalf of all, that which was threatening all? (45–46)[24]

Cicero first presents the image of the ship of state, then addresses its application. He pictures himself as sailing with friends in a ship that is suddenly attacked by pirates. This assault, the image for the assault of Clodius and the consuls, is certainly more apropos of the circumstances than would be a shipwreck that could be interpreted as an "act of God."[25] The fellow passengers who are willing to sacrifice themselves for Cicero provide an analogue for those "good men," the *boni*, who remained loyal to Cicero and the Republic.

In the application of the image we see the familiar picture of the ship of state, floating out to the deep amid storms of sedition and discord, its tiller torn from the hands of the Senate (its rightful helmsman), about to be attacked by an armed flotilla. Indeed, this most elaborate "allegory"[26] is a summary of all those previous nautical images—rather, of the entire thrust of the speech up to this point—and provides an almost poetic climax for Cicero's depiction of the status of the Republic in the hands of his and Sestius' enemies.

The most interesting and important portrait presented in this passage is that of Cicero the martyr, whose sacrifice redeemed the Republic from destruction. The sacrificial tone of the language and the emphasis on the theme "one for all" (*unus pro omnibus*, 46) would certainly have recalled to the Roman audience the noble and hallowed tradition of *devotio*: the option, open to a Roman general whose army was being bested in battle, to sacrifice himself or his representative in exchange for victory and the destruction of the enemy.[27] Here Cicero, through the symbolic death of his exile, sacrifices himself to ensure life and victory for the Republic.

That Cicero wishes to depict his exile as a *devotio pro re publica* is made clear only a few lines later, where he identifies himself with other martyrs who died *pro patria*, especially with P. Decius Mus and his son, whose *devotiones* were viewed by the people as legendary acts of heroism (48).[28] By portraying his exile as a *devotio pro re publica* and himself as the martyr who effected the sacrifice, Cicero makes creative use of both ethos and historical example. The idea of *devotio*, so important in the *Pro Sestio*, is in fact a recurrent and central theme in many of the *post reditum* speeches, representing a conscious effort by Cicero to rebuild his persona and recapture some of his lost dignity.

Cicero had introduced the theme of *devotio* in the first sentence of his first address to the people following his return:

> Fellow citizens: On the day when I vowed to sacrifice (*devovi*) myself and my fortunes on behalf of the cause of your safety, tranquility, and union, I prayed of Jupiter Optimus Maximus, and of all the other immortal gods . . . that if my earlier achievements had had the preservation of the community as their object, and if your welfare also had been the motive that led me to submit to the unhappy necessity of retirement, they should make me, and not the Republic and its loyal citizens, the exclusive mark of the pent-up hatred conceived by wicked and unscrupulous men. (*Post Red. ad Quir.* 1)[29]

Less than a month later, addressing the College of Pontiffs on the status of his house (*De Domo Sua*), Cicero elaborated on this role. As in the *Pro Sestio*, his identification with the sacrificial victim whose immolation saved the state comes primarily within the context of his longer justification for going into exile. The *unus pro omnibus* theme surfaces first in section 30.[30] Then the other arguments justifying Cicero's exile emerge (cf. also 63–64 and 96–99): that he had refused, out of consideration for the Republic and the *boni*, to resort to arms to maintain his position; that he and his destruction are somehow tied to or identified with the Republic; and that under these circumstances, he had voluntarily chosen to sacrifice himself on behalf of the commonweal.[31] Explicit reference is made to the *devotiones* of the Decii:[32]

> I had heard and had read how distinguished compatriots of ours had dashed into the thick of the foe upon indubitable death in order to save the army; and was I, when the safety of the whole Republic was to be won, to shrink from playing this part under better conditions than the Decii enjoyed, inasmuch as while they could not even hear of the fame they had won, I might have been in a position to be even the spectator of my own renown? (*De Domo Sua* 64)[33]

By casting his withdrawal from Rome in such a light, Cicero attempts cleverly to transform the disgrace of exile into the glory of saving the state. The ethos of the *dux togatus*, so important in the consular speeches, returns, bolstered now by his claim of having saved the state a second time: "Twice have I saved the Republic; first, when consul in the garb of peace I overcame armed forces, and next, when as a private citizen I gave ground before armed consuls" (*De Domo Sua* 99).[34]

To turn our discussion back to the *Pro Sestio*, Cicero makes this same claim more boldly after the description of his sacrifice. His symbolic *devotio* that saved the Republic and its citizens recovers for the former *Pater Patriae* some of the glory and dignity he had enjoyed at the time of his first saving act:

> So then I saved the Republic by my withdrawal, gentlemen; by my own grief and sorrow I kept off from you and your children devastation, fire, and rapine; I alone twice saved the Republic, once with glory, the second time with misery to myself. (49)[35]

The remainder of Cicero's account (55–70) centers on "the other iniquities of that year" (55). In terms of ethos, Cicero's flattering encomium of Marcus Cato (60–63), whose character the prosecution had attempted to sully, is most interesting. Pompey, another character enjoying great personal influence, is introduced as Cicero shows him taking up the cause of the Republic (Cicero's recall) (67). This picture provides a transition for the narrative to return in sections 71–77 to its avowed subject, the tribunate of Sestius. Here the tribune is similarly shown taking up the cause of the Republic, the *causa Ciceroniana* (72). Even here Cicero's ethos and the story of his return overshadow his client. At the end of that fatal year, "men seemed to breathe again, not yet in reality, but in the hope that the Republic would be restored" (71).[36] What he means to say is, of course, "in the hope that I would be restored"! The image of the ship recurs, this time emphasizing Cicero's role, as he reports a speech given on his behalf by Cotta:

> L. Cotta, asked first his opinion, said . . . that when right and justice were overthrown, when a great political upheaval was imminent, I had turned aside a little and, in the hope of finding calm hereafter, had avoided the stormy waves before me. Since by my absence I had saved the Republic from dangers as threatening as those from which I had once delivered it by my presence, it was therefore fitting that I should not merely be restored, but also honored by the Senate. (73)[37]

In this remarkable passage Cicero becomes the helmsman, or perhaps even the ship itself—the ship identified with the *res publica*, the state of Rome.

The narrative passes almost without notice into the refutation of the charge of violence (77–96), the formal and relevant *argumentatio* of the speech. Traditionally the main body of a forensic oration, the "proof" of the *Pro Sestio* is striking in its brevity, comprising only a fraction of the whole. Its short but central position in the speech, hidden as it were between the lengthy, "ethical" narrative and the extraordinary digression that follows it, reminds one of Demosthenes' treatment of the formal charge in his masterpiece, *On the Crown*.[38] Even in this portion of the speech ethos plays an important role. We see sketched through vivid narrative and description the portraits of the wounded, half-dead, yet still courageous Sestius (79), Milo, the champion of the state (and Cicero, 86–87), Piso and Gabinius, "who brought the state to the brink of ruin" (93–94), and the gladiator and fury, Clodius (88, 95).

This brief *argumentatio* concludes with a skillful introduction (96) to the *ethica digressio* (96–143). Unique among the speeches for its size and scope, this digression represents nothing less than the orator's plea for the forging of an ideal Optimate government, "an attempt at a constructive union of responsible conservative sentiment."[39] This harks back, although on a much broader scale, to Cicero's alliance between the Senate and the Roman knights during his consulship, the so-called *Concordia Ordinum*.[40] Taking his cue from the scornful question of the prosecutor—"What is the meaning of our 'nation of Optimates' (*natio optimatium*)?"—he first justifies the inclusion of such remarks and then proceeds, by developing the technique of definition, to sketch in some detail the character of the *optimates*, "who have acted so as to win by their policy the approval of all the best citizens," the character of himself as their chief spokesman, and the character of their adversaries, the *populares*, "who wished everything they did and said to be agreeable to the masses" (96).

This expansive excursus breaks into three rather distinct parts. A substantial central panel, in which the ethos of Cicero and the circumstances that surrounded his exile and recall are largely employed as illustrations, is devoted to demonstrating unanimity of public opinion; two equal portions concerned primarily with the ethos of the *optimates* (and *populares*) frame this panel. Far from being a "nation" or a "breed" as Vatinius had labeled them, the *optimates* in Cicero's estimation consist of "every good citizen" (*optimus quisque*), a phrase that can, with the exception of the few hostile and revolutionary *populares*, embrace the entire *populus Romanus*, including members of the senatorial order, municipal and rural citizens, businessmen and freedmen alike—"in short, no narrow oligarchy, but a union representative of all that was best in Italy, materially and morally" (97).[41]

To articulate the credo of the *optimates* Cicero once again resorts to nautical imagery:

> What then is the mark set before those who steer the ship of state, upon which they ought to keep their eyes and towards which they ought to direct their course? It is that which is far the best and the most desirable for all who are sound and good and prosperous, *cum dignitate otium*. (98)[42]

This *cum dignitate otium*, for Cicero a kind of tranquility linked with dignity in both the state and his own life,[43] has as its foundations the following elements: religious observances, the auspices, the powers of the magistrates, the authority of the Senate, the laws, ancestral custom, criminal and civil jurisdiction, financial credit, the provinces, the allies, the prestige of the government, the army, the treasury (98). When wicked men, bent on civil discord, assault these institutions and work for the ruin of the state, and "storms are aroused in the Republic," then "those who have claimed possession of the helm of the state must watch and strive with all their skill and diligence that they may be able, without any damage to those foundations and elements of which I have just spoken, to hold their course and reach the harbor of *otium cum dignitate*" (99).[44]

With this final occurrence of the image of the ship of state, Cicero, having woven the thread of the motif throughout the speech, now links it specifically to ethos and resolves the problem. The tiller of the ship is no longer in the hands of an unskilled, unscrupulous pilot like Gabinius (cf. 20), but rather under the control of the *optimates*, who, relying on their skill and diligence, and with an eye to the foundations of the Republic, hold their steady course into the safety of the harbor of *otium* and *dignitas*. The stability depicted here is a striking contrast to the ship's precarious existence in the hands of the *populares*, in previous uses of the image (e.g., 15, 20, 46): the Republic as a shipwreck, Piso and Gabinius as storms that buffet the state, the attack on the ship by pirates (Cicero's enemies). This contrast of character contributes in general to Cicero's vision of an alliance of "all best men" that would benevolently govern the Republic, and in particular to the defense of Sestius, who through his support of Cicero becomes implicitly identified with "the best men" and their efforts against "reckless and abandoned men" (100)—*populares* including Piso, Gabinius, Clodius, and the prosecutors—who work for the Republic's ruin.

After citing historical examples of noble *optimates* of the past and urging imitation of their conduct (101–105), Cicero moves to the second and central portion of the digression (106–127), devoted to showing that at present all citizens hold the same opinion in regard to public affairs (i.e., in keeping with the opinion of Cicero's union of *optimates*); moreover, those who claim to be "friends of the people" represent a tiny minority, a mere gang of hirelings (106). To illustrate this point he proposes three touchstones in public affairs that best indicate the sentiments of the people: a meeting (*contio*), an assembly (*comitia*), and a gathering for plays or gladiatorial shows (*ludorum gladiatorumque consessus*). Choosing the period of his own exile as the focal point of public opinion, he endeavors to show that the real, representative, "popular" opinion expressed in these three situations unanimously favored him and his recall, while those who opposed such measures, madmen and mercenaries, neither worked for the people's desires or advantage, nor indeed were favored by the people (114).

Various character sketches of such charlatan *populares* are presented throughout this part of the digression, including invectives against Gellius Poplicola, a witness against Sestius (110–111), Clodius (116), and Appius Claudius, brother of Clodius (126). Cicero's description of Clodius presents a good example of the biting tone that pervades these sketches:

> That arch-comedian himself, not merely a spectator, but an actor and a virtuoso, who knows all the pantomimic interludes of his sister, who is admitted into a gathering of women in the guise of a harp-girl, neither attended your games during that fiery tribunate of his, nor any others except once when he scarcely escaped alive. (116)[45]

Portrayal of ethos on the Optimate side is far from lacking, with the character of Cicero, of course, drawing the most attention. Identification of himself with the Republic remains explicit:

> But when there were proposals concerning my dignity [i.e., that he should be restored], no one thought himself sufficiently excused by ill health or old age from staying away; there was no one who did not feel that in recalling me he was recalling the Republic to its own home. (112)[46]

A clever and very subtle passage (120–124) describes the tragic actor Aesopus' presentation of lines of the Roman tragedian Accius, delivered in such a way that they seemed to refer to Cicero, and the people's dramatic and emotional response. That Cicero is only reporting hearsay in this account contributes to its effectiveness: "How on that occasion the whole audience indicated their feelings, how the whole Roman people declared their goodwill for a man who was not a *popularis*, I heard by report; those who were present can more readily estimate" (122).[47]

More blatant is the praise Cicero renders himself in the account of his triumphal return (127–131). Rhetorical questions highlighted by other rhetorical devices provide a powerful artistic means for the expression of Cicero's ethos, its *auctoritas*, and its effect upon the Roman people, the Senate, and all of Italy:

> Whom has the senate-house missed more? Whom has the Forum lamented more, for whom have the courts themselves longed as much? When I withdrew, all was deserted, grim, mute, full of grief and mourning. What place in Italy is there, in which there is not engraved on public monuments the zeal for my welfare and testimony of my dignity?[48]

The last character sketch (132–135) in this central portion of the digression is of Vatinius, an enemy of Cicero and Sestius, who Cicero claims is responsible for the pejorative label *natio optimatium*. By reintroducing (cf. 96), even by way of invective, the author of the term and the source for Cicero's remarks concerning the topic, the orator brings us full circle to the starting point of the discussion, the ethos of the *optimates*.

This return to the subject of the *optimates* forms the final part of the digression (136–143) and provides a frame around the central panel, resulting in an ABA arrangement. These concluding paragraphs of the digression represent nothing less than a eulogy of the "best men" along with an exhortation to young Romans to follow their example. It has been Cicero's goal throughout the speech to align Sestius and his political actions with himself and his own political philosophy in strong opposition and contrast to people like Clodius, Piso, Gabinius, and other *populares*. This alliance, a *concursus bonorum omnium*, crosses the barriers of birth and heritage to embrace all who, steeped in the *mos maiorum*, work to preserve and build up the foundations of the Republic. This is the only road to genuine glory and fame:

> Believe me, this is the one road to esteem, dignity, and office (honor): to deserve the praise and affection of loyal citizens who are wise and of a good natural disposition and to understand the organization of the state so wisely established by our ancestors. (137)[49]

The contrast between those who follow this road and those who choose another path is made quite explicit:

> But my entire speech is addressed to virtue, not to indolence; to dignity, not to desire, to those who consider themselves born for their country, for their fellow citizens, for esteem, for glory, not for sleep, for feasting, and for enjoyment. For if they are led astray by pleasures, and have given themselves up to the seductions of vice and the allurements of desire let them renounce public office, let them not touch the Republic, let them be content to enjoy their own ease and to owe it to the labor of brave men. (138)[50]

Such brave men who defend the principles of the Republic are *optimates*, regardless of their order or social status. Their path, Cicero concedes, is certainly a difficult one to tread, but many Romans, and even Greeks, have attained perpetual fame through such loyal service to their country (140–142). The digression ends with a passionate exhortation to emulate the past heroes of Rome; its emotional, declamatory style provides a fitting transition to the peroration (144–147), which itself begins with a *commiseratio* (144–145) and ends with a final identification of Cicero's cause with that of Sestius (cf. 31) and others who had supported him (145–146). The final words of the speech imprint upon the minds of the jury the stance Cicero's defense had actually taken throughout the speech: "Wherefore, I beg and beseech you, if you willed my salvation, to preserve those by whose efforts you have recovered me" (147).[51]

We know from Cicero's own testimony (*Ad Quint. Fr.* 2. 4. 1) that the entire defense of Sestius was a rousing success. Relying upon his colleagues' treatment of the formal charges, Cicero restricted his refutation of the charge of *vis* to a mere fraction of the whole (77–95), surrounding and almost concealing it with narratives and digressions that reveal the ethos of the individuals involved and of the groups they represent. As indicated by his final plea, Cicero's real strategy is to justify and glorify his own character and position and then, by explicitly identifying Sestius with himself, to exonerate him of all charges. The effectiveness of such a strategy was witnessed in the *Pro Sulla*; a more artistic application is evident here.

The long narrative that comprises the first half of the oration (6–77) contains a remarkable amount of character delineation, of Sestius, of Clodius, of Piso and Gabinius, but especially of Cicero. The persona that Cicero struggles to project, that of the self-sacrificing savior of the state for a second time, is greatly enhanced by the artistic manipulation of two themes that contribute some sort of persuasive quality, and therefore credibility, to Cicero's ethos. The first, a variation on traditional patron–client identification, is Cicero's identification of himself with the Republic and his *causa* (the effort for his recall) with the *causa rei publicae*. By explicitly identifying Sestius and his defense with himself and his *causa*, which is, in turn, identified with the Republic and its *causa*, Cicero imparts a special kind of *auctoritas* to his pleading. The second theme is Cicero's depiction of his exile as a sacrifice *pro omnibus*, a *devotio pro re publica*. Casting his exile in this light allows Cicero to corroborate the persona of the selfless leader he had projected years before and to regain some of his lost *dignitas* by enabling him to proclaim that he had saved the state a second time. Both these themes, so carefully wrought in this speech, recur in several other *post reditum* speeches and are obviously part of a network of resonances that Cicero appears to have consciously constructed upon his return in order to assuage the blow of exile and to transform it from a source of disgrace and ignominy to one of glory and fame.

Character portraits of Cicero's enemies abound; drawn as the pestilences that plague the Republic or the scourges that wound it, they provide an artistic complement to the metaphor of the afflicted or wounded Republic that can be identified with Cicero. His use of the image of the ship of state further underscores the *populares'* inability to govern the Republic and contributes substantially to constructing what, by this time, has become a familiar scenario in Ciceronian speeches: a conflict or antithetical juxtaposition of the parties involved. In this case, Cicero, Sestius, and the Republic stand in opposition to Clodius, Piso, Gabinius, and anarchy.

The long *ethica digressio* (96–143) serves as an expansion and formalization of this antithetical conflict as Cicero defines more closely the ethos of the *optimates* and *populares*. Considered in this light, Cicero's plan for an alliance of the "best men" actually represents a plea for support of himself, his client Sestius, and all who support the senatorial and constitutional government of the Republic against a band of gangsters and revolutionaries, supporters of men like Clodius, who call themselves *populares*. The use of the image of the ship of state, the dominant leitmotif of the speech, supports this interpretation as it acts as a unifying element in the discursive oration. Buffeted by storms of sedition and discord while in the hands of the so-called *populares* (in the first part of the speech), the ship in the hands of the *optimates* (in the digression) holds course and steers straight for the harbor of *otium cum dignitate*. The ethical portrait of two characters writ large, the juxtaposition of *optimates* versus *populares*, good versus evil embodied in Cicero and his supporters versus Clodius and his followers, enabled the jury to cast their lot with Cicero's forces and vote for acceptance of his ideal—which, of course, implied the acquittal of Publius Sestius.

## PRO M. CAELIO

Less than a month after the defense of Sestius, Cicero delivered before the same court, the *quaestio de vi*, a very different kind of oration on behalf of Marcus Caelius, who was charged on five counts, including violence and attempted poisoning. Faced with the rhetorical challenge of having little factual evidence to corroborate his case, the orator found his response in "the brilliant color, the entertaining irrelevancies, the vigor and self-assurance of the presentation, and the consular authority shed on Caelius by Cicero himself."[52] Delivered during the celebration in Rome of the Ludi Megalenses, Cicero's speech is in some ways his own theatrical production, a *ludus scaenicus*, a *fabula*, whose tone, characters, themes, and actions all recall, sometimes with amazing correspondence, the stock elements of a Roman comedy.[53] Under these circumstances ethos of course supplies a major source for persuasive material as Cicero disarms potentially dangerous charges by means of his cleverness, wit, and ability to portray character.[54]

In a highly stylized *exordium* (1–2) and in a manner reminiscent of a *prologus* who speaks at the beginning of a play, Cicero briefs his audience on the situation, reminds them of the festival atmosphere that should prevail during these days of the *ludi*, and introduces the actors in the case. First, there is Caelius, "a young man distinguished by his brilliant intellect, his industry, and his influence" (1). A veiled reference is next made to Clodia, Caelius' yet-to-be named antagonist, whom Cicero characterizes as a wanton prostitute (1–2). There is a brief reference to his audience, the "hard-working jurors" (1) and finally a picture of the two *patroni* of the case: Cicero, the understanding, avuncular advocate, and Atratinus, the counsel for the prosecution, Cicero's friend, "a most accomplished and humane young man" (2), who has, either through mistake or misguidance, chosen to undertake the prosecution.

In the next portion of the speech, which Austin labels a *praemunitio* (3–50),[55] Cicero sets out to demolish a number of charges and insinuations made by the prosecution, not through any systematic refutation or presentation of factual evidence or witnesses (cf. 22), but by means of his disarming, sometimes devastating wit, his clever ability to divert the direction of a charge, and, most important for our purposes, his artistic manipulation of ethos. In comic terms, Caelius is presented as the archetypical hero who at one time is identified with, and at another time is supported by, his *patronus* Cicero. The enemies, those accusers and adversaries who charge him and seek to rob him of his position (cf. 3), are all cast in the role of "blocking characters," who through their *severitas* impede in some way the hero's wishes or goals, in this case, his extrication from the charges—his acquittal.[56]

Atratinus, the young prosecutor, is handled roughly by Cicero. Although he claims *lenitas* as his guide, he projects an overbearing tone of condescension that must have caused even the bystanders to wince.[57] Employing the now familiar ethical tactic of portraying the *accusator* as an *amicus*,[58] he first identifies Atratinus as a friend, a *necessarius* (3), and then subjects him to a master-orator's judgment upon his character, his actions in this prosecution, and his oratorical abilities:

> With you Atratinus, I will deal more leniently. . . . I should like, however, to give you some advice: first, to let men form a correct opinion of you, so that, just as you are far from baseness in deed, you may keep yourself free from license in word; in the next place, not to bring charges against another which you would blush to hear brought falsely against yourself. For who is there who does not find that road open? Who is there who cannot make some scandalous attack as impudently as he pleases against your time of life and also against your dignity, even if without grounds for suspicion, yet not without some basis for accusation? But the blame for the part you have played rests with those who desired you to play it; the credit belongs to your scruples, because we saw with what reluctance you spoke, and to your ability, because you spoke with such grace and refinement. (7–8)[59]

L. Herennius Balbus, Atratinus' *subscriptor*, whose speech on behalf of the prosecution had railed against prodigality, lust, and the vices of youth (25), is cast in the role of an overstern censor of morals (25) and characterized by the Roman traits of *severitas* and *gravitas* in the extreme.[60] In the subsequent comparison (*synkrisis*) of fathers (37–38), borrowed from Roman comedy, Cicero corroborates this portrait as he suggests identification of Balbus with those stern, unbending, "iron-like fathers" (*ferrei patres*), guided by *auctoritas* and *severitas*, who scold their sons as fathers do in the comedies of Caecilius—from which he quotes:

> What am I to say? What am I to wish? Whate'er you do,
> By your disgraceful deeds you make my wishes vain. (37)[61]

The persona that Cicero's ethos assumes throughout the speech, particularly in this part, provides a foil to the harsh severity of the blocking characters.[62] He is to be identified with the "mild and indulgent father" of the *synkrisis*, whose attitude is epitomized by an apt quotation from Terence's *Adelphi* 120–121:

> He has broken a door, the wreck shall be made good;
> He has torn your clothes, they shall be mended up. (38)[63]

Cicero, who in most other contexts would have been counted a staunch supporter of *gravitas* and *auctoritas*, is now, in a spirit reminiscent of his handling of Cato in the *Pro Murena*, careful not to overstep the bounds of propriety in his advocacy of license. Rather, he concentrates on demonstrating the inflexibility and unreasonableness of Caelius' critics. "Boys will be boys," he says, "and their harmless peccadilloes, which we all enjoyed in our own time, should be winked at so long as they are within bounds":

> Let some sport be granted to age. Let youth be allowed greater freedom; let not pleasures always be forbidden; let not that upright and unbending reason always prevail; let desire and pleasure sometimes triumph over reason, provided that in such matters the following rule and limitation is observed: let a young man be mindful of his own repute and not a despoiler of another's . . . Finally, when he has listened to the voice of pleasure and given some time to the sport of youth and its empty desires, let him at length turn to the interests of home life, to activity in the Forum and the Republic, so that all those pursuits of vanity, which reason had previously failed to reveal, he may show that he has abandoned from satiety and found contemptible through experience. (42)[64]

In this same vein Cicero goes so far as to suggest, certainly tongue in cheek, that Caelius' affair with Clodia was an action that actually upheld the *mos maiorum*! "If there is anyone who believes that affairs with prostitutes have been off limits to youth, this man is undeniably severe. . . . This line of thinking is not only out of step with the license of the times but even with the practice of our ancestors" (48).[65]

Indeed, Cicero's portrayal of Caelius is aimed at presenting a young man who, although he has had his scrapes with *voluptas*, is now ready for more serious pursuits. Cicero projects the image of a Caelius who is in possession of an honorable heritage (3–5), a gifted intellect (cf. 1, 45), and the training (*disciplina*) and industry (*industria*) (cf. 1, 9, 11, 39, 45, 72, 74, 76) required for honorable pursuits. The Roman belief in the consistency of character is invoked as Cicero argues (45–47) that "a mind truly dedicated to passion and hindered by love, longing, and desire" (45) cannot be made to square with Caelius' *industria, disciplina*, and *ingenium*, which have been so vividly demonstrated in the young man's oratory and by his prosecutions (46–47). This contrast between the two styles of life, between two kinds of *mores*, reflects in some way the larger set of antitheses that Cicero works to establish throughout the speech, in Geffcken's words, "between *severitas* and *ludus*, between age and youth, between *industria* and *disciplina* in their due places and *voluptas* in its proper time."[66]

One of the strongest corroborating tactics that gives credence to this picture of Caelius' character is Cicero's identification with his client. The great consular orator, who claims that his own life and reputation have flowed from sources similar to those of Caelius (6), presents a slightly different kind of advocacy, that of a mentor, almost a father to his client:

> As soon as his father had given him the *toga virilis*—and here I will say nothing about myself (I will be content to leave that to your estimation)—I will only say that he was brought to me at once by his father. No one ever saw this young Marcus Caelius, while he was in that early youth, in the company of anyone but his father or myself, or in the irreproachable household of Marcus Crassus, while he was being trained in the most honorable pursuits. (9)[67]

As director of Caelius' *tirocinium fori*, Cicero becomes in a sense the custodian, the guarantor, of Caelius' character, the pledge that secures for the Roman people Caelius' honorable behavior (cf. 77, 80).[68]

In this regard, Cicero must next face the potentially damning charge of Caelius' association with Catiline (10–15). After emphatically insisting on Caelius' intimacy with himself and his way of thinking during his early career (cf. 10), he is forced to admit that Caelius had supported Catiline in his second candidacy for the consulship. Ethos, this time the character of Catiline, again supplies material to neutralize the charge. The portrait that Cicero sketches of the villain is partly familiar from the *Catilinarians*, and partly new as he forges together those wicked and lurid aspects of character with those that were most alluring in his old adversary. The result is the creation of an ethos (12–14) that defies by its very duplicity the Roman conception of character to such a degree that Catiline, in this regard, cannot be considered a human being, but rather some strange, unique monster or portent:

> No, I do not believe that there has ever existed on earth such a monster, such a fusion of natural tastes and desires that were contradictory, divergent, and at war among themselves. (12)[69]

It was precisely owing to this uncharacteristic character, so uniquely defiant of Roman assumptions about ethos, that Caelius, and along with him many other good men, were tricked into supporting this "monster." Even Cicero was almost bamboozled:

> I myself, yes, I say, I was once myself nearly deceived by him, when I took him for a loyal citizen, eager for the acquaintance of all the best men, and for a true and faithful friend. I had to see his crimes before I believed them, and to have my hands on them before I even suspected them. If Caelius also was among his crowds of friends, there is more reason why he should himself be troubled at his mistake, just as I too sometimes regret my own with regard to this same man, than that he should be in fear of such a friendship being made a matter of accusation. (14)[70]

This rather breathtaking confession, coming from the consul who had claimed so often to have discovered the villainy of Catiline, provides a kind of capstone to his identification with his client and a compelling argument for Caelius' innocent error in this regard.

The most detailed, witty, and artful use of ethos in this portion of the speech is, of course, Cicero's treatment of Clodia, whom he endeavors to portray as Caelius' chief antagonist and the source of all trouble and complaint. With the first, rather oblique, reference to Clodia in the speech, where he asserts that Caelius is being "besieged by the forces of a prostitute" (1), Cicero has already introduced the two major comic character themes that he will employ at her expense. We have seen in previous speeches Cicero's portrayal of characters in terms of stock, comic traits.[71] The portrait of the prostitute (*meretrix*) who, as a kind of *dux femina* (i.e., a female general, a *miles gloriosa*), assails her innocent victim recurs throughout this speech to play a central part in Cicero's unstaged comedy.[72]

In another oblique but telling reference (18), Cicero builds the suspense as he blames all of Caelius' troubles on some "Medea of the Palatine," who will remain unnamed until sections 30–31. There Clodia is finally pronounced as the source of the charges, "a woman not only of noble birth (*nobilis*), but also of notoriety (*nota*)" (31). With this pun, he begins to sketch the portrait of Clodia, the immoral, wanton woman, free with her favors—even with her brother:[73]

> And that I should do even more vehemently, were I not hindered by my personal enmity to that woman's husband—I meant to say brother; I always make that mistake. As it is, I will act with moderation. . . . For indeed I never thought that

I should have to engage in quarrels with women, still less with a woman whom everyone has always thought to be everyone's friend rather than anyone's enemy. (32)[74]

Cicero next presents a masterful display of dramatic ethos, unparalleled in any of his speeches, as he introduces two *prosopopoeiae*, or impersonations of character, who each, in his turn, castigates Clodia and contributes to her portrait. Heightening the effect is the fact that Cicero chooses as his dramatis personae members of the noble Claudian family who, albeit at different ends of the spectrum in terms of time, age, and morals, both upbraid their relative for her behavior.[75]

On the one side stands Appius Claudius Caecus, censor in 312, consul in 307 and 296, builder of the Appian Way, paragon of Roman virtue, the very incarnation of *gravitas* and *auctoritas*. His "speech" is a curious mixture of the plain with the grand, meant to set in sharp contrast the glories of the Claudian *gens* (of himself in particular) with the "virtues" of Clodia (34):

> "Was it for this that I struck down the peace with Pyrrhus, so that you could daily strike up treaties of foulest love? Did I bring water to Rome so that you could use it incestuously? Did I build up a road so that you could walk it accompanied by other women's husbands?"[76]

At the other end of the spectrum is Clodia's youngest brother, Clodius, whom Cicero labels *urbanissimus* (36), the antithesis of that harsh, almost uncouth Caecus. With the severe persona of Caecus removed, Cicero introduces the persona of Clodius in his own character (35–36), admonishing Clodia that she will be held accountable for her familiarity with Caelius. The tone of the orator's narrative changes from the lofty to the low as he introduces a bedroom scene in which the chief actors are brother and sister.[77]

> I will choose [to personify] your youngest brother . . . who loves you most dearly; who, I suppose, being a prey to a sort of nervousness and certain idle terrors at night, always when a little fellow used to sleep with you, his elder sister. (36)[78]

Clodius' ensuing "speech" to his sister, reminiscent of the advice offered by pimps or bawds in comedy,[79] reveals much about Clodia's character and its manifestations in regard to Caelius. Her libidinous desire, her possessive impulsiveness, Caelius' unwillingness, Clodia's allurements, and her manifold opportunities for assignations are disclosed in only a few lines. The striking contrast between the personae of the ancestral Caecus and the living Clodius and the style and tone of their speeches is circumscribed by the consonance of their message to Clodia: forget about Caelius. Appius' solution is based on his call to Clodia for morality; Clodius' answer is based on his exhortation to his sister to extend the province of her immorality beyond Caelius.[80]

Quintilian (11.1.39) assures us that Cicero changed his tone and manner of presentation to suit each character, in a performance that must have brought not a little hilarity to the *corona* of the courtroom. We have noted elsewhere, in other contexts, the effectiveness of portraying character by introducing direct speech into the narrative. In this case, under a carefully wrought dramatic illusion, Cicero presents relatives of Clodia, speaking in their own character, each of whom in his own way castigates her while lending valuable insight into her ethos, at least as Cicero would have it portrayed. Although the *prosopopoeiae* are illusions, they nevertheless provide a more effective means of chastising Clodia's *mores* than would a straightforward sermon by the orator and a more subtle manner of characterization than invective or labeling.

These impersonations, in fact, prepare the audience for the reemergence of the *meretrix* theme. Cicero has been careful not to use the actual word, but rather to sketch the ethos of Clodia in such terms. After the brief comparison (37–38) between the severe, unfeeling father who epitomizes Balbus' approach to the case and the lenient, merciful father representing his own viewpoint, Cicero brands Clodia all the more deeply with the mark of the *meretrix* through his own insistent denial that he is referring to her at all:

> I am not now saying anything against that woman, but suppose it were someone quite unlike her—a woman who made herself common to all, who openly had some special lover every day, into whose gardens, house, and place at Baiae the passions of all come and go at will, who even supported young men, and made their fathers' stinginess bearable at her own expense; if a widow were casting off restraints, a frisky widow living frivolously, a rich widow living extravagantly, a wanton widow living whorishly, should I regard any man guilty of misconduct if he had been somewhat free in his attentions to her? (38)[81]

Only ten sections later (48–49), Cicero virtually repeats this sketch. These two passages, considered together, function as a kind of frame around the intervening portion of the speech, which is devoted to molding Cicero's persona as a forgiving father (esp. 39–42), presenting *exempla* to illustrate his argument, promoting the character of Caelius, and calling for the indulgence for youth that has always been granted, even by the *mos maiorum* (48). By following this sanction of indulgence with another vivid portrait of Clodia as a *meretrix*, Cicero implies that Caelius' involvement in the affair was entirely within the normal bounds of youthful behavior, whereas his lover's rapacious demands amounted to preying on his innocence and good nature.[82]

Once again Cicero employs the tactic of denying identification: "I will name no woman" (48). The life of the prostitute, the parties, the gardens, and Baiae return to the scene. The personal marks of a prostitute, however, spice this portrait: her bearing, her dress, her provocative eyes, her freedom of speech, even her embraces and caresses, betray not merely the ethos of a whore, but a "shameless and wanton whore" (49). Under such circumstances, does a youth who takes advantage of this situation, Cicero asks that severe Balbus (49), seem to assail this woman's chastity or simply gratify her passions?

Having established this scenario, Cicero claims to have laid the foundations for his defense. As he tells us (51), his speech has made its way "out of the shallows, escaped the reefs, and now faces only clear sailing ahead."[83] Indeed, he has established through character the basis for his defense. Although he has not as yet dealt systematically with the charges, he has skillfully placed all the characters of this production onstage: the hero Caelius, the indulgent father Cicero, Balbus, the epitome of *severitas*, and the wanton *meretrix* Clodia—all stock comic characters who create not only a comic atmosphere but the expectation among Cicero's audience for the stock comic denouement, the extrication of the hero.

At section 51 Cicero begins the formal *argumentatio* with a discussion of the charge that Caelius stole gold from Clodia (*crimen auri*). The argument is chiefly based on probability, and ethos supplies much of its material. Caelius' character is incompatible with such a crime and, barring that, too intelligent to have executed so great a crime so foolishly (53). Clodia is still the whore marked by an excessive degree of *familiaritas*,[84] toward Caelius (cf. 33, 53), her slaves, and with the exchange of a *quadrans*, even toward the public bathman (62)! With this last reference, Cicero reminds his audience of Clodia's meretricious nickname, *quadrantaria*, to which he will later refer (69).[85] Even the "prostitute's" house, which had figured prominently in earlier descriptions (cf. 38, 47, 52), begins to assume the character of its mistress and to become identified with her: "The whole charge arises from a hostile, infamous, cruel, crime-stained, lust-stained house" (55; cf. 57).[86] Juxtaposed to this is the house implicated in the charge, a house "full of integrity, dignity, duty, and piety" (55), the house of L. Lucceius, "a most virtuous man and a most honorable witness" (54). Under such circumstances, the validity of the *crimen auri* can, according to Cicero's standards, be determined simply by a comparison of character:

> The question to be decided is easy to settle—whether a rash, wanton, and angry woman seems to have trumped up this charge, or whether a man of sobriety, wisdom, and restraint seems to have given conscientious evidence. (55)[87]

The final part of Cicero's *argumentatio* (56–69), which deals with the charge of poisoning, also presents Cicero's finale to his "comedy," a *fabula* or *mimus balnearum* in which Clodia acts the leading role, but this time cast as a *dux femina*, an *imperatrix*, a kind of *miles gloriosa*.[88] The orator prefaces his narration of his mock-epic battle at the baths with a short but solemn eulogy (59–60) of Q. Metellus Celer, Roman patriot, supporter of Cicero and the Republic, and, incidentally, husband of Clodia, rumored to be the victim of this *Quadrantaria Clytaemnestra*. The movement from the heroic and sublime, as represented by Celer, to the mock-heroic and absurd, as seen in Clodia, emphatically underscores her own familiarity with poison as a murder weapon, recognition of which she did not bargain for in her charge against Caelius.

According to Cicero, the entire scene at the baths was Clodia's strategem: she designated the baths as a meeting place, posted the troops, set the ambush, planned the attack (63). Clodia, the *meretrix*, the *spoliatrix* (52), has now become the *imperatrix* (67):

> My mind is athrill at the idea of seeing, in the first place, these young dandies, intimate friends of a rich and noble woman, and, then again, those valiant warriors, posted by their commandress in ambush and in garrison at the baths. I intend to ask them how or where they concealed themselves; whether it was a bathtub, or a "Trojan Horse," which received and protected so many invincible warriors, waging war for a woman.[89]

Cicero has taken the *fabella* of Clodia, "the poetess of many such plays" (64), and through skillful narration and character portrayal has reduced it to absurdity, to a travesty, actually to a mime that, having no substantial material, no suitable plot, nor a proper ending, collapses (just as the charges against Caelius have done) in confusion and failure:

> So, then, we have the finale of a mime, not of a proper play; the sort of thing where, when no fit ending can be found, someone escapes from someone's clutches, off go the clappers and we get the curtain. (65)[90]

The peroration that concludes the speech (70–80) reiterates several of the themes and character portrayals found earlier in the oration. There is Clodia, the wanton force behind the prosecution (70); there is Cicero, servant of the state, who now guarantees Caelius' allegiance (77); but most importantly, there is Caelius (72–77), restored from the vagaries of youth, ready to live up to his true ethos, which is marked most deeply by its *disciplina* and *industria* (cf. 72, 73, 74, 76). Acquittal today, Cicero argues, is an investment in the Republic's future:

> If you restore Caelius in safety to me, to his own people, to the Republic, you will find in him one pledged, devoted, and bound to you and to your children; and it is you above all, gentlemen, who will reap the rich and lasting fruits of all his exertions and labors. (80)[91]

The *Pro Caelio* is unique among the speeches in the Ciceronian corpus for its widespread and very carefully wrought use of dramatic ethos. Each major character assumes the persona of a stock figure of Roman comedy; when combined, these produce a *fabula* worthy of the Ludi Megalenses. By casting the characters of the speech in such roles, Cicero can rely not only on his disarming wit to conciliate and ingratiate the jury to his case but also on his audience's preconceived notions of such comic roles to reinforce the portraits he has presented. In this regard, the characters of Clodia—the wanton whore and/or *miles gloriosa* who assails Caelius, the innocent, unsuspecting, promise-filled youth—are most important.

Unlike most of the *post reditum* speeches, the *Pro Caelio*, whose political ramifications are minimal, says little about Cicero, his exile, and his public role in the state. Traces of the anxious and humiliating struggle to regain his *dignitas* are absent from the speech. The consular ethos is there, to be sure, but presented ever so subtly. Atratinus, the prosecutor, is devastatingly dismissed as a neophyte. Caelius, the client, and his efforts are identified with

Cicero, the *patronus*, who, as the great consular orator, guarantees the young man's allegiance to the state. Through this identification Cicero speaks for Caelius and, in a sense, becomes Caelius, working as the comic hero who searches for extrication from his troubles and victory over those who would oppose him. Cicero's persona as the understanding, supportive, and merciful father is an extension of this role and works to effect the same result.

The extraordinary *prosopopoeiae* of Appius Claudius Caecus and Publius Clodius add yet another dimension to the use of ethos in the speech. Their characters, by nature so antipathetic, are nevertheless bound to one another by their common mission of admonishing their relative, Clodia. Although Cicero's audience must have split their sides in laughter, their laughter would certainly not have blinded them to Cicero's message as conveyed by these personae.

The speech, so successful at the time of its delivery, endures for us today as one of Cicero's finest efforts. For persuasion through sheer delight (recall that Cicero identifies *delectare* with ethos), the *Pro Caelio* stands unchallenged. Once again Cicero has shown us, in this magnificent rhetorical tour de force, the importance and effectiveness of ethos as a source for persuasive material.

## PRO CN. PLANCIO

The ethos and *auctoritas* of Cicero once again reemerge as the protagonists of the drama in the speech on behalf of Gnaeus Plancius, who, four years earlier, while serving as quaestor in Macedonia, had provided Cicero succor and friendship during the dark hours of his exile. Analogous in many respects to the speech on behalf of Sestius,[92] the *Pro Plancio* displays a collection of Ciceronian tactics whose source of persuasion resides in ethos. The actual charge (*ambitus*, bribery to influence an election), as we have seen happen in so many Ciceronian speeches, retreats into the backround, taking cover under the ethos of Cicero, his deeds, and his *auctoritas* and becoming further obscured by the presentation of the characters of the others involved in the case.

Allusions to the bonds between Cicero and his client, Cicero and the jury, and Cicero and the prosecutor introduce the speech (1–2). Plancius, whose exceptional loyalty toward Cicero during his exile accounted for the eager support of so many patriots at the polls, is now threatened, and dangerously so, because of that very loyalty and support; this situation evokes Cicero's grief (1). The jury, all of whom had prized the orator's safety, evoke Cicero's confidence (2); the prosecutor Laterensis, who himself had been so solicitous for the orator's dignity and safety (2), now evokes Cicero's surprise by launching this attack on Plancius. Patron–client identification is immediate and explicit, and Plancius' defense becomes the defense of Cicero:

> The labors involved in my present advocacy are already greater than those of the general run of cases; but I must go beyond these, and take upon myself the further burden of speaking, not only on behalf of Gnaeus Plancius, whose safety I am in duty bound to protect no less carefully than my own, but also on behalf of myself, for our opponents have said almost more about me than about my client and his case. (3)[93]

As he has done on other occasions,[94] Cicero here explains the large role that his ethos plays in the proceedings as being only his necessary, almost required response to charges of the prosecution. Indeed, his subsequent treatment reveals that many of Laterensis' arguments and those of L. Cassius, his *subscriptor*, were aimed at the great orator's ethos in an attempt to undermine his *auctoritas* (cf., e.g., 4, 72–77, 83–104). Such methods of prosecution may at first glance seem odd, or at best irrelevant; but considering the importance of ethos and authority in the Roman judicial setting, which is corroborated by the evidence we have seen thus far in Ciceronian oratory, the use of such tactics would not have seemed out of the ordinary in a Republican court of law. Recall that as a young pleader, Cicero had complained vigorously and repeatedly about his opponents' *auctoritas* as an obstacle to his defense. Now, with the tables turned, the *accusatores* of Plancius must have felt the weight of Cicero's *auctoritas* so strongly that they deemed it necessary to go to great lengths in their attempt to neutralize it.

Cicero, of course, denies the existence of any such advantage: "I do not have so good a conceit of myself as to presume to imagine that Plancius' services to me entitle him to exemption from all prosecution."[95] Plancius' own shining life and spotless character will secure his acquittal (3); nevertheless, the very prominence of Cicero's ethos throughout the speech, and the tack his argumentation takes later in the speech, belie his less than vigorous disavowals.

The *contentio dignitatis*, standard fare in a charge of *ambitus*, is next introduced (5–6). Cicero expresses his great consternation at being torn in opposite directions by two friends, one the prosecutor, the other the defendant, and admits his hesitancy in pursuing such a comparison between them (6). Manipulation of ethos is skillful in this part of the speech. Cicero emphasizes his close friendship with Laterensis (5), as well as the common ground that both he and Plancius shared with himself—the concern for Cicero's interests and welfare. Cicero carefully acknowledges Laterensis' virtuous character, his self-control, industry, patriotism, courage, integrity, honor, and devotion, but ascribes his electoral defeat to the impulse and caprice of the people, who are swayed more often by the personal efforts and popularity of the candidates, especially in the less important elections, than by such endowments as Laterensis possesses (9). Cicero breathes life into the *populus Romanus*, whom he personifies to give advice, in direct speech, to Laterensis:

> "I have not preferred Plancius to you, Laterensis, but, since there was no choice between you as good patriots, I chose to bestow my favors upon the man who importuned me for them, rather than upon the man who refused to supplicate me for them. . . . But, if you would attain to those high honors which your merit deserves, I suggest that you learn to do me a more earnest homage." (12–13)[96]

The persona Cicero assumes throughout this portion of the speech is that of a concerned friend and also a friendly mentor. Himself a successful veteran of the polls, he can counsel Laterensis, as he had Sulpicius in the *Pro Murena*, on the proper methods of canvass, the mistakes he made, and the spirit with which he should accept the outcome. Cicero throughout advocates a kind of philosophical approach to the people's mandate and a resigned acceptance of the rules of the political game:

> We too have our part to play; tossed as we are upon the stormy billows of popular favor, we must be content with the people's will, win it to ourselves when it is estranged, grapple it to us when we have won it, and pacify it when it is in turmoil. If we set no great store by its awards, we are not called upon to do it homage; but if we set our hearts upon them, we must not grow weary in courting its favor. (11)[97]

As the speech proceeds, identification of *patronus* with client becomes more explicit, particularly in the sections that deal with Plancius' election despite his lower social standing as an *eques* (17–24). Laterensis, basing his assumptions on Roman respect for character and authority, had argued that his *nobilitas* should have secured the office for him.[98] Cicero, like Plancius a Roman knight by origin (17), concedes the primacy of the prosecutor's heritage but is quick to point out that the nobility of his competitors proved ineffectual against his own bid for the consulship and other offices (18). Indeed, Laterensis' heritage, Cicero construes cleverly, proved a liability to his candidacy (19–24). Tusculum, his native town, is so packed with consular families that Laterensis' nobility and his candidacy went practically unnoticed (19); Plancius, on the other hand, a favorite son of Atina, became in his canvass a celebrity, a source of pride to townsmen and the surrounding population, who turned out en masse in his support. Cicero himself stands as an authority for such a phenomenon, along with C. Marius, for both rose to office as favorite sons of a similar hometown, Arpinum (20).

The most extraordinary instance of patron–client identification in this part of the speech occurs in Cicero's proclamation of his own contribution to Plancius' election (24–26). In an interesting twist of a tactic so popular under the conventions of the rhetoric of advocacy, he claims that Plancius' cause was supported not by the influence of the pleader, but by the motive of the plea (24). Plancius was supported by the people because the people supported Cicero's cause, which Plancius had taken up:

> I was canvassing for him, not because he was my friend or my neighbor, nor because I had been on very intimate terms with his father, but rather because he was, in a sense, the only begetter and savior of my life. It was no personal ascendancy, but the motive of my appeal that won men's hearts. No one was glad at my restoration or grieved at my injury who did not feel gratitude to Plancius because he had shown me pity. And if before my return loyal citizens came forward and spontaneously offered their services to Plancius when he was seeking the tribunate, can you believe that my prayers availed him nothing, when my name, even my absence, was a recommendation to him? (25–26)[99]

This argument for supporting Plancius because of his role as a supporter of Cicero will become increasingly important as the defense progresses.

In the final part of the *contentio dignitatis* (27–35) Cicero turns specifically to the character and life of Plancius. In a standard and summary fashion he sketches the portrait of an honorable, self-controlled, and dutiful young man, both in his public career as a soldier, military tribune, and quaestor (27–28) and in his private life (29–30). He then dismisses a few charges against Plancius' character as sullying insinuations (30–31) and finally defends the actions and ethos of Plancius' father (32–35). Cicero's use of "character witnesses" in the presentation of Plancius' ethos is quite effective. Appeal to the character and authority of such witnesses and their explicit identification with his client is again the favored technique. For example, Plancius not only reveres his father as a god, but identifies with him as "a companion, a brother, a comrade in years"; C. Saturninus, "a most accomplished man," joins Plancius in a "fellowship of grief"; Cicero, Plancius' *patronus*, becomes in this case Plancius' fellow-defendant (*mihi in huius periculo reus esse videor*, 29). These are the kinds of proofs, Cicero argues, whose source lies in character and whose authority resides in character, that are incontrovertible, fashioned in flesh not words:

> Yes, proofs such as these, gentlemen, are substantial and indubitable; they are tributes to integrity which are not colored by the hues of specious rhetoric, but stamped with the inalienable characters of truth. . . . Can you wonder, then, that a man was elected aedile who, though in respect of name and fame he may be inferior to yourself, is nevertheless your superior in the support given to him by his townsfolk, his neighbors, his associates, and in his connection with me in the crisis of my life, is your equal in virtue, integrity, and self-mastery, and is adorned with every quality which lends intrinsic as well as extrinsic worth? (29–30)[100]

At section 36 Cicero claims that he is at last turning to the question at issue. He endeavors here, as he had earlier in the speech (cf. 5, 6, 16, esp. 17), to impress upon the jury his desire to stick to the facts of the case. That this demand is less than sincere is indicated not only by the brevity of what might be called the formal *probatio* of the case (36–57) but also by its content. Neither much time nor much effort is expended in denying the charge;[101] rather, Cicero concentrates on complaining about Laterensis' method of jury selection (36–46)[102] and deflecting accusations about *sodalicia* (46–48) and *coitio* (53–54).

Even in this phase of the speech Cicero's argumentation finds itself moving back into the realm of ethos. Laterensis is still portrayed as the upright noble, marked by the traditional virtues of *gravitas* and *magnitudo animi* (50); now, however, these virtues are given an ironic twist: Cicero blames Laterensis' ultimate failure at the polls on these stellar qualities. It was precisely his magnanimity and loftiness of character that had prevented him from supplicating the Roman people on his knees, obtaining a postponement, and thereby securing election as so many nobles before him had done:

> I have not the least doubt that the whole populace would have come over to your side. Almost never has it happened that nobility, above all a nobility which is blameless and irreproachable, has been, when a suppliant, rejected by the Roman people. (50)[103]

As he had done so cleverly in the *Pro Murena*, Cicero converts his opponent's strength of character, normally a decisive advantage, into a liability that stands as the ultimate cause for his failure in the election.

Irony in connection with Laterensis' nobility continues. In answer to the query of what Laterensis might reply to his ancestral busts (*imagines*) and to his late father, a most excellent and accomplished man, Cicero catalogues a long list of nobles who were defeated for the aedileship but were afterwards elected consuls. Laterensis is merely following their example; he should be encouraged by it; in fact his defeat, if interpreted rightly, could be construed as a recognition of his merit (52)! By cleverly toying with the noble ethos of Laterensis, Cicero has managed to convert the disgrace of the election into a moral victory that has its basis in that very nobility and, in doing so, to neutralize to a large extent the advantage that *nobilitas* would have certainly lent the plaintiff in this case.

Cicero next addresses L. Cassius, junior *subscriptor* to Laterensis, in a refutation of charges (58–71) that dealt primarily with Cicero and Plancius' connection to him. From this point in the speech to its conclusion, the ethos of Cicero plays an increasingly significant role. Cicero assumes the by now familiar role of friend (*familiaris*, 57) and advisor to Cassius. His tone is gentlemanly and civil but not without a subtle edge of irony and condescension.[104] After praising his speech for its elegance and grace (58), Cicero turns the tables on his opponent, implying that Cassius, unlike Plancius, is really not conscious of his own oratorical limitations (62). Next he deflates the impact of Cassius' encomium of Laterensis by agreeing with it entirely—even though it is irrelevant to the case (63).[105] But he goes a step further and converts Cassius' praise of Laterensis into a source of censure: "Not merely do I grant that the highest endowments are to be found in Laterensis, but I would even find fault with you for gathering specious and trivial qualities, instead of enumerating the solid endowments he possesses" (63). The final stroke that completes this subtle yet devastating squelch of the *subscriptor* is Cicero's vignette of the student Cassius, who spends his leisure studying the speeches of his friend (and teacher) Cicero—who himself spends his private hours writing them: "absolute leisure was a thing I never knew" (66).

The treatment of Plancius' character in this part of the speech is interesting. Cicero attempts to compensate for his client's rather embarrassingly scanty list of public qualifications by dwelling on his worthy character traits. No glorious soldier, no orator or juris-consult,[106] Plancius nevertheless exhibits the moral qualities necessary for a candidate: "uprightness, honesty, incorruptibility, not a glib tongue, professional skill, a deep knowledge" (62). Like slaves bought to manage estates, magistrates are "stewards (*vilici*) of the Republic" who need only to excel in frugality, industry, and vigilance. If a candidate possesses any special expertise, the Roman people are certainly pleased, but an ethos marked by upright-ness (*virtus*) and integrity (*innocentia*) is really the only require-ment (62). Such a line of argument issuing from Cicero, a *novus homo* certainly possessed of *virtus* and *industria*, but one who ad-mittedly attributed his political successes to his great oratorical skill, must have sounded as incredible to the Roman jury as it does to us today.

Plancius' qualifications are, of course, bolstered by Cicero's identification with him. Born from similar roots, Cicero, a "new man," climbed the steps to the highest honors. Plancius (and La-terensis for that matter), if he follows the correct path, can do the same. The lively narrative concerning Cicero's quaestorship in Sic-ily and its general anonymity among citizens in Rome works quite effectively in this regard. From that embarrassing experience Cic-ero had learned how important it was for an aspiring politician to stay in Rome, a lesson that Plancius, in turn, learned from his friend and *patronus* Cicero:

> He had not the same qualifications as others may have had; but qualifications he nevertheless had, qualifications of steady application, of attentive service to friends, of generosity. He lived in the public view, he stood for office, and his life gener-

ally was guided by those principles which have enabled very many "new men" to rise untraduced to the same honors. (67)[107]

As the discussion turns to Cicero's debt to Plancius and the identification of *patronus* with client becomes more explicit (68–82), the ethos of Laterensis returns to the stage. Cicero once again uses a clever interpretation of events to demonstrate his debt to Plancius and to debilitate the prosecutor's attacks. Employing an interesting variation on the tactic of the *accusator* as *amicus*,[108] he here portrays his "friend" Laterensis as a traitor to the cause that both he and Plancius had shared: the succor of Cicero in his time of need. Laterensis' support in that crisis had led Cicero to assume that his support and gratitude would extend to anyone who had helped the exile's cause. The prosecution of Plancius represents nothing less than a renunciation of that gratitude and, in a sense, a rebuff of Cicero himself:

> When you were on terms of closest friendship with me, when you were willing even to risk your life at my side, when in the bitter, heart-rending hour of my departure you had put, not merely your tears, but your powers, mental, bodily, and material, at my service, when you had defended my wife and children in my absence with your succor and your substance, in all your dealings with me you led me to believe that you readily granted me full permission to devote all my efforts to promoting Plancius' advancement, because, as you alleged, you yourself viewed with gratitude his services to me. (73)[109]

Only under a system of advocacy, and one relying heavily upon character, could patron–client identification be so prominent, could issues become so commingled, could a *patronus'* cause so totally overshadow the *causa* pertinent to the courtroom. In fact the issue of Cicero's gratitude results in a profession of his grateful feelings toward Laterensis (78), followed by a type of *contentio* between Laterensis and Plancius for Cicero's gratitude (79) and culminating in a *locus* (80–82) on the importance of gratitude and its place in Cicero's ethos.

By section 86 it becomes apparent that Cicero regards the attack on Plancius and the criticism of his defense as actually an attack on himself and ultimately upon his exile. Cicero's character, which has for some time been in the foreground, now becomes the focal point of the speech. Once again the actors in Cicero's tragedy step onstage: the vile and degraded consuls, the debauched Clodius, the powerful triumvirs, the Senate in mourning, the betrayed patriots, and, of course, the drama's protagonist, Cicero himself (86–87). The persona of the self-sacrificing patriot is again assumed as Cicero justifies his actions with an explanation by now familiar to his audience: that he, like Q. Metellus Numidicus, could have prevailed, had he resorted to arms;[110] but for the safety and welfare of the state and her loyal citizens, he refused an armed confrontation and chose to retire; that he and his fortune were somehow linked or identified with the Republic and its fortune; and that for these reasons he chose to withdraw voluntarily, sacrificing himself for the state (87–90).[111]

The features of this persona continue to be defined in the next portion of the speech, which attempts to justify Cicero's actions on behalf of the triumvirs and his "palinode" (91–94). The Republic's "address" (in *oratio obliqua*) to Cicero, the patriot, states clearly his relationship to her and the qualities of his ethos that deserve to be rewarded:

> The Republic herself, could she speak, would plead with me in this way, and say that since I have always served her, and never myself, and since the wage I have won from that service has been not joy and wealth, as it should have been, but a cup of bitter grief, I should now for once serve myself and think of my dear ones; her fear is not that my services to her have been insufficient, but rather that the return that she has made to me has been too little and out of all measure with the extent of my service. (92)[112]

The wise politician and the true patriot are marked not by a stubborn, adamantine tenacity of opinion, but by a certain moderation whose course is determined by the interest and well-being of the state and public tranquility (cf. 93–94).

Transference of this persona of the patriot to the persuasive persona of a *patronus* lies but a step away, through the identification of Cicero with his client Plancius and Plancius' support of the patriot. This connection Cicero effects in the final sections of the speech. In a very dramatic narrative (96–100) that describes the darkest days of Cicero's travail, Plancius' ethos is revealed in terms of its relationship to Cicero. When word first reached Plancius that Cicero had landed at Dyrrhachium, "he immediately dismissed his lictors, discarded his official insignia, doffed his official robes" (98),[113] and set out to meet him. Cicero's friendship, his well-being, and the *officium* Plancius felt toward him took precedence even over his official position and duties. (Of course, Cicero might argue, given his justification of exile and his importance to the Republic for its survival, that Plancius *was* performing his "official duties.") Indeed, throughout this time, Plancius discarded the persona of a quaestor to assume that of a comrade (100).

The portrait of the loyal, diligent, unselfish, and sympathetic friend extends into the very emotional peroration, which offers an excellent example of ethos transgressing its bounds and being transported to the heights of pathos:

> O the misery of your lonely watches, Plancius! O those lamentable vigils! O those bitter nights! O pitiful prop of my existence! Wretched, indeed, if I, now living, cannot help you whom perhaps I might have helped by my death! Never, never, while I live, shall I forget that night! You took no rest; you never left my side, you grieved with me when I, miserable and induced by some false hope, made false and empty promises. (101)[114]

These promises, of course, were for expressions of Cicero's gratitude; if death or some other disaster should have prevented Cicero's return, then certainly those who supported his cause with their aid, their sorrow, their indignation, and their tears would repay the debt; now the opportunity to display their gratitude on behalf of Cicero presents itself. Patron–client identification becomes complete, as it had in the *Pro Sestio*. Support for Plancius is support for Cicero; tears shed for Plancius are tears for Cicero (cf. 104); acquittal for Plancius is acquittal for Cicero and his exile:

> For what can I do . . . except to link you with my salvation? Only those who gave salvation to me can render it to you. Come what may . . . I shall hold onto you and embrace you, and I shall avow myself to be not merely the intercessor for your fortunes, but your partner and your comrade; and none, I trust, will be so heartless or so insensible, so forgetful, I will not say of my services to loyal citizens, but of their services to me, as to tear from my side the savior of my person, and take him from me. (102)[115]

The persuasive technique of the *Pro Plancio* is interesting. It would appear that Cicero's opponents, recognizing the strength that an ethos in possession of considerable *auctoritas* might exert in the courtroom, chose to concentrate much of their prosecution on the task of disarming the orator's *auctoritas*. Given the apparently weak factual status of Cicero's defense and the opportunity such a gambit offered to the *patronus* for justifying (yet again) his exile, for explaining his current political position, and for repaying a debt to his friend, the prosecution appears to have played right into his hands. His presence in the case thus justified, Cicero makes the most of ethos from the *exordium* onwards, identifying himself with his client, portraying the *accusator* as his *amicus*, drawing the characters of Plancius, himself, Laterensis, and Cassius with features supportive of his defense.

Laterensis' insistence on a *contentio dignitatis* allows Cicero to turn back upon the prosecutor several of his own points, and it is here that we see, perhaps, the most clever manipulation of ethos in the speech. Laterensis' *nobilitas*, proffered by him as an advantage for election, is craftily converted by Cicero into a cause for his defeat; the support and friendship that he exhibited toward Cicero and his supporters at the time of Cicero's exile is used as a vantage point to contrast the ungrateful and unsupportive attitude now revealed by his prosecution of Plancius. In the same vein, the *subscriptor* Cassius' encomium of Laterensis is defused, not by Cicero's refutation of its content, but rather by his assertion that it did not do its subject justice!

The efficacy of ethos in this speech is greatly enhanced by its disposition. Under other circumstances—for example, if he had possessed overwhelming evidence in support of Plancius—Cicero might have addressed the charges against himself first, clearing the way for the *contentio dignitatis* and the factual refutation of the charges. In this situation, however, he wisely chose first to reveal the characters proper to the drama in a *contentio*; he then slipped in the formal refutation of the charge, only to take up last the charges against himself, which were technically irrelevant to the case. This disposition enabled him to return to his relationship with Plancius, and once there, never to depart from it. As the account moves from Cicero's ethos and his *apologia pro suo exsilio* to the narrative of Plancius' service toward Cicero and his character as revealed by that service, the speech's intensity gradually heightens, ethos is transformed into pathos, and the courtroom is lit by a burst of emotion whose flame is extinguished only by the termination of the speech.

The *post reditum* speeches span some of the most difficult years of Cicero's life and career. His return from humiliating exile, his struggle to repair his private fortune and his personal *dignitas*, the horrible year of Luca and the *De Provinciis Consularibus*, all exerted a profound effect upon him, his oratory, and his use of ethos in that oratory. In certain respects, Cicero's situation in these speeches is similar to that of his early speeches. Once again he is searching for a persona, struggling to reassert his authority in the state. The speeches considered in detail here, the *Pro Sestio* and the *Pro Plancio*, as well as the other *post reditum* speeches (the *Pro Caelio* is, of course, the notable exception) are products of this situation and their use of ethos reflects this fact. Cicero is, at least in his own eyes, as much on trial as are his clients. Their support of him during his exile is tantamount to support of the Republic. This fact alone, according to his line of reasoning, should secure them acquittal, and it is to this line of argument that he resorts time and time again.

The tone of these orations is at times strident, grating, and unappealing. We actually seem to feel the feelings of a man who appears to be grasping almost desperately in his attempt to regain his self-confidence and his public persona. Reading passages from these speeches or others written in this same period (e.g., *In Pisonem*) can be an embarrassing and uncomfortable ordeal. In terms of our study of ethos in Ciceronian and Roman oratory, however, such reading is enlightening, for it illustrates brilliantly how character and its artistic manipulation abide as important, if not primary, oratorical weapons, even for a man whose sense of desperation on various occasions during that period nearly overwhelmed him.

# V

# THE FINAL YEARS

*The Loss and Recovery of Independence,*

*and the Ethos of a Patriot*

In such an upheaval, in such confusion of events, we must look to situations, not customary procedures. (*Philippics* 11.27)

An eloquent man, my boy, eloquent and a lover of his country. (Plutarch *Cicero* 49)

"Oratory is both an instrument and an emblem of *civitas*, and Rome was no longer a *civitas*."[1] This statement succinctly describes the oratorical and political situation in which Cicero operated during the last decade or so of his life and career. The extraordinary political upheaval, the brutal politics of those in power, and the general chaos that resulted during the 50s and 40s had a profound effect on the Roman Republic and on its oratory, a genre inextricably bound to historical and political events, "an art in which *dignitas* and *humanitas* are of the essence."[2] Character as a source of persuasive material nevertheless remains important; in fact, ethos in a speech composed under these circumstances is often granted an added dimension. The character of the power or powers that be, looms over the persuasive process; it can stand aloof, actively enter in, or intimidate from afar. At any rate, its presence is felt and the response that the orator makes to it is more often than not based in ethos or in its close relative, pathos.

Cicero, the Republic's premier orator, suffered not a little humiliation and anxiety as an unsympathetic and less than willing pawn at the hands of the Roman autocrats. He struggled throughout this time to maintain, without overstepping his bounds, an ethos in possession of some *dignitas*.[3] Once the fetters of the dictatorship had been loosed on the Ides of March in 44, however, the orator again found himself involved in the crisis, a crisis tantamount to a fight for existence, both for himself and the Republic.[4]

The character he presents so forcefully throughout the *Philippics* is that of a Roman patriot in full stature, "a great, vigorous, and memorable man,"[5] a man who is "eloquent and a lover of his country."[6]

The portrait of his antagonist, Antony, set in diametric opposition to his own, is the denial of all that is Roman and human. These two characters, writ large, present the Roman audience with a choice, hard and fast, between right and wrong, good and evil, light and darkness, Roman and un-Roman, freedom and slavery.[7] As a result of the overwhelming emphasis that he places on this juxtaposition, it is perhaps here, in his final speeches, that ethos is granted its freest rein as a source for persuasive material in the oratory of Cicero.

## PRO T. ANNIO MILONE

Cicero's speech on behalf of Milo, who as tribune in 57 had worked for Cicero's recall and at whose hands Clodius, Cicero's archenemy, had been slain, presages several of the conditions of oratory under the eye of a dictator or emperor.[8] Pompey, extraconstitutionally the sole consul of 52, sat aloof on the steps of the Treasury, his true sentiments unknown to the people and to the pleader. The Forum was crowded and Pompey's armed guard surrounded him. Their weapons, glittering in the sunlight, cast a strange, unaccustomed light on the proceedings.[9] Cicero, sole counsel for Milo, was forced to speak his defense under a legal procedure, enacted by Pompey, that was novel and restrictive for the speaker. The Republican orator, visibly shaken by the strangeness of these circumstances, lost confidence and the delivery of his speech was not equal to the challenge.[10] Milo was convicted.

The speech as transmitted to us is an extraordinary rhetorical composition,[11] often relying upon presentation of character for its effectiveness. As we have come to expect, Cicero introduces the major characters of the drama immediately. Milo, "the bravest of men" (1), is marked by patriotism and greatness of spirit (16); he is a loyal supporter of Cicero and the *boni* (5). The orator himself confesses his uneasiness at the sight of the Forum (2), but expresses his confidence in his case, and in the wisdom of Pompey, whom he characterizes as "a most wise and upright man" (2). Polarization of the two conflicting sides begins immediately as Cicero identifies himself (cf. also 5) and the onlookers with Milo; their interests, their families, their fortunes, their lives, are no less at stake than the defendant's (3). On the other side stand that small minority, fed by the fury of their dead leader Clodius (3). This *furor* will become the distinguishing mark of Clodius and his followers in the speech, to be contrasted, as it is here, with the calm disdain with which Milo ignores it.

Before entering upon the main body of the speech, Cicero includes a preliminary refutation (7–23) designed to disarm the prejudicial charges made by the prosecution against his case. Milo's opponents had claimed that the Senate and Pompey, by their actions, had already judged Milo to be guilty. Such a charge, of course, presented a serious obstacle to Cicero's case, seeing that the ethos of Pompey was, at that time, in possession of supreme *auctoritas* and *dignitas*; the support of such a powerful man might easily sway the decision in either direction.

Pompey is again presented as an eminently wise man in possession of a "profound and almost godlike endowment of soul" (21). Most importantly, he is, according to Cicero, the friend of Milo and the enemy of Clodius, a man who in reality shares the sentiments of Cicero and the *boni* about Clodius (21–22). The ethos of Clodius, the "mad (*furiosus*) tribune" (14), lurks in the backround. This "cut-throat and parricide" (8) had even dared to attempt the assassination of Pompey, on whose life the commonwealth reposed, and of Cicero, who managed through some good fortune to escape his bloody hands (18–20).

Such character delineation continues in the next portion of the speech (24–30), which purports to be a simple statement of the facts (24). In reality, this brief passage represents one of the finest ethical narratives in Ciceronian oratory, calculated to paint characters of Clodius and Milo that demand the facts just as Cicero has interpreted them. The first clause of the first sentence is indicative of Cicero's technique: "When P. Clodius had determined to harass the Republic during his praetorship by every kind of crime . . . " (24). Ethos, internalized (Clodius' thought processes) and externalized (epithets, description) sets the backround of the case.[12]

The important contrast between characters is emphasized in the account, then interpreted as the motivational cause for actions:

> When Clodius, a man most alert for every chance of evil-doing, saw a man most brave, his bitterest foe, would most certainly be consul, when he realized that this had been clearly intimated not only by the talk but also by the votes of the Roman people, then he began to work openly and declare in plain terms that Milo must be slain. (25)[13]

This contrast continues into the description of the fateful day when Clodius and Milo met on the Appian Way (27–29). Clodius, still characterized by his *furor*, left "an uproarious public meeting" to set the ambush (27). Milo, on the other hand, spent a routine day in the Senate, returned home for some last-minute packing, and was even forced to wait for his wife while she finished her toilette (28). The juxtaposition of the ethos of the highwayman preparing an ambuscade with that of the domestic couple preparing for a business trip is striking and effective.

At section 31 Cicero poses what he claims is the crucial question: "Which of the two plotted against the other?" He has already indicated that his major line of defense will be a plea of self-defense (*constitutio legitima* or *definitiva*): Milo, although responsible for the death of Clodius, acted in self-defense and thus under circumstances that made his action "legal." The *argumentatio* that follows (32–71) is concerned primarily with demonstrating that Clodius premeditatedly attacked Milo, who was then forced to defend himself.

Cicero's previous character assassination of Clodius in the narration and preliminary refutation is, of course, the foundation upon which he now argues his case.[14] Considering the motives of the parties (32–35), Cicero first argues that Clodius, a "bold, impious beast," is the kind of creature ruled by self-interest, whereas a good man will never be driven to crime (32). In fact, as the supporter of Cicero and the state, Milo's own interests were severely impaired by Clodius' death; now there is no longer an arena open to display his virtue in suppressing the vice of Clodius (34–35)!

Next Cicero considers the "natural disposition and habits" of the antagonists (36–43). Deeds, which in Roman terms are dictated by one's character and nature, reveal ethos, and Clodius' and Milo's actions support the characters that Cicero has thus far sketched. Clodius, the mad, bloodthirsty, wild beast (cf. 35, 40) is the heir to Catiline's dagger, with which he sought the lives of great citizens:

When did his dagger, which Catiline had bequeathed to him, rest in its sheath? That it is which has threatened us; to that I have not allowed you to be exposed on my behalf; that lay in wait for Pompey; that drenched with the life-blood of Papirius the Appian Way which perpetuates its wielder's name; that too was many years later once again aimed at me. (37)[15]

Milo, the defender of Cicero, the vexer of Clodius' madness, the vanquisher of his weapons, and his accuser (35), has, in contrast, used violence only to thwart such nefarious attempts by Clodius. He had, moreover, foregone countless opportunities to slay Clodius with impunity, particularly at the time of Cicero's recall (38–41). Ethical narrative is especially effective here:

> Again at the elections in the Campus, how often he had the chance!—when Clodius had rushed into the enclosures and had given orders for the drawing of swords and the hurling of stones, and then, cowed by Milo's sudden glance, was fleeing toward the Tiber, while you and all loyal citizens prayed that Milo might give free play to his own valor. (41)[16]

The ethos of the brave, patriotic, and dauntless hero who with only a glance sent the cowardly Clodius packing, needs no explication.

In rhetorical textbook fashion, Cicero next considers the circumstances of time, place, and means at the disposal of the combatants, and demonstrates in each instance that the facts suggest that it was indeed Clodius who had planned the ambush (44–56). In considering the circumstances following the slaying (61–66), Milo's ethos is again prominently paraded. His conscience free from guilt, the patriot returned and entrusted himself to the people and the Senate: "how prompt was his return, how impressive his entry into the forum . . . , how superb was his magnanimity, his mien, and his tone." (61).[17]

Cicero's treatment of Pompey and his relationship with Milo is very interesting in this part of the speech. The orator does his best to minimize the rumor of Milo's plot against Pompey and the precautions Pompey took against it (65–66). In doing so, Cicero finds himself in an awkward position. Recalling all that we have said about the impact that an ethos in possession of *auctoritas* could exert on Roman society and the Roman judicial system, it is obvious that Pompey and his ethos, in his extraordinary role as sole consul, under circumstances that made him more than a disinterested bystander, would have had much influence on the outcome of the trial. Both prosecution and defense recognized this, a fact made clear by the charge that Pompey had already prejudged Milo's guilt as well as by Cicero's efforts at refutation (15–22). Now Cicero must disarm the rumor of the plot without making Pompey's actions look ridiculous; he does so by praising his vigilance (*diligentia*) in regard to the Republic: "I was unable to suspect of cowardice a man of Pompey's surpassing courage; I was thinking that in a man who bore the whole burden of the Republic, no vigilance could be excessive" (66).[18]

In the final part of the *argumentatio* (67–71), Cicero goes a step further in dealing with the ethos of Pompey. In nearly every speech since the time of his consulship he had displayed an efficacious identification of client with *patronus* that imparted a measure of the *patronus'* dignity and authority to the case of the client. Such identification has proven, and will continue to prove, a factor in this speech; but here the orator recognizes that his own authority, dignity, and reputation are eclipsed by the sole consul's, and in an attempt to garner further conviction for his defense, he identifies Milo and himself and their efforts with Pompey:

> But if Milo had been granted the opportunity, he would assuredly have proved to your own satisfaction that never had man been dearer to fellow man than you to himself, that never had he shunned any danger on behalf of your dignity, that again and again he had contended with that most foul pestilence [Clodius] on behalf of your glory; that his tribunate had, under your advice, been directed to my restoration which had been especially dear to you; that later he had himself been defended by you when his civil privileges were in danger, and had by you been assisted in his candidature for the praetorship; that he had hoped always to possess two most sure friends—you, because of your good offices to him, me, because of his own to me. (68)[19]

This extraordinary version of the rhetoric of advocacy reaches its climax in the next section (69) with a *prosopopoeia* of Milo, who "speaks" to Pompey. Overstepping the bounds of the rhetoric of advocacy, Cicero speaks as his client in first person, a technique that brings immediacy to the plea, reveals the ethos of a resigned, loyal, and determined Milo, and corroborates his bond with the powerful Pompey:

> "See how full of change and diversity is life's course, how wayward and wanton is fortune, what time-serving hypocrisies, what desertions and faint-heartedness between loved ones in the hour of danger! Surely, surely a time will come, and a day will dawn when you . . . shall sigh in vain for the affection of a most faithful friend and the loyalty of a most steadfast man and the magnanimity of one whose valor has no equal in human history!" (69)[20]

The identification of Milo with Pompey and the picture of the two as close supporters and friends of one another are calculated not merely to enhance the ethos of Milo but also to place an additional onus upon the jury: in order to condemn Cicero's client, according to the scenario that the orator has staged, they must condemn Pompey's friend.

At this point in the speech, Cicero has concluded his formal plea of self-defense. Instead of concluding his speech, however, he chooses to digress in a *pars extra causam* (as he calls it in section 92), an *ethica digressio* (72–91) that argues the justice of Clodius' death on the grounds that he was a criminal. Although this line of defense was strongly recommended by Marcus Brutus,[21] Cicero appears to have thought that his plea of self-defense would prove stronger as a primary plea. This stance (*constitutio generalis* or *iuridicialis*, i.e., qualitative) could then serve as a supplemental line of defense that would corroborate his cause primarily by offering him wider scope for the characterization of the dramatis personae and providing an opportunity to raise the emotional pitch to a perorational height.[22]

The artistic arrangement of the digression's presentation of character is striking. Cicero immediately introduces the qualitative *stasis*. Once again he speaks in first person *as* his client. Milo's "boastful lie" that he killed Clodius (72) begins one of the longest periods in Ciceronian oratory (72–75), which has as its subject the atrocities committed by the villain Clodius against gods and man. Cicero's aim is to characterize Clodius through his actions, to portray him as a monster who has, by his crimes, belied his descent from his noble *gens*, his *Romanitas*, and even his humanity! A pounding, relentless anaphora of *eum qui*, "a man who," underscores the catalogue, of which the following is a brief example:

> . . . a man who by the weapons of slaves had expatriated a citizen whom the Senate, the people of Rome, and all nations had declared to be the preserver of the city and the life of the citizens; a man who had bestowed and taken away thrones, and allotted the world to whomsoever he wished; a man who, after working many a deed of carnage in the Forum, had by armed violence driven within his own doors a citizen of peerless valor and renown; a man who considered no evil deed, no impure desire as sinful . . . a man, in fine, who had ceased to regard statute, law, or landmark. (73)[23]

Somehow the Roman state endured these outrages, Cicero explains, but if that madman had lived and obtained power he would have made himself master of all (76). Therefore, the destruction of such a pestilence averted disaster; Milo stands as the "greatest public benefactor in history," the savior of law, liberty, and honor who, if he so chose, could boast in this fashion:

"Stand by me, citizens, and listen: I have slain Publius Clodius! With this blade and this right hand have I warded from your neck the frenzy (*furores*) of one whom we could no longer restrain by any laws or courts, so that it might be through me alone that justice, equity, law, liberty, honor, and decency might yet dwell in the state!" (77)[24]

The second part of the digression (78–83) continues to develop the portrait of Milo as benefactor of the Republic. Cicero proposes to acquit Milo on the condition of bringing Clodius back to life. Neither Pompey nor the judges would permit such a resurrection, a tacit but certain sign that they admit the justice of Clodius' death. In fact, Milo should be judged a tyrannicide and accorded the honors shared by such men in Athens and in other cities in Greece (80). Like Cicero himself, who in the face of danger dared to crush the Catilinarian conspiracy, Milo, by not hesitating to slay a despot, has proven himself a true hero (82). This conscious identification of client with *patronus*, as well as with other great benefactors of the Republic such as Ahala, Nasica, Opimius, and Marius (83), enables Milo's case to benefit from their authority.

In the next part of the digression (83–86) Cicero advances his portrait of Milo a step further, as he depicts his client as an instrument of the gods working for the salvation of Rome: "It is this very power [the divine], which has often shed upon this city incredible wealth and blessings, that has now uprooted and abolished this scourge, having first roused such a mood in him that he dared to provoke with violence and challenge with the sword the bravest of men." (84).[25] The emotional tenor of the passage continues to increase until it reaches its climax with the orator's apostrophe to the Sanctities who witnessed Clodius' demise. The character themes of madness and inhumanity that have marked Cicero's descriptions of Clodius throughout the speech are here in prominence:

Surely the very Sanctities who witnessed the beast's fall must have bestirred themselves and asserted their rights in his ruin. For to ye now, hills and groves of Alba, to ye, I say, I appeal and pray; and to ye, ruined altars of the folk of Alba . . . which that madman, after hewing down and leveling the most hallowed groves, had buried beneath the maniacal masses of his underground buildings. It was your altars and your sanctities that put forth on that day their strength. (85)[26]

The fact that Clodius fell before the shrine of the Bona Dea, the very goddess whose secret rites he had so flagrantly violated a decade earlier, corroborates the presence of a *vis divina*, Cicero claims, as do also the crazed actions of Clodius' mobsters, who, struck by madness from the gods (86), deprived his corpse of a decent and proper funeral.

From the picture of Milo as an instrument of the gods, Cicero returns the emphasis to Clodius' character as illustrated once again by his actions, which have been dictated by it (87–88). This, the central portion of the digression, recalls the opening catalogue of Clodian atrocities and also works to maintain in Cicero's audience the level of outrage felt against Milo's adversary. Like the first catalogue, this list is highlighted by an emphatic rhetorical device, in this instance, the homoeoteleuton of *-erat*, the pluperfect verb ending:

> He had polluted by unchastity the most hallowed sanctities; he had smashed the most solemn decrees of the Senate; he had brazenly bought himself off from the juries that were to try him; he had harassed the Senate in his tribunate; he had canceled measures taken for the security of the Republic and endorsed by the consent of all the orders; he had banished me from my country, had plundered my property, had burned my house, had persecuted my children and my wife; he had declared an unholy war against Pompey. . . . The state, Italy, the provinces, the subject-kingdoms could not contain his madness. (87)[27]

Against outrages such as these the solitary figure of Milo stood forth (88). The portrait sketched is reminiscent of the scene painted by Demosthenes in the famous narrative on the fall of Elatea in *On the Crown* (169–173), where he alone of all the statesmen came forward to speak what was best for Athens. Here Milo alone came forth to thwart the destructive pestilence embodied in P. Clodius. The contrast between the ethos of the criminal and that of the patriot is noteworthy.

This juxtaposition between protagonist and antagonist is continued in the next part of the digression (88–89), which briefly returns to the theme of the *vis divina*; the gods certainly instilled into the mind of that madman (*furiosus*, 88) the notion of attacking Milo. Cicero makes the contrast between the effeminate Clodius and the brave Milo explicit even in the startling chiastic arrangement of words: *ut homo effeminatus fortissimum virum conaretur occidere* (89).

This is immediately followed by the final part of the digression (90–91), which once again casts Clodius in the role of tyrant, Milo in the role of tyrant-slayer, and proposes again to call Clodius back from the dead: "Raise him up, raise him up from the dead, if you can! Will you break the onset of him while living whose frenzy you can hardly endure when unburied?" (91).[28] These last two parts of the *ethica digressio* frame the central panel of Clodius' crimes, reflecting in reverse order the topics of Milo the tyrannicide, and of the *vis divina*:

A 72–78: Crimes of Clodius (anaphora of *eum qui*)
B 78–83: Milo as tyrannicide; resurrection of Clodius
C 83–86: The *vis divina*: Milo is instrument of the gods
A 87–88: Crimes of Clodius (homoeoteleuton of *-erat*)
C 88–89: The *vis divina*: Milo is instrument of the gods
B 90–91: Milo as tyrannicide; resurrection of Clodius.

An equally elaborate, five-part peroration (92–105), which sustains the high pitch of ethos and pathos introduced in the digression, concludes the oration. The first part (92) is introductory; it explains the role of restraint that Milo is to play and begins the emotional appeal by Cicero. This actually represents the employment of one of the numerous perorational "commonplaces," by which "we show that our soul is full of mercy for others, but still is noble, lofty, and patient of misfortune and will be so whatever may happen" (*De Inv.* 1.109). Here, however, the orator develops the *locus* in a distincly dramatic and Ciceronian way through a contrast between his own emotions and those of Milo. We have seen this technique, a product of the rhetoric of advocacy, employed successfully before (for example, in the speech for Roscius Amerinus); here it allows Cicero himself to engage in a pathetic *commiseratio* pleading for the acquittal of his client and at the same time to portray Milo as the proud patriot who refuses to partake in such undignified emotional appeal.

The second and longest part of the peroration (93–98) consists of Milo's "speech" to Cicero. We have often noted the effectiveness, in character portrayal, of introducing first-person speech into an oration delivered by a patron on behalf of a client. The choices that one makes, even in speech, reveal character. In this oration Cicero has relied heavily upon the personification of Milo. The character revealed has been consistent: that of the self-sacrificing patriot, willing even to undergo his fellow citizens' ingratitude for his services toward them:

"Farewell, farewell, my fellow citizens! Security, success, prosperity be theirs! Long may this city, my beloved fatherland, remain glorious, however ill she may have treated me! May my countrymen rest in full and peaceful enjoyment of the Republic, an enjoyment from which, since I may not share it, I shall stand aloof, but which none the less is owed to me!" (93)[29]

The "speech" then shifts to indirect discourse in a passage that is less dramatic, less personal, and more prosaic (95–97). Milo is here made to dwell upon his efforts to control Clodius—a specific example of his service to the state—and his near election to the consulship. A return to the more dramatic direct discourse frames the central section and concludes the "speech" (98). The positive tone of this part complements the rather negative tone of the first: Milo here reflects on the everlasting glory and fame his deed has won for him.

Cicero's reply (99), a much shorter address, comprises the third element of the peroration. He appears to accept the exile of Milo but expresses his dismay at the ironic fact that his own dearest friends, not his enemies, are bringing about this tragedy. This introduces the fourth part of the peroration (99–100), in which Cicero elaborates on his own ethos and its relationship to his friend Milo:

To you . . . there is no service of love, zeal, or duty that I have failed to render. It was I who on your behalf courted the enmity of the great; it was I who often exposed my person and my life to the weapons of your foes; it was I who cringed a suppliant at the feet of many for you. I have staked my goods, my fortunes, and those of my children, to share alike in all of your crises; in fine, upon this very day, if any violence awaits you, any life and death struggle, I claim it for myself. (100)[30]

Finally the *patronus* draws his entire oration to a close with an empassioned *commiseratio* (101–105) in which, among other things, he laments, much as he did in his defense of Sestius (*Pro Sest.* 145–146), that he cannot now repay the debt of salvation owed to Milo, which harks back to his recall from exile. The topic that had figured so prominently in the *ethica digressio*, that of recalling Clodius to life, appears for the last time, here quite emotionally (103). The character of Milo, however, will not entertain such talk, and he interrupts to offer himself again for his country (104). Cicero solves the problem of ending such an extended emotional appeal by using a tactic familiar from other orations: his tears impede his pleading, and Milo forbids that tears should defend him.[31] The speech ends with the reintroduction of the powerful figure of Pompey, who will approve of Milo's acquittal by judges who are the best, the wisest, and the most brave (105).

As is obvious from the foregoing analysis, ethos plays a prominent role in the persuasive process of this speech. Cicero makes few statements and presents few arguments that are not based in or predicated upon the characters of those involved in the case. The techniques used for the manipulation of ethos are, for the most part, familiar. Clodius and Milo are painted in bold, vivid strokes in a disjunctive mode that places them at opposite ends of the spectrum. The madness of Clodius, his disregard for the *mos maiorum* and things sacred and hallowed to the Romans, and his ultimate bestiality are set in sharp contrast with the calm deliberateness of Milo, the unflinching, proud patriot who is willing to sacrifice himself for his country and its citizens.

Ethical narratives and numerous personifications in which Milo "speaks" for himself are effective means of revealing character in the speech. The beautifully constructed ethical digression presents perhaps the most concentrated and detailed picture of the antagonists. Much of the credibility of Cicero's plea of self-defense was based upon the undergirding premise that the characters of Clodius and Milo made it probable that it was Clodius and not Milo who planned the ambush. Thus Cicero provides the jury with a legal escape of self-defense; in the digression, whose persuasive force relies almost entirely upon ethos (and its close relative, pathos), Cicero offers the jury a patriotic reason for using that escape, by showing Clodius to be an un-Roman, criminal beast. The ethos, so vigorously expressed in the digression, is easily converted into the rousing pathos of the peroration.

Patron–client identification is present, but in variation. Cicero was the first to acknowledge that under the circumstances of the trial, his own dignity and authority were eclipsed by Pompey's. He therefore labors not only to dissolve all possible prejudice that Pompey's previous actions might have imputed to his case but also to identify and ally the sole consul with his client by portraying them as friends, mutual supporters, and preservers of the Republic. He can then add himself to the equation and thus invest his own ethos and Milo's ethos with persuasion garnered from the support of Pompey's *dignitas*.

Despite the highly artistic use of ethos, the near-perfect arrangement of material, and the compelling intensification of emotion found in this speech, the *Pro Milone* seems to leave the student of Ciceronian oratory wanting something more. Without agreeing absolutely with W. R. Johnson's description of the speech as "a lifeless, utterly unreal perfection,"[32] one must still acknowledge that the speech on behalf of Milo has an element of unreality about it. I believe that this is attributable, at least in part, to the circumstances of the speech, which in many ways must have seemed very strange to the Republican orator. When the focal point, or at least one of the focal points, of the speech becomes the ethos and authority of an autocrat, the immediacy of the persuasive process is somewhat distanced from the real issue at hand. The style begins to assume an artificiality that looks forward to imperial rhetoric and oratory; the *Pro Milone*, with its penchant for personification and emotionalism, presages in many ways the "unreality" of the declamatory style of the Empire. For an orator who had spent thirty-five years pleading in Republican courtrooms, the unreality of the circumstances must have seemed very real indeed.

## PRO Q. LIGARIO

If the *Pro Milone* had, in some way, presaged the conditions of oratory under a monarchy, Cicero's so-called Caesarian speeches realize that prophecy in full dimension. In his new role as dictator Caesar had assumed judicial powers, and Cicero found himself pleading cases in which the dictator acted as both judge and jury, at times even presiding within the confines of his private home. Such circumstances obviously had an effect on oratory and the orator.[33] Submission to another's will, compromise of one's principles, and loss of independence are discomforting sights to behold and embarrassing ordeals to endure. A decade earlier, seeing a rift develop between the triumvirs and harboring hope for the Republic, Cicero had spoken out. Soon after Luca he had felt the bit of restraint pulled tight; his speech *On the Consular Provinces* was the result. Now, in 46, heartened by the amnesty offered to M. Marcellus and again envisioning (rather naively) a resurrected Republic, Cicero abandoned his long-standing resolve to hold silence and eulogized Caesar in the *Pro Marcello*, an action that he later described ruefully to his friend Sulpicius:

> I imagined I saw before me some vision of the Republic rising, as it were, from the dead. . . . On being asked my opinion I

changed my resolution; for I had determined, not, I assure you, from indolence, but from despair of regaining my former dignity, never to speak again. Caesar's magnanimity and the Senate's devotion broke this determination; and so I expressed my thanks to Caesar at great length; and I am afraid that now in every respect I have deprived myself of that dignified retirement which was my one solace in my troubles. Still, now that I have avoided offending one who might have thought that my unbroken silence meant that I considered the Republic extinct, I shall act in that respect with moderation, or even keep on the safe side of moderation, in order to serve his will as well as my own inclinations. (*Ad Fam.* 4.4.3–4)[34]

Whether the defense of Ligarius, who was charged in 46 with supporting King Juba of Numidia and the Africans against the Roman people (i.e., *perduellio*), was an act calculated to serve Caesar's will or Cicero's "own inclinations," or whether it represents some sort of combination of these two situations, is ultimately an insoluble question.[35] What can be stated with certainty, however, is that Cicero, the Republican orator par excellence, pleading before the dictator as sole judge in the Forum, was faced with an unaccustomed oratorical situation. These unique circumstances presented peculiar rhetorical challenges to which Cicero as orator had to respond.[36] In terms of the presentation of character, the subject of this study, Cicero's primary response was a change in focus, a change we noted in its incipient stage in the *Pro Milone*. The ethos of the litigants, the *patroni*, the judge, and the audience had been considerations in almost every Ciceronian oration. Now, however, when the verdict was taken out of the hands of a jury of citizens and placed entirely at the discretion of the authoritative figure of the dictator, the emphasis shifted. The authority, dignity, and reputation of the *patronus*, no matter how great, had been eclipsed by the ethos of the dictator; as a result, the personal influence that the *patronus* could wield was greatly impaired. Praise of the client's character and of one's own character had to be tempered, set in proportion to, rather in the shadow of, the judge's ethos. The character of the audience, at least in terms of persuasion, was subsumed by the character of the judge. Opponents were to be censured, not so much in reference to themselves or their adversary, as to the dictator and his actions. A closer examination of the use of ethos in the *Pro Ligario* will illustrate these points.

Subtle presentation of character and of the close relationships between characters marks the first part of the speech. Q. Tubero, the prosecutor, is termed Cicero's "kinsman" (*propinquus*), a statement that emphasizes the natural bond between the two and establishes the *accusator* as an *amicus*. A sarcastic reference to Tubero's diligence in framing the charge is an omen of treatment to come. C. Pansa, "a man of outstanding intellect" and Cicero's fellow *patronus* and close friend (*necessarius*), is further distinguished by his *familiaritas* to Caesar. Cicero presents himself ironically, as a *patronus* at a loss for words; his defensive strategy of taking advantage of Caesar's ignorance has been foiled by the revelation of the "strange and unheard-of charge" leveled against Ligarius: "that he was in Africa." This charge, of course, he admits without qualification and must, therefore, appeal to Caesar's character, distinguished as it is for its compassion and clemency. In this way Cicero introduces the only *deprecatio* extant among his speeches; that the speech is a *deprecatio* with qualification, however, soon becomes evident.[37]

Having ironically conceded Ligarius' "crime," he turns from his role and his predicament in that role to the role of Tubero as prosecutor and presents him with a more serious dilemma:

> You have then, Tubero, the benefit of what is the greatest hope for a prosecutor, a defendant who pleads guilty, but guilty of having been on the same side as you, Tubero, and as that gentleman worthy of every kind of praise, your father. (2)[38]

In one sentence Cicero has changed his posture as pleader from defensive to offensive, implicating not only the prosecutor but the honorable elder Tubero in the same charge.[39] "The orator who a few seconds earlier was throwing up his hands in desperation, who had been robbed of a line of defense is no longer at a loss: much of the rest of this speech will be a strong, sometimes vicious attack on Ligarius' accusers."[40] This shift from the defensive to offensive also marks a distinctive shift or variation in the rhetoric of advocacy. Cicero *patronus* commonly identifies his client with himself to advantage; here his client is identified with the opposing counsel to that counsel's disadvantage. Such clever use and variation of the rhetoric of advocacy is one of the most effective means of persuasion in the speech.

The brief statement of facts (2–5) continues this subtle characterization, here concentrating on the ethos of Ligarius, which is sketched through effective ethical narrative. Ligarius and all of his actions are associated with peace and disassociated with war.[41] When he set out for Africa, there was no hint of war (2). When Considius left, Ligarius accepted command unwillingly but administered the province honorably in time of peace. When war burst out, Ligarius longed for home; he retired from the scene upon the arrival of Varus, whose greedy assumption of power (3) contrasts starkly with Ligarius' previously mentioned hesitation. Indeed, Ligarius' every action was informed by peace:

> So far from leaving his home at the call of war, he left when there was not the remotest suspicion of war; he went out as legate in time of peace, and in an utterly peaceable province he so bore himself that peace was his highest interest. (4)[42]

In sum, Ligarius would have much preferred to have been in Rome, removed from the conflict and reunited with his brothers (both good Caesarians, incidentally), to whom he was continually drawn by an almost inconceivable affection (5).

This portrait of Ligarius as a nursling of peace, preferring his Caesarian brothers' company to war in Africa, presents Caesar with Ligarius' personal reactions to the events and works to establish character and intention as the basis for judgment; it also lays the foundation for Cicero's next argument. Resorting again to clever uses of the rhetoric of advocacy, Cicero first separates himself from his client and manages at the same time to extol Caesar's merciful character:

> You have then, Caesar, up to this point no evidence of any clash of wills between Ligarius and yourself; and note, I pray, with what loyalty I defend his cause; I am betraying my own. O admirable clemency worthy to be adorned by the praise, commendation, literature, and monuments of all! When Marcus Cicero maintains in your presence that another was not an adherent of the cause which he admits that he himself embraced, . . . he does not shudder at what thoughts about himself may occur to you as you listen to his defense of that other. (6)[43]

The orator then continues in the same vein to praise the gracious clemency of the dictator, especially in regard to himself and to detail the special considerations Caesar showed toward him (6–7).

Having drawn the distinction between himself and his client, Cicero's next step is to identify himself with the prosecutor Tubero. This he effects in a bold and dramatic manner:

When your sword was unsheathed on the battle line at Pharsalus, what was its object, whose breast did its point seek,
what was the meaning of your weapons, what were your
mind, your eyes, your hands, your fiery spirit seeking? What
were you desiring? I am too insistent; my young friend betrays embarrassment; I will return to myself. I fought upon
the same side. (9)[44]

This extraordinary identification with the prosecutor confirms the
relationship of the *accusator* as *amicus* (cf. 1, 8, 21); Cicero and
Tubero, as well as Tubero's father, were all supporters of Pompey
who had subsequently benefited from Caesar's clemency. Cicero
differs from them in that now he pleads for that clemency to be
extended to another, while the Tuberos call for the condemnation
of a man whose actions toward Caesar were less culpable than
their own (10). "[The] device here becomes central to the argumentative strategy because it implies that one could do nothing
worse than be a supporter of Pompeius, a crime which has already
found forgiveness."[45] Caesar pardoned Cicero and the Tuberos,
who wanted to fight against him; *a fortiori*, how much more ought
he to pardon Ligarius, who had no such will? This line of argument, of course, conveniently disregards (as Cicero does throughout the speech) the distinction made by the prosecution between
those who fought at Pharsalus and those who held out against
Caesar in Africa.[46]

Cicero's *vituperatio Tuberonis* in this part of the speech reaches its
climax in section 11, with his characterization of Tubero as an un-
Roman barbarian. By pressing the prosecution of Ligarius to such
a degree, in essence calling for his death, Tubero had exceeded the
limits of cruelty: "No Roman citizen has ever done this before you.
This is the character of foreigners, either of fickle Greeks or inhuman barbarians" (11).[47] Such cruelty, Cicero claims, far exceeds
that of Sulla (12). We have often seen Cicero's attempt to paint his
adversary's character black, showing it to be a denial of things
Roman and, on the contrary, barbaric and even inhuman. In this
instance, perhaps out of consideration for his relationship to the
Tuberos, he retreats and retracts his statement: "I know you, I
know your father, I know your house and name, the ardor of your
family and your household for virtue, humanity, and learning . . .
and so I am perfectly aware that you do not aim at bloodshed"
(12–13).[48] This perhaps softens the insult, but like the taste that
remains in the mouth after swallowing a bitter pill, the portrait of
Tubero as a cruel barbarian lingers.

In fact, despite this disclaimer, Cicero continues to characterize his adversary in terms of his lack of humanity (13–16). The ethos of Caesar, marked by *humanitas, lenitas, misericordia,* and *clementia,* stands in vivid contrast to the character of Tubero, who by his act of prosecution is actually urging Caesar to abandon those virtues.[49] Cicero's direct address to the dictator in the voice of Tubero states the case all the more emphatically (14): "If, when we were doing at [Caesar's] home what we have actually, and I trust not vainly done and now do, you had suddenly burst in upon us and raised the cry, 'Gaius Caesar, take care not to forgive! take care not to pity these brothers appealing for a brother's deliverance!' would you not have divested yourself of every bit of humanity?"[50] That Tubero makes such a plea in public, in the Forum (14), only exacerbates the situation. Indeed, "his" words, "do not forgive," disqualify him from humanity:

> These are not the words of a human being, nor would human voice utter them. He who utters them in your presence, Gaius Caesar, is sooner likely to cast humanity from his own heart than to tear it from yours. (16)[51]

This portrait of Tubero as a creature devoid of humanity, the foil to Caesar, although admittedly exaggerated and distorted, is central to Cicero's presentation of the case.

This line of distorted argumentation and prejudicial character portrayal reaches its culmination in Cicero's next assertion: Ligarius, whom he is throwing upon the mercy of the court, has really done nothing wrong; there has been no *scelus* (17–19).[52] By continuing his misconstrued interpretation of Tubero's charge as simply adherence to the Pompeian cause, Cicero exonerates his client of all guilt and places him in the same status as himself, the prosecutors, and countless others who fought against the cause that "even the gods assisted" (19).

The remaining sections of the *argumentatio* (20–29) expand upon themes introduced previously. The common lot of Ligarius and the Tuberos is again underscored when Cicero censures the prosecution for attacking Ligarius for following the same course as they followed (20). Cicero's own connection with the elder Tubero, a relationship that figured prominently in the early part (6–7) of the speech, is reaffirmed (21). Finally he continues his distortion of the charges by turning the tables on Tubero's complaint that he was barred by Ligarius from entering the province (23–25). This charge Cicero converts to his client's profit, pointing out that Ligarius' action saved Tubero from sinning against Caesar:

And what complaint is this to bring to Caesar's ears—plaintively to arraign the man who debarred you from waging war against Caesar! In this connection I give you full leave to boast, even with lies if you will, that you would have handed the province over to Caesar. Even if you were excluded by Varus and others, still I will readily avow that the blame belongs to Ligarius for having robbed you of the opportunity of winning so rich a glory. (25)[53]

The irony of this rendering of the charge bursts into full-blown sarcasm in the next and final portion of the argument (26–29). Cicero now chooses to dwell upon Tubero's *constantia*, a virtue that under normal circumstances would contribute favorably to the portrait of one's ethos. He here turns this virtue, if not into a vice, at least into a source for embarrassment before Caesar, for Tubero's constancy manifested itself in his adherence to the Pompeian cause versus Caesar:

> But observe, I beg you, Caesar, the constancy of this gifted man, which however much I respected it myself, as I do respect it, I still should not refer to, had I not known that it is a virtue which meets with your special commendation. What constancy so great, then, was ever found in any man? Constancy, do I call it? Surely long-suffering were the better term! For how few would have acted thus!—to return to the very party by which at a time of civil dissension he had been cruelly rejected! There is real greatness of soul in such an act—the act of a hero whom no affront, no constraint, and no peril can make to swerve from the cause he has embraced and the ideal he has set before him! (26)[54]

That the coup de grace of Cicero's argument should take this form is fitting. Throughout his speech he has attempted to blur the distinctions between the Pompeians, ignore Ligarius' association with King Juba, and throw prosecutors, defendant, and advocate into the same class. Now, by contorting the facts, he distinguishes Tubero by his character's constancy, constancy to the cause against Caesar. The whole presentation is further undercut by another level of irony: Tubero had deserted the Pompeian cause immediately after Pharsalus.

A sizable peroration (29–38) concludes the speech. The character of Caesar, marked by his extraordinary clemency, demands the focus and dominates the plea. The tone of *deprecatio* is dominant: "Every word I have spoken I would have referred to one single head—to your humanity or your clemency or your mercy" (29; cf. 31).[55] The most interesting portion of this peroration is Cicero's reaffirmation of the bond between Ligarius and his Caesarian brothers (33–36).[56] Cicero links them in a kind of patron–client identification and, in this conclusion to what has been a rather powerful theme in the speech, makes explicit what he had previously implied: that Ligarius, in his heart, was always, like his brothers, a supporter of Caesar!

> And could you but see clearly the concord that binds the Ligarii, you would judge that all the brothers had been on your side. Or can you doubt that, had it been possible for Ligarius to remain in Italy, his views would have been the same as those his brothers held? . . . In their wills they were all with you; the storm broke and swept away one; and if he had acted of set purpose, he would be like those whom you have determined, in spite of all, to preserve. (34)[57]

Despite Cicero's claim at the beginning of the peroration that his entire speech has been aimed at Caesar's clemency (29), we have seen that the oration depends on persuasive strategy more than a strict *deprecatio* would, and that much of that strategy is in turn rooted in ethos. The character of Caesar, the dictator and sole judge, has taken center stage; his clemency and humanity become the points of reference for other characters, most especially Tubero, whose supporting role in the drama is extremely important. Cicero casts Tubero as the implacable Pompeian, unwilling to share Caesar's mercy with others. He is the foil to Caesar, the un-Roman, even inhuman, point of contrast that emphasizes, by effective juxtaposition, the *humanitas*, *misericordia*, and *clementia* of the dictator all the more.

The leitmotif of peace that surrounds the initial portrayal of the ethos of Ligarius is effective both for Cicero's presentation of the facts and for the general impression of Ligarius that he wishes to imprint upon the mind of Caesar. A victim of unfortunate circumstances, Ligarius acted no differently than many who had already been forgiven (especially the Tuberos and Cicero); his real wish was to have remained at home in the company of his two brothers, who are staunch stays of the Caesarian regime. This bond between brothers is another recurrent theme in the speech and functions almost as patron–client identification would, enhancing the defendant's position because of his association with an influential *patronus*.

The cleverest and most artistic use of ethos in the speech is

Cicero's skillful manipulation of the rhetoric of advocacy. In the *exordium* (1–3), by confessing his client's guilt—the guilt of having fought on the same side as the prosecutor—he turns his defensive stance into an offensive one. This identification of client with adversary works to Ligarius' advantage as well as Tubero's disadvantage. Shortly thereafter (6–12), Cicero separates himself from his client Ligarius and his intentions and identifies himself with the Tuberos, his adversaries. Their intentions were hostile toward Caesar; Ligarius' were not. Since both Cicero and the Tuberos have benefited from Caesar's mercy and now stand fully reinstated, it is only proper and fitting that Ligarius should be reprieved in a similar manner.[58] This posture deflects the Tuberos' anger from Cicero, who places himself in the same position and, more importantly, sets up the prosecutor for the devastating *vituperatio Tuberonis*, which characterizes him as a person selfish and self-serving, compassionless toward his fellows, anti-Caesarian in spirit, almost devoid of humanity.

Cicero's interpretation of the prosecution as well as the prosecutor is certainly a distorted misrepresentation. Nevertheless, by refusing to recognize Tubero's distinctions, he has painted a canvas half white and half black, half good, half evil, half clement and humane, half pitiless and inhuman. He has left the dictator with only one expedient, and therefore one feasible choice. In choosing the "good" side, Caesar can preserve both Ligarius and his own image, which has been drawn so favorably by Cicero throughout the speech.

## THE THIRD PHILIPPIC

The euphoria enjoyed by Cicero and other Republican supporters at the assassination of Caesar was short-lived. As Antony fortified his position and ran roughshod over the Senate's decisions, Cicero found himself once again despairing of his hope for a resurrected Republic. Resigned to "waiting out" Antony's consulship, the orator was about to retire to his studies and to Greece when he received encouraging news from Rome about Antony's waning support. His turn back to the capital marked the final turning point of his life, "the final phase of his career, the most glorious and courageous of his life, a period in which he put forth all his talents and all his energy in one last desperate attempt to save the republic to which he had dedicated so much of his life and from which he had derived most of his reputation."[59]

The fourteen speeches against Antony, the *Philippics*, are the oratorical and literary legacy that Cicero left to us from this period. Marked by "extreme clarity of vision, purposefulness, vividness, and rapidity of presentation,"[60] these orations are the products of public and personal crisis, speeches that rely upon ethos and pathos as predominant sources for persuasion.[61] The point at issue throughout the speeches is reduced, in a way, to a conflict between two characters writ large: Antony, who personifies the forces of despotism, madness, evil, darkness, hostility, and inhumanity; and Cicero, who represents constitutionality, the Republic, and the forces of tradition, goodness, and right.

We have seen Cicero establish such antithetical juxtapositions in many of his cases. The goal of employing this "disjunctive mode"[62] of character presentation is, of course, to present his audience with two clear-cut, mutually exclusive alternatives, which in reality leave little room for choice. The devolution that characterizes Antony's ethos is the same that characterized the ethos of Cicero's and the Republic's other great enemies, Catiline and Clodius: from a Roman to one who denies his *Romanitas*, to an anti-Roman *hostis*, to an inhuman monster or beast.[63] Such a portrait, drawn with bold strokes, admitting none of the finer distinctions and acknowledging none of the "gray areas," placed in stark contrast to that of Cicero and other loyal Romans, not only prejudices the audience's interpretation of the facts but almost demands (recalling the particularly strong influence of character in Roman society) a foregone conclusion to the issue at hand.

Throughout the *Philippics* the ethos of Cicero is that of a true, unfailing patriot, willing to put his life on the line for the Republic and its cause. The immediacy of his presentation makes this portrait overwhelmingly convincing. For more than twenty years he had held fast to the cause of the Republic; his role, however, has now changed. Formerly the *dux togatus*, the "nursling of peace" (*pacis alumnus*), he has now become the *princeps sumendorum sagorum*, the "leader in the putting on of military cloaks," as he faces his opponent with the only real weapon that he ever wielded, his eloquence. That such a weapon proved more than a passing threat, that it could deal more than a glancing blow, the orator's severed head and hands nailed to the Rostra eloquently, if somewhat gruesomely, came to testify.[64]

The Third Philippic, in which Cicero urges the Romans to seize the opportunity offered them by the supportive actions of Octavian and Decimus Brutus, essentially presents the dichotomy between characters found throughout the *Philippics*. The tone of urgency that characterizes this speech is in evidence from the outset.[65] Contributing to this feeling are the brief but pointed sketches of the characters involved. Antony appears immediately, a profligate and ruined man who wages a nefarious war against the heart of Rome, her altars and hearths (1). Almost within the same breath, Cicero introduces a foil to Antony: D. Brutus, "an eminent and distinguished man" (1). In doing so, he reveals a basic method of operation for the manipulation of ethos in the speech, particularly in its first half. By alternating the black warp of Antony's character with the white weft of the ethos of the Republic's loyal supporters, Cicero weaves a tapestry of vividly contrasting hues that sets off the villain Antony from the Romans and their Republic.[66]

The madness and cruelty of Antony, important leitmotifs of his character portrait, are introduced immediately (cf. 2). These are first offset by the courage and foresight of the consuls-elect, "men of the best intentions, of the highest judgment, and of remarkable agreement," then by Octavian's almost divine intelligence and courage:

> C. Caesar, a young man, or rather almost a boy, but one of incredible and, as it were, superhuman spirit and energy, at the very time when Antonius' frenzy was at its greatest heat . . . collected a very strong army of veteran soldiers who had never known defeat. (3)[67]

A return to the madness and cruelty of Antony (4) is then underscored by a brief but effective ethical narrative describing the occasion when "he commanded, under his host's roof at Brundisium, the butchery of the bravest men and best citizens, with whose blood, as they were dying at his feet, it was well known his wife's face was sprinkled" (4).[68] Indeed, had Octavian not withstood the madman's assaults, the Republic would have fallen (5). The picture of Antony's insane cruelty toward Roman citizens and the Republic itself, effected so vividly within such a short space, has begun the characterization of his ethos as un-Roman, the first step in Cicero's account of the devolution of his enemy's character.

The legions that defected from Antony provide the next foil to his ethos. The Martian Legion, braver and more friendly to the Republic than any individual, "refused to be party to his madness" (6). The Fourth Legion, emulating such courage, attached itself to the army of Octavian—who is again praised, by way of summary and proposal, for saving the state.[69]

Cicero continues his depiction of Antony's ethos as un-Roman in the next part of the speech, where he paints Antony as a tyrant eager to enslave the Roman people. The foil is again found in D. Brutus; unlike Antony, he is "a citizen born to serve the Republic, mindful of the name he bears, and an imitator of his ancestors!" (8).[70] The mention of the Republic, his name, and the ancestors is, of course, important for establishing Brutus' *Romanitas*, as is Cicero's favorable comparison of him to Lucius Brutus, who had expelled Tarquin. To mirror this image, Antony is compared unfavorably to that last king of Rome:

> Tarquin, whom our ancestors would not endure, was not considered and called cruel, not impious, but "The Proud," a fault which we have often borne in private citizens, but which our ancestors could not brook even in a king. Lucius Brutus did not brook a proud king; shall Decimus Brutus endure the reign of a felon and traitor? What single act did Tarquin ever do to compare with the innumerable acts Antonius is both doing and has done? (9)[71]

The comparison continues to the detriment of Antony and to the benefit of Decimus. Much as the brief ethical narrative of the slaughter at Brundisium had provided the capstone to an earlier description of Antony, his disgraceful behavior at the Lupercalia provides the climax to his portrait as an un-Roman who by his character and actions has denied his consulship and his *Romanitas*:

> Indeed, you ought not to have thought M. Antonius a consul after the Feast of the Lupercal. For on the day when, before the eyes of the Roman people, he made a public speech while naked, oiled, and drunk, and aimed at placing a diadem on his colleague's head—on that day he abdicated, not his consulship only, but also his personal freedom. (12)[72]

Cicero's concluding comment about the incident provides a summary of his argument as well as an outline for its future course, the demonstration of the devolution of Antony's ethos:

> Am I then to consider this man a consul, this man a Roman citizen, this man a free man, in a word, this man a human being, who on that foul and iniquitous day showed what he could endure while Caesar was alive, and equally what he wished to gain for himself when that man was dead? (12)[73]

Cicero then pauses to contrast this picture of Antony once again with loyal supporters of the constitution, this time the province of Cisalpine Gaul, "the flower of Italy, the mainstay of the empire of the Roman people, the ornament of its dignity" (13). This sets the stage for the central point in the speech,[74] which proposes to brand Antony as an enemy (*hostis*), a word that implies he is no longer a Roman citizen.[75] Cicero here uses the same argument he had employed against Catiline and his followers in his portrayal of them as public enemies: Antony, by his character and his actions, has renounced his *Romanitas* and therefore has forfeited all the rights and privileges accorded a Roman citizen.[76] The portrayal of Antony as *hostis* (implicitly or explicitly), central in this oration, is continued throughout the *Philippics* (e.g., 4.15; 5.25; 6.6; 7.8; 13.21, 22, 26; 14.9).

There follows (15–18) a renewal of the attack on Antony's character. The epithet *barbarus* (15) immediately reminds us of his alienation from *Romanitas*, as does the by now familiar juxtaposition of Antony with the loyal supporters of the state, here Octavian:

> First of all he has heaped on Caesar abuse culled from the recollection of his own indecency and licentiousness. For who is more chaste than this young man? Who more modest? What brighter example among youth have we of ancient purity? Who, on the contrary, is more unchaste than the calumniator? (15)[77]

Character assassination continues (19–21) as Cicero details how Antony's depraved ethos has dictated his reprehensible actions, culminating with a reassertion that Antony is, by his own confession, a public enemy (21).

At section 22, Cicero begins his description of the final stage in the devolution of Antony's character: inhumanity. Here he denies his enemy even the faculty of coherent speech, which most separates man from beast.[78] "Who talks like that? . . . Would it not be better to be dumb than to say what no one understands?"[79] The characterization continues (23–24) as Cicero distinguishes between Antony's behavior in the Senate and the edicts he has issued; the description is presented in terms of bestial behavior: "What I ask is this—why he was so tame in the Senate, although in his edicts he had been so wild?" (23).[80] Later the comparison is more direct: "What a fine guardian—the proverbial wolf to guard the sheep! Would Antonius be the guardian of the city or its plunderer and harasser?" (27). Finally comes outright identification:

But this hideous beast—who can bear him, and how? What is there in Antonius save lust, cruelty, insolence, audacity? Of these qualities he is wholly compacted; nothing shows in him of talent, nothing of moderation, nothing of modesty, nothing of chastity. (28)[81]

This identification establishes an important character theme not merely for this speech but for the portrait of Antony that Cicero wishes to project throughout the *Philippics*.[82]

Cicero's own ethos comes into the foreground here, really for the first time in the speech. Like the other foils to Antonius in the oration, he is a loyal supporter of the Republic, but he also assumes for himself the unique role of the *defensor conservatorque libertatis*: "Today for the first time, Members of the Senate, after a long interval we set our feet in possession of liberty; of which I, so far as I could, have been, not the mere defender, but even the savior" (28).[83] Cicero has thus become the *patronus* of freedom and the Republic, their defender in both the general and the specific sense. Here is the ethos of a patriot par excellence, the antonym of Antony, the loyalist linking the ancestral past with the potentially glorious present:

> Therefore, since matters have been brought to the point that we must decide whether he should pay penalties to the Republic or we be slaves, by the immortal gods! Members of the Senate, let us put on our fathers' spirit and courage, so that either we may recover the native liberty of the Roman race and name, or prefer death to slavery. (29)[84]

This noble and stirring portrait of the patriot is followed immediately, in fine disjunctive fashion, by a catalogue of the crimes of Antony and his brother (29–32). The list of atrocities recalls the catalogue of Clodian crimes set forth in the *Pro Milone* (*Pro Mil.* 87) and is, in fact, characterized by the same rhetorical device of homoeoteleuton, this time the perfect subjunctive verbal ending *-erit*. Antony's brutality and inhumanity are revealed vividly through a narration of dastardly actions and emphasized by a return to the theme of madness: "Even in his broken fortunes he does not abate his audacity or cease his mad rush and frenzy" (31).[85] His brother is honored with a similar list of evil deeds (31), and Cicero concludes by linking these as well to Antony himself: "These same things, wherever he led his army, were done by Marcus Antonius."[86]

A return to the ethos of Cicero as the savior of liberty and defender of the Republic (32–34) brackets the catalogue of Antonian atrocities:

> I will let no moment pass, by day or night, without thought for the liberty of the Roman people and your dignity where thought is required; where action and deeds, I will not only not refuse, I will even seek and demand to act and do. (33)[87]

As he has done throughout the speech, Cicero gives the Romans two choices: slavery under tyranny of Antony, or freedom under the Republic with him and the other loyal supporters of the constitution. As he had done earlier in the speech, as well as in the First and Second Philippics (e.g., 1.13; 2.18), Cicero here presents himself as the patriot, a leader prepared not merely to take up the cause, but to die for it. His exhortation is bolstered by the introduction of the immortal gods (34, 36), who have provided this unique opportunity and by the intensification of the tone of urgency that (by recalling the *exordium*) brings the speech full circle.[88] Cicero's formal proposals (37–39) conclude the oration.

Writing to a friend about a month after the delivery of this speech, Cicero described its impact in this way:

> I embraced the entire Republic, and speaking with intense fervor, more by force of spirit than of eloquence, I recalled a drooping and weary Senate to its ancient and traditional fortitude. This day, my exertion, and my pleading for the first time brought to the Roman people the hope of recovering their liberty. (*Ad Fam.* 10.28.2)[89]

Indeed, Cicero claimed (*Phil.* 5.30; cf. 6.2) to have "laid the foundation of the Republic" on the day of the Third and Fourth Philippics. It was also on that day, 20 December, that the people hailed him "with one mind and one voice" as savior of the Republic for a second time. What he had hoped for and hoped to persuade the people of upon his return from exile many years before was realized in his fight against Antony for the Republic.

It is interesting to note that this speech, which so moved the Senate and people of Rome, finds its source for persuasion chiefly in ethos, the effective presentation of character. Juxtaposing two mutually exclusive portraits in a disjunctive style that reflects their antithesis, Cicero presents the Roman people with a choice that really offers no choice: cruelty, tyranny, slavery, and evil, personified in Antony, his brother, and his followers; or humanity, constitutionality, and freedom, personified in Cicero, Octavian, Brutus, and the loyal supporters of the Republic. This argument is founded on probability, but a probability that is based almost entirely upon character and the actions that, according to Roman beliefs, have been dictated by character.

Essential to the polarization of these two parties is Cicero's vivid depiction of the devolution or degeneration of Antony's ethos—a devolution that similarly characterized other Ciceronian enemies —from noble Roman (consul), to un-Roman, to no Roman (*hostis*), to inhuman. Themes that support this portrait, and its juxtaposition to the portrait of the loyal Roman Cicero and his compatriots, are responsible for much of the power, not only of this speech, but of the other speeches of the *Philippics*. The new foundations laid by Cicero and the Senate with this speech ultimately proved too weak to support the sagging structure of the Republic. The foundations of character that the orator had laid, however, would prove strong enough to support all the subsequent contentions that he could manage to stack upon them.

## THE TWELFTH PHILIPPIC

It is fitting that we conclude our survey of ethos in Ciceronian oratory with a brief examination of the orator's own character as he presents it in the *Philippics*. We have already alluded to the ethos of the patriot, which is prevalent throughout these speeches, and have witnessed its effectiveness when used as a point of contrast to the ethos of Antony and his brother as presented in the Third Philippic. The Twelfth Philippic, in which Cicero speaks out against the idea of an embassy to Antony and particularly against his own participation in that embassy, presents the most detailed portrait, excepting that found in the undelivered Second Philippic. Like the Second, the Twelfth Philippic attempts to broaden the gulf between the two antagonistic factions through effective manipulation of ethos, to unleash once again the storm of hatred against the Antonii, which perhaps had begun to subside.[90] "Cicero's tactic in this speech, as it was in the first half of *Philippic II*, . . . was to focus attention on himself, especially his importance to the survival of the state, and to arouse sympathy for himself by emphasizing the personal danger that he has always risked in defending the Republic (cf. *Philippic II* 1)."[91]

The speech takes its *exordium* from the person of Cicero, the statesman whose advice on most weighty matters the Senate is wont to follow, but who in this particular instance has erred (1). The orator is faced with the rhetorical challenge of "apologizing" for his mistake of earlier supporting the idea of an embassy and then accounting for his change of mind. Cicero pleads guilty to his error but mitigates it by identifying with the consul Pansa, a man marked by extraordinary prudence, courage, and magnanimity, who made the same error (2; cf. 6). Out of concern for D. Brutus and deceived by a fallacious hope of honorable peace (cf. 7), Cicero (and Pansa, and other patriots) saw the situation through rose-colored glasses: "This indeed I saw, but I saw it through a fog; my anxiety for Decimus Brutus had blurred my vision" (3). It is of the human condition to err, but a wise man can and will correct his mistakes:

> To a man of sense everything is open that can be corrected. Every man is liable to err; it is the part only of a fool to persevere in error; for second thoughts, as the saying goes, are usually the wiser. That mist has been dispelled I spoke of just now; light has broken, the case is clear, we see everything, nor with our eyes only, but we are warned by our friends. (5)[92]

The persona of the statesman who watches out for the welfare of the Republic and its loyal supporters, who passionately hopes for an honorable peace, who frankly admits his mistakes but is quick to remedy them is thus effectively molded in the early sections of the speech and clears the way for Cicero's arguments against the embassy.

These arguments are, for the most part, points that Cicero had made previously, particularly in the Fifth Philippic, in which he had opposed the first embassy to Antony.[93] Although character description bolsters these arguments, notably that of the Capuans (7), the Martian and Fourth Legions (8), Hirtius and Octavian (9), the people of Cisalpine Gaul (9), and the Antonii (12–15), the ethos of Cicero does not fully reemerge until the second half of the speech, in which he deals specifically with his own role in the embassy and in this conflict in general.

Perhaps recalling the embassy to Philip in which Demosthenes was so humiliated, Cicero begins by outlining the compromised position into which he, of all people, would be thrust if forced to become a member of the delegation. His own reputation (*existimatio*), so important to himself and to the status of his ethos, is at stake:

Am *I* to be one of this embassy, or to mix myself up with that policy in which the Roman people will not even know if I dissent from the rest? The result will be that, if anything is allowed or conceded, the wrongdoing of Antonius will always be at my risk, since the power of doing wrong will appear to have been conceded to him by me. (16)[94]

It is clear from these words that Cicero considers himself the chief representative of the Republic in its fight against Antony, the state's spokesman, almost the state itself.[95] We recall that such identification was crucial to the persona that Cicero attempted to fashion in the *post reditum* speeches. In this speech, identification of himself with the Republic functions in a similarly important manner.

Explicit reference to Cicero as the Republic's chief representative in its struggle with Antony occurs in the next two sections of the speech (17–18). His role throughout the conflict is capsulized in a moving and emphatic manifesto of his persona (note the anaphora of *ego*, "I"):

It was I who never thought envoys should be sent; I who, before the return of the embassy, ventured to say that even if they brought Peace herself, since under the name of peace lurked war, she should be rejected; I took the lead in the putting on of military cloaks; I always called him a public enemy when others called him an adversary; I always called this a war when others called it a tumult. And this not only in the Senate; I always used the same language before the people; and not only against Antonius himself have I always inveighed, but also against his allies and agents in crime, both those here and those with him, in a word against the whole house of Marcus Antonius. (17)[96]

Twenty years earlier Cicero had assumed the "war" with Catiline and his followers and the persona of the *dux togatus*; now he assumes the "war" against the Antonii and a different persona, that of the *princeps sumendorum sagorum*, "the leader in the putting on of military cloaks."[97] Formerly considered the "nursling of peace" (*pacis alumnus, Phil.* 7.8), here and throughout the *Philippics* he assumes the character of the man first girt for war. In the Fifth Philippic (31) he had proposed that men should don the *sagum*, the garb that to the Romans symbolized a state of war (as the toga did peace).

In the Seventh Philippic, Cicero proclaims this exchange of roles in a tortuous, halting, but extraodinarily effective and emphatic period:[98]

> I, therefore, who have always been an advocate of peace, and to whom peace, especially domestic peace, although dear to all loyal men, has been particularly dear—for the whole course of my career has been spent in the Forum, in the senate-house, in repelling danger from my friends, from which source I have won the highest honors, moderate wealth, and such dignity as I possess—I then, the nursling, so to speak, of peace, who certainly would not have been whatever I am —for I claim nothing for myself—without domestic peace— these are dangerous words: I shrink from the thought of how you will take it, Members of the Senate, but in return for my unfaltering desire to maintain and increase your dignity, I ask and beseech you, Members of the Senate, that first of all, even if it seems harsh or incredible to hear it said by Marcus Cicero, you receive what I shall say without offense and secondly that you not reject it before I explain its meaning—I—I will say it again—I, who have always been the encomiast, always the advocate of peace, refuse to support a peace with Marcus Antonius. (*Phil.* 7.7–8)[99]

The halting hesitancy and degree of qualification that characterize this period perhaps physically demonstrate the difficulty with which Cicero announces to the Senate his shocking volte-face. Here is the *dux togatus* of the Catilinarian affair, the patriot who, as he himself so many times had declared, withdrew into voluntary exile to avoid an armed conflict with Clodius that would have had grave repercussions on the Republic and its loyal supporters, now rejecting peace with Antony as a dangerous, disgraceful, impossible course of action. Once assumed, this is a persona that he never lays aside, a stance from which he never retreats.

In the Eighth Philippic (32) he announces his personal decision to forego his privilege, as a consular, of wearing the toga and to assume, with his fellow citizens, the *sagum*, the garb of war. In the Twelfth Philippic, as we have noted, he dubs himself *princeps sumendorum sagorum* (12.17; cf. 10.19), and in the final Philippic (14.1–3), he pleads powerfully against the proposal to return to wearing the toga. This singleness of purpose, this consistency of persona, contributes powerfully to the positive portrait of Cicero the patriot, the chief representative of the Republic, the protagonist against whom in sharp relief is set the antagonist Antony, whom Cicero here and throughout endeavors to paint as a public enemy (*hostis*) waging a full-scale war (*bellum*) against the Republic.

Cicero attempts to stir sympathy for himself through a clever rhetorical conceit: his eyes will not endure to look upon men like the Antonii (19–20). This line of argument enables him again to emphasize Antony's status as an enemy (19), his brother's cruelty, the wickedness of their followers, and, of course, Cicero's own love of the Republic: "I cannot see with a calm spirit so many savage, wicked enemies, and that not because of any squeamishness on my part, but from love of the Republic" (20).[100]

This leads naturally into a passage in which Cicero describes in detail the dangers that would threaten him as an ambassador to Antony (21–24). It is in this part of the speech that his identification of himself with the Republic reemerges as a major theme:[101]

> But to you and to the Roman people my life should not be cheap. For I am the man, unless perhaps I deceive myself, who, by my vigils, anxieties, votes, and even by the many perils I have faced on account of the most bitter hatred towards me of all wicked men, have contrived not to be harmful to the Republic—lest I seem to speak too arrogantly. This being so, do you think I should have no thought of my danger? (21–22)[102]

As is clear from this passage, Cicero, as he had more than a decade before, following his return from exile, considers himself, if not the embodiment, at least the symbol of the state. His dangers are her dangers, his safety her safety, his survival the survival of the Republic. For this reason, he argues, he should remain in the city and, as he has always done, protect it from its enemies (24). His bond with the Republic is then made even more explicit, as he links his present role with his role in the past:

> Facts are eloquent. It is now twenty years that every criminal has made me his single aim. And so they have paid the penalty, I will not say to me, but to the Republic; my safety the Republic has up to now ensured to secure its own. This I will say with some timidity, for I know that to a man anything may happen—but anyhow: I was never taken unawares, though on one occasion, surrounded by the massed strength of some very powerful people, I fell deliberately, knowing that I would be able to rise again with the utmost honor. (24)[103]

The oblique references to his role in the Catilinarian affair, his sacrificial exile on behalf of the Republic, and his identification with the state invest Cicero's ethos with an added dimension of authority and serve to align him and his supporters with the Republic, constitutionality, right, and Roman tradition, against the Antonii, who personify the antipathy of such ideals. The projection of the persona of the patriot and the identification of this character with the Republic are, and have long been, Ciceronian methods of winning persuasion through sources rooted in ethos. It is perhaps their sincerity and extraordinary intensity that distinguish them in this context.

Even if Cicero were to reach the conference safely, he argues, he would be forced to meet and speak with Antony, who would scarcely keep himself from laying hands upon him, hands that, because they seek the destruction of the Republic through the destruction of its chief representative, are here labeled sacrilegious and impious:

> I scarcely think I shall be safe. I know the man's fury, I know his unbridled violence. The bitterness of his character and the savagery of his nature do not usually soften even when tempered with wine. When this man is inflamed with wrath and madness, and his brother Lucius, that most horrible beast, stands with him, he will assuredly never keep his sacrilegious and impious hands from me. (26)[104]

The details of the Antonian ethos are familiar: insane madness, violence, bitterness of character, and drunken, demented, angry bestiality separate these villains from Cicero, the Republic, and the whole human race—not to mention other "noble" enemies in Roman history who have received embassies in a civilized fashion (27).

As the speech nears its conclusion, Cicero summarizes his plea with a final request that emphasizes one last time his position and the portrait of himself that he has projected throughout this speech and the *Philippics* in general: "Let my life, therefore, be guarded for the Republic, and let it be preserved, so far as dignity or nature shall allow, for my country" (30).[105]

Cicero's use of ethos in the selections from the *Philippics* examined here presents little that is new or different from his methods in previous speeches. There is, to be sure, the change of roles from *dux togatus* to *princeps sumendorum sagorum*, but the ethos of Cicero is essentially the ethos of the patriot, which was already evident in his fight against Catiline and in his battle with Clodius. He is, as he had portrayed himself more than a decade earlier, the personification of the Republic, upon whose survival rests the survival of the state. He is Rome incarnate just as his enemies are the denial of all things Roman and even human. Such devolution of character described Catiline, Clodius, and others before Antony, and its shocking, disjunctive disposition against Cicero and the forces of good and of Rome is a common Ciceronian manipulation of ethos.

The difference between the treatment of ethos in the *Philippics* and in other Ciceronian speeches is one of scale, one of intensity, one of sincerity. This *is* a rhetoric of crisis, a crisis that in some way Cicero seems to have realized would be his last; this *is* his finest hour.[106] These are characters writ large, locked in a titanic struggle for existence. The ethos of Cicero as patriot is not a new portrait, but rather one retouched with new intensity, sincerity, and purpose, which, when stripped of all its excess political coloration, reveals a depth that is even reflected in the style of its presentation. Here is an ethos that has power to move hearts, for good and for ill; that it exercised this power, historical fact attests.

Caesar Augustus, an ultimate if not entirely willing collaborator in the destruction of Cicero and the Republic, perhaps most succinctly and most accurately described his character. Many years after the orator's death, the emperor found his grandson secretly reading a book of Cicero's works. "Seeing it, he took it from the boy and read a great portion; then giving it back to the lad, he said, 'An eloquent man, my boy, eloquent and a lover of his country.' "[107]

# VI

## CONCLUSION

Further, there is such authority in all that he says that his audience feel ashamed to disagree with him, and the zeal of the advocate is so transfigured that it has the effect of the sworn evidence of a witness, or the verdict of a judge. And at the same time all these excellences, of which scarce one could be attained by the ordinary man even by the most concentrated effort, flow from him with every appearance of spontaneity, and his style, although no fairer has ever fallen on the ears of men, nonetheless displays the utmost felicity and ease. It was not, therefore, without good reason that his own contemporaries spoke of his "sovereignty" in the courts, and that for posterity the name of Cicero has come to be regarded not as the name of a man, but as the name of eloquence itself. (Quintilian *Institutiones Oratoriae* 10. 1.111–112)

Oratory, by its very nature, involves character. Verbal persuasion of any sort always implies the presentation of a persona by the speaker that can effect its audience for good or for ill. In the foregoing analysis of Ciceronian oratory, I have attempted to demonstrate the role and the extent of Cicero's use of rhetorical ethos and its effects on persuasion. Unfortunately the ravages of time and fortune, and perhaps Cicero's own greatness as an orator, have made it impossible for us to compare his oratory to that of his countrymen and contemporaries. Nevertheless, a thorough examination of his extant speeches and his use of rhetorical ethos in them has provided us with some tenable hypotheses about this extraordinarily effective source for persuasion.

Although it is not unusual to find character playing a role in oratory, it is perhaps surprising to discover both the extent to which Cicero utilizes it as a persuasive tool and the variety of methods he employs in its application. The sociopolitical circumstances in Republican Rome are largely responsible for this. The importance of individual character in such a society must not be underestimated. For the Romans, a man's character remained essentially constant from birth, even from generation to generation of the same family. It was almost impossible to change or to disguise one's ethos. A man's actions were a direct result of his character; indeed, character determined actions. Under such circumstances, a man's deeds along with his family's military or political accomplishments were important. Those who excelled in these areas amassed influence, glory, reputation, authority, and dignity. Under such a system a close-knit and very exclusive cadre of nobles emerged who guarded their privileges and jealously protected admission to their ranks. Roman Republican history has often testified to the power that such individuals could and did exert upon society.

It was into such a social and political milieu that the young *novus homo*, Cicero, found himself thrust in the early part of the first century B.C. As an orator working under the Roman convention of advocacy, it was absolutely necessary that he deal not only with the characters of his client and his opponent, but also with his own ethos and that of opposing counsel. In large part, the study of ethos in Ciceronian oratory is the story of the orator's struggle to establish an ethos of authority, to exert it when once established, to reestablish it when it had been diminished, and finally to reexert it with the courage of a true patriot when the very ideals for which it was established tottered on the brink of collapse.

The preceding chapters of this study have attempted to chronicle this struggle. Investigation not only has revealed the artistic applications of Cicero's rhetorical ethos but also has brought to light broader observations about Ciceronian oratory and Republican Roman oratory in general. Internal evidence in the speeches overwhelmingly confirms the thesis that a man in possession of *auctoritas, gratia, dignitas*, and a sterling *existimatio* could wield immense influence in a Roman court of law. Cases involving the charge of election bribery (*ambitus*) are particularly informative about the importance of ethos in Roman society and, more specifically, in a Roman court. Priority of election at the polls, previous offices held, degree of nobility, and ancestral achievements all find their way into court cases and are granted by the litigants, to the astonishment of modern audiences, the status of worthy, even necessary arguments and proofs.

In the early speeches, such as the *Pro Quinctio*, *Pro Roscio Amerino*, and the *Verrines*, Cicero is often preoccupied with defusing his opponents' influence, complaining about their unfair advantage, and establishing himself as the sympathetic underdog. The persona he projects is that of the young, somewhat inexperienced, yet intelligent and capable champion of the downtrodden, fighting in the face of unscrupulous influence and power. The orations against Verres reveal to us firsthand the plight of the *novus homo*, his struggle to gain the coveted rank of *nobilitas*, his bitterness over the situation, and the grudging envy of nobles who disdained the industry and hard work of new men. These speeches, perhaps more than any other works of Cicero's, disclose the pain he suffered, in greater or lesser degree, throughout his entire career, realizing but refusing to accept that despite his glorious accomplishments he would always live under the shadow of being a new man, never entirely accepted by his noble peers. This rejection certainly appears to have provided the psychological motivation for many of Cicero's actions and accounts for his poignant, sometimes pathetic, and ultimately futile struggle for recognition from his associates, which by its very nature was unachievable for a *novus homo*.

The prominence of Cicero's own ethos is perhaps the most characteristic feature of the consular orations. In these speeches Cicero exerts the weight of his position and accomplishments both without mercy and without end. The consular orator exercises the full range of the *auctoritas* and *dignitas* of his office, which had been enhanced dramatically by his quick and effective handling of the Catilinarian affair. As the threat of exile moves closer, his defense of his clients is often coupled with a defense of his own actions, and it is common to find the *Pater Patriae* demanding the acquittal of his client almost solely on the basis of his own authority and position in the Republic.

In the *post reditum* speeches Cicero finds himself in a situation similar to that of his early speeches. Once again he is searching for a persona, struggling now to reassert his authority in the state, working to regain his damaged *dignitas*. His glorious recall from exile and his claim to have saved the state a second time by his withdrawal become the main grist for his rhetorical mill. Although at times marked by turgidity and shrillness, these orations are replete with effective applications of ethos, particularly the ethos of the orator. Cicero identifies himself with the state; the Republic becomes his advocate. He is the self-sacrificing patriot who offered himself as a *devotio* for the survival of Rome. Portrayed in sharply contrasting hues, the characters of Cicero's enemies, the enemies of the state, are likewise prominent.

In the final speeches, when the Republic came into the hands of autocrats, we find Cicero, at least for a time, operating under circumstances antithetical to oratory and free speech. The role of ethos, however, is adapted and remains prominent. Men like Pompey and Caesar, whose authority eclipses that of others, including Cicero himself, are invoked to lend weight to his cases. Their characters take on major parts, and Cicero's ethos and that of his client move into the background accordingly. The *Philippics* mark perhaps Cicero's finest hour and certainly find much of their persuasive effectiveness in ethos. The difference between the treatment of character in these and other Ciceronian orations is one of scale and intensity. These speeches are largely concerned with two antithetical characters writ large: Cicero, the unfailing patriot, the *princeps sumendorum sagorum*, a Roman representing Romans, the Republic, and the forces of good; and Antony, the public enemy, the abnegation of all things Roman, the force of evil in the state. Such portraits are certainly not entirely new, but rather have been retouched, highlighted by new intensity, sincerity, and purpose, painted on a grand scale. Here is presentation of character that borders continually on the emotional and, like pathos, has the power to move men's hearts.

It is perhaps noteworthy that in the speeches following his consulship, Cicero's younger and less prestigious adversaries find themselves in the predicament that the elder Cicero had, at least outwardly, long since forgotten: that of pleading a case while in possession of less *auctoritas* than one's opponent. They seem to have directed much of their zeal and their speeches toward neutralizing his advantage, as in the *Pro Plancio*. Cicero's air of kindly condescension toward these young orators—which permits a lightning change to devastating quips—suggests that he remembered the dynamics of inequity all too well. After his return from exile, when the solidity of his own *auctoritas* was undermined, the opportunity to reinforce its outward signs easily at the expense of his younger opponents would become a welcome strategy.

Given such situations, it is easy to see why an ethos in possession of traditional Roman virtues was an important, even essential part of one's case, as was the demonstration that an opponent's character lacked such virtues. This set of circumstances also helps to explain much of Ciceronian egotism, so repulsive to many modern readers. For Roman politicians and pleaders, a good measure of egotism and braggadocio was expected, almost required. This is not, of course, to exonerate Cicero from what must have seemed excessive boasting even to the Romans; but when we consider Cicero's own powerful personality, enhanced by his feat of breaking the barrier of the nobility, the Roman orator's penchant for relying on character as an important source for persuasion, and the goal that the advocate must always have in mind—securing a forensic victory—we can perhaps arrive at a conclusion closer to the truth.[1]

Having come to appreciate the importance of character in Roman society and in the courts of the Republic, we can easily understand why ethos became for Roman orators such a vital source for persuasion. In the hands of a master orator with the skill and personality of Cicero, the effective presentation of character becomes not only a powerful persuasive weapon but also a vehicle for artistic expression in the speech.

In Ciceronian oratory we find an artistic application of rhetorical ethos that far outstrips anything known in Greek oratory or in the severely fragmented oratory of his predecessors. With the rhetoric of advocacy in practice, the actors in the drama are multiplied: Cicero skillfully deals with the character of his client, the opposing litigant, himself, and the opposing counsel, as well as others who often have only a very tenuous connection with the case. Sometimes he identifies with, at other times he separates himself from, his client. On yet other occasions he even identifies himself with the opponent or portrays the *accusator* as his *amicus*, all to his own benefit. Character descriptions and sketches, sometimes based on stock comic or tragic counterparts, are only the most prosaic of his methods of expressing character. He is particularly adept at personification, *prosopopoeia*, and "ethical narrative"; one of his favorite tactics is the use of imaginary speech or dialogue to characterize the principals in the case.

The thrust or purpose of Cicero's presentation of character in almost every instance is to establish mutually exclusive, radically antithetical alternatives from which the jury can choose. On Cicero's side stand justice, truth, equity, the Republic, constitutionality, Rome herself; on the other side stand their opposites, injustice, falsehood, cupidity, the anti-Republican forces that by their actions and desires deny their *Romanitas* and seek to overthrow Rome. By presenting the judges with such mutually exclusive choices in a disjunctive mode, he in reality allows no choice but to side with him and the forces of good and the Republic.

Cicero's goal in presenting character in such a way is, of course, to lay a moral, or "ethical," foundation upon which to argue the probability of his defense. If his client's character, for example, can be shown to be entirely inconsistent with the charge, the orator has, in Roman terms, gone a long way in establishing the improbability of the accusation. For this reason the character of those involved in the case generally appears, at least in outline form, immediately at the opening of the speech. But following Aristotle's advice, Cicero then diffuses his presentation of ethos throughout the speech, "like blood in a body" (*De Or.* 2.310). He interweaves proof by character with proof by other means and, depending on the guilt or innocence of his client, the strength of his case, and the amount of proof that can be established by rational argumentation, employs rhetorical ethos accordingly. Where compelling, logical proofs are lacking, proof based on character often fills the breach, overshadowing the real facts of the case and often becoming the focal point of the speech.[2]

On many occasions we find Cicero inserting a digression, between proof and peroration, that has as its subject not any arguments directly related to the charge, but rather the character of people involved in the case. This "ethical digression," rooted in Greek oratory, is brought to perfection by Cicero and often serves to link the formal proof of the case with an emotional conclusion, in a corresponding movement of intensity from logos to ethos to pathos. This movement becomes more comprehensible once we come to understand the connection between ethos and pathos in Roman oratory. Ethos, for the Romans, represented a milder form of pathos, the presentation of the gentler emotions. Thus when ethos is vigorously and emotionally expressed, it yields to pathos, and the courtroom, to use Cicero's own words, is transformed from a *iudicium* into an *incendium* (*De Or.* 2.202), inflaming the souls of the orator's audience and moving them where he wills.

The suppleness and ease with which Cicero manipulates all of these aspects of rhetorical ethos is astonishing. In his assessment of Ciceronian oratory a century later, Quintilian (10.1.112) observes that the virtues of Cicero's oratory, any one of which someone might achieve only by applying the most intense care, flow from him unlabored, that his oratory displays a happy felicity. The same could be said of Cicero's handling of rhetorical ethos in the speeches. Aristotle's dictum (*Rhet.* 1.2.1356a13) that under certain circumstances ethos can prove to be the most efficacious source of persuasion found its full realization in Ciceronian oratory.

By his practice as well as by his own admission, Cicero preferred to speak for the defense. In the *Pro Murena* (59) he claims that power, extraordinary authority, and excessive influence, all components of a character prized by the Romans, should be reserved for defense of those who are weak, helpless, and in trouble. Certainly the primary sphere for the exercise of Cicero's rhetorical ethos is the defense speech. Nevertheless, it is noteworthy that for Cicero the best defense often proved to be a powerful, even ruthless offense; some of the most effective uses of ethos in the speeches occur when it is used as an offensive weapon—including, of course, attacks on opponents when the orator is appearing for the defense. The assaults on the characters of Verres, Catiline, Clodius, and Antony certainly come to mind; yet more effective, subtle, and artistic are those brought against Cato in the *Pro Murena*, or Tubero in the *Pro Ligario*. In the latter, Cicero remarkably transforms the desperation of a *deprecatio* into a strong, sometimes vicious attack on the prosecutor.

The blatant and indiscriminate use of rhetorical ethos evidenced in Cicero's orations perhaps seems unjustifiable, either logically or morally, to a modern audience. Our courts would find most of Cicero's proof based on character totally irrelevant and therefore inadmissible as evidence. But because character is inherent in the art of verbal persuasion, the ethos of litigants and lawyers, politicians and presidents still plays its part in persuasion for good and for ill. The forum of the Congress or the arena of the political campaign are still replete with methods for manipulating ethos to one's advantage. Although we try in some ways to control the effect of character on our decisions, ethos continues to wield a tremendous weight. The Romans certainly understood the power of character in their society and recognized the problems that such power could create. Still, they seemed to accept that power as part of their existence, preferring to trust in the manifestation of a person's nature, his family's collective ethos and achievements, touchstones that seemed truer and less susceptible to change and deception than facts, which could more easily be distorted and disguised.

Ciceronian ethos is a product of the meeting of Roman traditions, of Cicero's own personality, and of some features of Greek and earlier Roman oratory. The first of these factors, Roman tradition, is perhaps the most important. Such traditions conditioned Cicero's audience, and without understanding such conditioning, Cicero (or any public speaker) was doomed to failure. Yet oratory, more than any other literary genre of antiquity, deals with constantly changing circumstances, with different rhetorical challenges. An orator's success or failure, as well as the artistic quality of his orations, were largely the direct results of the responses he made to such circumstances and such challenges. Acutely aware of his audience and their traditions and endowed with a strong personality that was enhanced by the Roman virtues of authority, dignity, and influence and steeped in the rhetorical traditions of his predecessors, Cicero employed rhetorical ethos as a source of persuasion with uncanny success. Certainly there were failures; but these (e.g., the *Pro Milone*) seemed to occur mostly because of some external factor and not the failure of Cicero's rhetorical ethos or oratorical art. Even Cicero's critics for the most part grant him his successes and admit that his oratory possesses the power to move men, perhaps as powerfully as any oratory throughout the ages.

Surely it would be rash to suggest that Cicero's use of rhetorical ethos is the sole, or even major, factor in his success. The effectiveness of his oratory lies in myriad converging factors that include not only his genius as an orator but also the circumstances of the time and the occasions of his speeches. Nonetheless, the orations themselves bear witness that ethos played a major role in almost every Ciceronian speech; that his audience and their daily lives were conditioned by their beliefs about character; that his rhetorical ethos, handled with great skill and originality, could and often did become his major source for persuasion. Almost within his own lifetime (so Quintilian tells us), Cicero's name became a word synonymous with eloquence, *non hominis nomen sed eloquentiae*. It is both interesting and important that a good portion of that reputation is based in the eloquence of Cicero's rhetorical ethos.

# NOTES

## CHAPTER I

1 For an explanation of "traditional" and "conceptual" rhetoric, see Kennedy, *Classical Rhetoric*, 3–17.

2 See Kennedy, *Art of Persuasion*, 35–39, and *Classical Rhetoric*, 9–15.

3 It is not within the scope of this study to consider the role of ethos in the Greek tradition. Wilhelm Süss, *Ethos*, has attempted, with varying degrees of success, a detailed examination of the concept in Greek rhetoric and oratory.

4 See, e.g., *Phaedr.* 269d–274a, *Leg.* 722–723, *Gorg.* 500–504; *Lysis* 210a–d; cf. Sattler, "Conceptions of Ethos," 55–65; Solmsen, "Aristotle and Cicero," 390–404, esp. 402–404.

5 Cf. *Phaedr.* 261a, 270b, 271a–d.

6 Aristotle's conception of a thing's organic unity, as illustrated, e.g., in *Metaph.* 6.17.1041b11–13, seems to have been responsible for his decision to analyze a speech, not as being composed of discrete parts, but as being a whole in which proof, style, and disposition play discrete roles. See Solmsen, "Aristotelian Tradition," 35–50, 169–190; cf. idem, "Aristotle and Cicero," 390–404; Sattler, "Conceptions of Ethos," 57.

7 *Rhet.* 1.2.1356a1 4. See Grimaldi, "A Note on the πίστεις," 188–192; idem, *Studies*, esp. 53–68, and *Commentary*, 19–20, 349–356; in these passages Grimaldi distinguishes the various uses of the word *pisteis* by Aristotle in the *Rhetoric*, arguing convincingly that the *pisteis* of the passage in question represent "source material for demonstrative proof, whereas the πίστεις as modes of demonstration are ἐνθύμημα and παράδειγμα" ("A Note," 190).

8 Kennedy, *Classical Rhetoric*, 68.

9 Grimaldi, *Studies*, 62; *Commentary*, 39–40. He prefers the name *to pragma* (based on the testimony of Dionysius of Halicarnassus *Lysias* 19) for the third source of persuasion, which is not to be identified with *enthymēma*; rather, "the three pisteis as sources for rhetorical demonstration are informed or ordered by the demonstrative process, i.e. the inferential process of deductive and inductive reasoning, namely enthymeme and example" ("A Note," 191).

10 Cf. Cope, *Introduction*, 108–113; see also the relevant passages in Cope's *Commentary*; Kennedy, *Art of Persuasion*, 91–93. For slightly different conceptions of ethos, cf. Süss, *Ethos*, esp. 1–2, and Sattler, "Conceptions of Ethos," esp. 55–56.

11  Sattler's diagram of ethos, "Conceptions of Ethos," 58, illustrates the important connection between this source of persuasion and *proairesis*.

12  Solmsen, "Aristotle and Cicero," 404, concludes that Aristotle is certainly indebted to Plato "for his new conception of rhetoric in general and ψυχαγωγία in particular, but that he is independent of Plato in the methods of its execution." See above, n. 4.

13  Cf. Solmsen, "Aristotelian Tradition," 46–50, 178–179; and "Aristotle and Cicero," 390–402.

14  See, e.g., *Rhet. Her.* 1.8, 11, 2.5; *De Inv.* 1.22, 26, 29; cf. Solmsen, "Aristotelian Tradition," 178.

15  Solmsen, "Aristotle and Cicero," 397–402; cf. his "Aristotelian Tradition," 179.

16  *Ad Fam.* 1.9.23; cf. *De Or.* 2.152, 160.

17  The *affectus* are treated in 2.185–211; the technical passage is 2.206–211. Cf. Solmsen, "Aristotle and Cicero," 396–402.

18  Cf. *De Or.* 2.310, also 2.80–82, 322.

19  "Valet igitur multum ad vincendum probari mores et instituta et facta et vitam eorum, qui agent causas, et eorum, pro quibus, et item improbari adversariorum, animosque eorum, apud quos agetur, conciliari quam maxime ad benevolentiam cum erga oratorem tum erga illum, pro quo dicet orator. Conciliantur autem animi dignitate hominis, rebus gestis, existimatione vitae; quae facilius ornari possunt, si modo sunt, quam fingi, si nulla sunt. Sed haec adiuvant in oratore: lenitas vocis, vultus pudor[is significatio], verborum comitas; si quid persequare acrius, ut invitus et coactus facere videare. Facilitatis, liberalitatis, mansuetudinis, pietatis, grati animi, non appetentis, non avidi signa proferre perutile est; eaque omnia, quae proborum, demissorum, non acrium, non pertinacium, non litigiosorum, non acerborum sunt, valde benevolentiam conciliant abalienantque ab eis, in quibus haec non sunt; itaque eadem sunt in adversarios ex contrario conferenda." Antonius' theorizing about ethos is likely to have been slightly out of step with the way ethos was being used by Roman orators; the tendency of rhetorical theory to lag behind practice, at times by a substantial margin, has often been noted. Cf. Kennedy's comment on the theory and practice of ethos in "Rhetoric of Advocacy," 436.

20  This usage seems to occur commonly in Latin; cf., e.g., Sallust's introduction to his character description of Cato and Caesar, *Cat.* 53.6: "quin utriusque naturam et mores, quantum ingenio possum, aperirem."

21  Fantham, "*Conciliare* and *Ethos*," 271.

22  Ibid., 272–275.

23  See *Brut.* 185, 187–188, 197, 276; *Opt. Gen.* 3; *Orator* 69; *Part. Or.* 22. Cf. Fantham, "*Conciliare* and *Ethos*," 273–275.

24  Cf. Solmsen, "Aristotle and Cicero," 399–400.

25  Cf. McClintock, "Cicero's Narrative Technique," 38–41.

26  See Cicero *De Off.* 1.107–114.

27  Cf. Cicero *Pro Sulla* 69, 79; *De Am.* 32; *De Off.* 1.110; *Pro Rosc. Am.* 68. Tacitus' description of Tiberius' volte-face (*Ann.* 6.51), not as a change but rather a revelation of his true ethos, which he had disguised for so many years, reflects similar beliefs about character.

28  References to Cato and other early orators in this chapter are to *Oratorum Romanorum Fragmenta (ORF)*, ed. Malcovati.

29  Thus narration of deeds provides biography, and "biography becomes proof" (McClintock, "Cicero's Narrative Technique," 40).

30 Cf. Heinze, "Auctoritas," 348–366, esp. 363–366.

31 The influence Pericles exercised among the Athenians was extraordinary and, judging from the import of Thucydides' words (2.65.6–13), seems to have been the exception rather than the rule for Athenian statesmen. Cf. Plut. *Per.* 15.4–5.

32 As happened to Socrates on the day the Athenians debated the fate of the generals who had served at the battle of Arginusae (Plato *Apol.* 32b; cf. Xenophon *Mem.* 4.4.2).

33 Heinze, "Auctoritas," 351–366, esp. 358, 363–366. Cf. Cicero *De Or.* 3.133 for a vivid description of a man possessed of great *auctoritas*, M'. Manilius.

34 For these concepts see, e.g., Cicero *De Inv.* 2.34, 166; *Top.* 73; *Pro Leg. Man.* 43–46; *De Off.* 2.31–51; *Acad.* 2.62–64; *De Or.* 2.334. Cf. Heinze, "Auctoritas," 348–366; Balsdon, "*Auctoritas, Dignitas, Otium*," 43–50; Carpino, "*Dignitas* in Cicerone," 253–267; Wirszubski, "Cicero's *cum dignitate otium*," 1–13; Dorey, "Honesty in Roman Politics," 41–42, n. 21.

35 Throughout this study the term *novus homo* is used in its special sense, to mean the first man of a family "to attain the consulate and hence *nobilitas*," especially one who "rose from outside the Senate straight to the consulship," (*Oxford Classical Dictionary*, s.v.); cf. Wiseman's definition, *New Men*, 1: "a senator whose forebears had been of equestrian status and had not entered the Senate at all," i.e., "a senator with no senatorial antecedents in his family." In the period 366–63 B.C., only fifteen *novi homines* reached the consulship. Cf. Scullard, "The Political Career of a "Novus Homo'," 2: "Thus the 200 consuls between 232 and 133 B.C. belonged to 58 families, but 159 of them came from only 26 of the families, and half the total came from only ten." See also Sallust's comment on the nobility's attitude toward a "new man," *Cat.* 23.5–6; Mitchell, *Cicero*, 95–98; Wiseman, *New Men*, 100–107; Gelzer, *Roman Nobility*, 50–53.

36 For similar anecdotes cf. also *Brut.* 54–55; *De Or.* 1.38, 214.

37 Quintilian (10.1.111) said much the same thing about Cicero's *auctoritas*.

38 Cf. Livy 38.50–51 for an account of the same episode and the debate among the Romans concerning the power of authority that preceded it.

39 If Cicero's feelings are representative, the Romans were certainly more sympathetic to the defendant and the role of defender than to the plaintiff and the role of the prosecutor. For this sentiment cf. *Verrines*, passim; *Pro Mur.* 59; *De Off.* 2.49–51. Cicero, to be sure, attempts to disarm the character and authority of Cato in the same way in the *Pro Murena*, although here and elsewhere he is never chary of exerting the weight of his own authority to effect persuasion.

40 For the importance of ethos in Roman oratory see Kennedy, *Art of Rhetoric*, 41–42, 57, 100–101.

41 McClintock, "Cicero's Narrative Technique," 41.

42 Cf. Douglas's comment in "Ciceronian Contribution," 25: "Characteristically Roman and Ciceronian is the adaptation of Aristotle's appeal to ἤθη solely through the medium of the speech so as to take into account the *auctoritas* possessed by the orator even before he begins to speak." Cf. Cope on Aristotle *Rhet.* 1.2.4 in *Commentary*, 1:29–30. This is not to deny, of course, that the reputation of the speaker played a part in actual Greek rhetorical practice; cf., e.g., Isoc. *Antid.* 278. One need only to open the speeches of Lysias, Aeschines, or Demosthenes to see ethos utilized in such a manner. Nevertheless, when compared to a Roman orator, the Greek's reliance upon his own

authority for persuasive material is far more limited. Cf. Süss, *Ethos*, 116–119.

43 See Kennedy, "Rhetoric of Advocacy," 419–436; *Art of Rhetoric*, 12–14.

44 This practice probably stems from the traditional patron–client relationship at Rome, which is closely bound to the Roman custom of submitting proposed courses of action to a competent *auctor* for counsel—behavior that served, as we have seen, as the basis for the strong respect and reliance upon *auctoritas* in Roman society. Cf. Heinze, "Auctoritas," 351–366; Kennedy, *Art of Rhetoric*, 12–14; "The Rhetoric of Advocacy," 428–429; Taylor, *Party Politics*, 41–42.

45 "Valet igitur multum vincendum probari mores et instituta et facta et vitam eorum, qui agent causas, et eorum, pro quibus, et item improbari adversariorum, animosque eorum, apud quos agetur, conciliari quam maxime ad benevolentiam cum ergo oratorem tum erga illum, pro quo dicet orator."

46 Cf. Kennedy, "Rhetoric of Advocacy," 436.

47 Kennedy, *Art of Rhetoric*, 42.

48 Cf. Kennedy, "Rhetoric of Advocacy," 429: "The Roman patron often plays a role which approaches that of a judge and character witness rolled into one"; also 430–431.

49 See *De Or.* 2.182–214, esp. 185, 212; *Orat.* 128–133; Quint. 6.2.8–17. Even in Aristotle, both *ēthos* and *pathos* are, in some way, concerned with the emotions and are aimed (*pros ton dikastēn* or *akroatēn*) at *psychagōgia*. Hendrickson, "Origin and Meaning," 249–290, has argued for an Aristotelian conception of proof that displays two aspects, *en autōi tōi pragmati* and *pros ton diakastēn*, and a Peripatetic tradition that assigned a twofold, rather than threefold, function to the orator. Cf. Solmsen, "Aristotelian Tradition," 179–180; Süss, *Ethos*, 147–173; Voit, Δεινότης, 132ff. The Roman conception of ethos and pathos reflects in spirit a twofold division with emphasis on the emotional: "Ethos, vigorously expressed, produces pathos, and both of these elements came more easily to the Roman character than did extensive or intricate logical argumentation" (Kennedy, *Art of Rhetoric*, 41).

50 Johnson, "Varieties of Narrative," 34–41, observes this liability in terms of its effect on Cicero's narrative technique.

51 Cf. Gotoff, *Cicero's Elegant Style*, 4–9; idem, "Cicero's Analysis of Prosecution Speeches," 123–124.

# CHAPTER II

1 Cf. Wiseman, *New Men*, 100–107, esp. 102–103; Mitchell, *Cicero*, 94–98; Scullard, "The Political Career of a 'Novus Homo,'" 1–25. See also *Commentariolum Petitionis* 2, 13.

2 Cf. Scullard, "The Political Career of a 'Novus Homo,'" 1, 15–25.

3 "Quae res in civitate duae plurimum possunt, eae contra nos ambae faciunt in hoc tempore, summa gratia et eloquentia."

4 For the details of this complicated case see Kinsey's commentary in his *M. Tulli Ciceronis Pro P. Quinctio Oratio*, 3–4; Greenidge, *Legal Procedure*, 531–541; and Craig, "Role of Rational Argumentation," 16–19.

5 Wooten, *Cicero's Philippics*, 58–86, notes the use of this rhetorical tactic of juxtaposing mutually exclusive, fundamentally opposed systems. This "disjunctive mode" marks the orator's speeches throughout his career.

6 Cf. McClintock, "Cicero's Narrative Technique," 60–75.

7 Horace *Ep.* 1.11.27, expresses a similar sentiment.

8 Cicero's use of these abusive terms throughout the speech seems certainly to be dictated by more than rhetorical convention (*pace* Kinsey, *Pro Quinctio*, 65). By introducing stock comic characteristics into his description of Naevius, he evokes from his audience a preconceived notion of such an ethos. For *praeco*, cf., e.g., Plaut. *Poen.* 11–14; *Bacch.* 815; Cic. *Ad Fam.* 6.18.1; Horace *Ars Poet.* 419–421; for *scurra*, see Plaut. *Epid.* 15; *Trin.* 199–202; *Rhet. ad Her.* 4.14; Cic. *De Or.* 2.247; Horace *Sat.* 1.5.52–70; *Ep.* 1.15.26–32; 1.18.2–8.

9 Kinsey, *Pro Quinctio*, 5–6; Craig, "Role of Rational Argumentation," 19.

10 For a detailed analysis of these arguments see Craig, "Role of Rational Argumentation," 21–34.

11 "Huic tum molestus esse videlicet noluisti quem nunc respirare libere non sinis; quem nunc interficere nefarie cupis, eum tum pudenter appellare nolebas. Ita credo; hominem propinquium, tui observantem, virum bonum, pudentem, maiorem natu nolebas aut non audebas appellare; saepe, ut fit, cum ipse te confirmasses, cum statuisses mentionem de pecunia facere, cum paratus meditatusque venisses, homo timidus virginali verecundia subito ipse te retinebas; excidebat repente oratio; cum cuperes appellare, non audebas, ne invitus audiret. Id erat profecto."

12 "Restat ut aut summa neglegentia tibi obstiterit aut unica liberalitas. Si neglegentiam dices [Naevius], mirabimur, si bonitatem, ridebimus."

13 "'De fortunis omnibus P. Quinctius deturbandus est; potentes, diserti, nobiles omnes advocandi sunt; adhibenda vis est veritati, minae iactentur, pericula intendantur, formidines opponantur, ut his rebus aliquando victus et perterritus ipse se dedat?'"

14 "Quid mihi," inquit, "cum ista summa sanctimonia ac diligentia? Viderint," inquit, "cum ista officia viri boni, de me autem ita considerent: non quid habeam sed quibus rebus invenerim quaerant, et quem ad modum natus et quo pacto educatus sim. Memini; vetus est, 'de scurra multo facilius divitem quam patrem familias fieri posse.'"

15 "'Pro me pugnabit L. Philippus, eloquentia, gravitate, honore florentissimus civitatis, dicet Hortensius, excellens ingenio, nobilitate, existimatione, aderunt autem homines nobilissimi ac potentissimi, ut eorum frequentiam et consessum non modo P. Quinctius qui de capite decernit, sed quivis qui extra periculum sit perhorrescat.'"

16 Craig, "Role of Rational Argumentation," 41.

17 *Pace* Canter, "Irony," 461.

18 Cf. Davies, "Cicero, *pro Quinctio* 77," 156–157, and Kinsey's reply, "Cicero, Hortensius and Philippus," 737–738.

19 The speciousness and irrelevancy of the point are noticed by Kinsey, "Cicero, Hortensius and Philippus," 737, and Craig, "Role of Rational Argumentation," 54.

20 "Est quaedam tamen ita perspicua veritas, ut eam infirmare nulla res possit."

21 "Omnia sunt, C. Aquili, eius modi, quivis ut perspicere possit in hac causa improbitatem et gratiam cum inopia et veritate contendere." Cf. 79.

22 "Ea res nunc enim in discrimine versatur, utrum possitne se contra luxuriem ac licentiam rusticana illa atque inculta parsimonia defendere an deformata atque ornamentis omnibus spoliata nuda cupiditati petulantiaeque addicatur. Non comparat se tecum gratia P. Quinctius, Sex. Naevi, non opibus, non facultate contendit; omnis tuas artis quibus tu magnus es tibi concedit; fatetur se non belle dicere, non ad voluntatem loqui posse, non ab adflicta amicitia transfugere atque ad florentem aliam devolare, non profusis sumptibus vi-

vere, non ornare magnifice splendideque convivium, non habere domum clausam pudori et sanctimoniae, patentem atque adeo expositam cupiditati et voluptatibus; contra sibi ait officium, fidem, diligentiam, vitam omnino semper horridam.atque aridam cordi fuisse. Ista superiora esse ac plurimum posse his moribus sentit."

23 See Craig, "Role of Rational Argumentation," 16–54.

24 See Kennedy, "Rhetoric of Advocacy," 429–432; my treatment of this speech is indebted to his fine analysis.

25 Cf. Imholz, "Gladiatorial Metaphors," 228–230.

26 "Accusant ei qui in fortunas huius invaserunt, causam dicit is cui praeter calamitatem nihil reliquerunt; accusant ei quibus occidi patrem Sex. Rosci bono fuit, causam dicit is cui non modo luctum mors patris attulit verum etiam egestatem; accusant ei qui hunc ipsum iugulare summe cupierunt, causam dicit is qui etiam ad hoc ipsum iudicium cum praesidio venit ne hic ibidem ante oculos vestros trucidetur; denique accusant ei quos populus poscit, causam dicit is qui unus relictus ex illorum nefaria caede restat."

27 Solmsen, "Cicero's First Speeches," 549, notes the continual presence of two subjects in the speech "which may indeed be described as the thread running through the oration from the beginning to the end. The two subjects stand in sharp contrast to each other. The one is the greed, corruption, and unscrupulous wickedness of Sextus' adversaries; the other is Sextus' own modest and honest life, old-fashioned, but in keeping with the best Roman traditions."

28 "Alter [Capito] plurimarum palmarum vetus ac nobilis gladiator habetur, hic [Magnus] autem nuper se ad eum lanistam contulit, quique ante hanc pugnam tiro esset quod sciam, facile ipsum magistrum scelere audaciaque superavit."

29 "Certum est deliberatumque quae ad causam pertinere arbitror, omnia non modo dicere verum etiam libenter audacter libereque dicere; nulla res tanta exsistet, iudices, ut possit vim mihi maiorem adhibere metus quam fides."

30 Kennedy, "Rhetoric of Advocacy," 430.

31 "Etenim quis tam dissoluto animo est qui haec cum videat tacere ac neglegere possit?"

32 "Patrem meum, cum proscriptus non esset, iugulastis, occisum in proscriptorum numerum rettulistis, me domo mea per vim expulistis, patrimonium meum possidetis. Quid voltis amplius?"

33 That Cicero considered character the most important source of proof in such cases is also expressed in sections 68 and 75.

34 "Quibus tandem tu, C. Eruci, argumentis accusatorem censes uti oportere? Nonne et audaciam eius qui in crimen vocetur singularem ostendere et mores feros immanemque naturam et vitam vitiis flagitiisque omnibus deditam, denique omnia ad perniciem profligata atque perdita? Quorum tu nihil in Sex. Roscium ne obiciendi quidem causa contulisti."

35 Recall Aristotle's directive (Rhet. 3.16.1417a16), ēthikēn de chrē tēn diēgēsin einai ("It is necessary for the narrative to be of a moral character"). This is an excellent example of the third type of Aristotelian ethos, dramatic ethos, used to portray the character of a third party.

36 "Ita neglegens esse coepit ut, cum in mentem veniret ei, resideret, deinde spatiaretur, non numquam etiam puerum vocaret, credo, cui cenam imperaret, prorsus ut vestro consessu et hoc conventu pro summa solicitudine abuteretur."

37 "Quem simul atque attigi, statim homo se erexit, mirari visus est. Intellexi

quid eum pepugisset. Iterum ac tertio nominavi. Postea homines cursare ultro et citro non destiterunt, credo, qui Chrysogono nuntiarent esse aliquem in civitate qui contra voluntatem eius dicere auderet."

38  Perhaps Cicero's role as sole defender of Sextus is faintly reminiscent of Demosthenes' courageous action at the announcement of the fall of Elatea (*On the Crown* 169), when he alone stepped forward to speak what was best for Athens.

39  See above, n. 33.

40  "Quod mihi maximo argumento ad huius innocentiam poterat esse, in rusticis moribus, in victu arido, in hac horrida incultaque vita istius modi maleficia gigni non solere. Ut non omnem frugem neque arborem in omni agro reperire possis, sic non omne facinus in omni vita nascitur. In urbe luxuries creatur, ex luxuria exsistat avaritia necesse est, ex avaritia erumpat audacia, inde omnia scelera ac maleficia gignuntur; vita autem haec rustica quam tu agrestem vocas parsimoniae, diligentiae, iustitiae magistra est."

41  "Dices: 'Quid postea, si Romae adsiduus fui?' Respondebo: 'At ego omnino non fui.' 'Fateor me sectorem esse, verum et alii multi.' 'At ego, ut tute arguis, agricola et rusticus.' 'Non continuo, si me in gregem sicariorum contuli, sum sicarius.' 'At ego profecto qui ne novi quidem quemquam sicarium longe absum ab eius modi crimine.' "

42  "Verum quaeso a vobis, iudices, ut haec pauca quae restant ita audiatis ut partim me dicere pro me ipso putetis, partim pro Sex. Roscio. Quae enim mihi ipsi indigna et intolerabilia videntur quaeque ad omnis, nisi providemus, arbitror pertinere, ea pro me, ipso ex animi mei sensu ac dolore pronuntio; quae ad huius vitae casum causamque pertinent et quid hic pro se dici velit et qua condicione contentus sit iam in extrema oratione nostra, iudices, audietis."

43  Kennedy, "Rhetoric of Advocacy," 431.

44  "Verum haec omnis oratio, ut iam ante dixi, mea est, qua me uti res publica et dolor meus et istorum iniuria coegit. Sex. Roscius horum nihil indignum putat, neminem accusat, nihil de suo patrimonio queritur. Putat homo imperitus morum, agricola et rusticus, ista omnia quae vos per Sullam gesta esse dicitis more, lege, iure gentium facta; culpa liberatus et crimine nefario solutus cupit a vobis discedere; si hac indigna suscipione careat, animo aequo se carere suis omnibus commodis dicit." Kennedy, "Rhetoric of Advocacy," 432, aptly describes the advantages that accrue to Cicero and his defense as a result of the skillful use of this stratagem: "Sympathy is won for the unsuspecting Roscius, and he is partially protected from the powerful anger which Cicero may call down upon himself. The emotional tone is again heightened. At the same time, admiration is awakened for Cicero's courage and for his self-sacrifice in taking on himself what is really the danger of society. Cicero clearly saw in the occasion an opportunity to bring himself in the full light of the public stage as a candidate for many future roles." Cf. Stroh, *Taxis und Taktik*, 76–77.

45  For a detailed account of the use of this type of digression and its tradition in Greek and Roman rhetoric and oratory see May, "The *Ethica Digressio* in Cicero's Judicial Speeches"; cf. idem, "The *Ethica Digressio* and Cicero's *Pro Milone*," 240–246; Kennedy, *Classical Rhetoric*, 44, 94; Stroh, *Taxis und Taktik*, 75–76.

46  On Theodorus see Radermacher, "Artium scriptores," B.xii; cf. Plato *Phaedr.* 226e and Arist. *Rhet.* 3.13.1414b13–15. On Licymnius see Radermacher, "Ar-

tium scriptores," B.xvi; cf. Arist. *Rhet.* 3.13.1414b16–18 and an anonymous rhetor's comment on this passage, Radermacher, B.xvi.6. At one point Aristotle appears to regard the *epilogos* as merely recapitulatory, simply a brief conclusion (cf. *Rhet.* 3.13.1414b4–13 and at the conclusion of the *Rhetoric*, 1420a6–8); however, at another point (3.19.1419b10–1420a8) he describes a four-part *epilogos*, of which recapitulation is only the fourth part. The other three—praise of oneself and censure of one's adversary, amplification, and appeal to pathos—remarkably resemble the attributes of the *ethica digressio*.

47 Often *graphai paranomōn*; cf., e.g., Lycurgus' *Against Leocrates* 75–148; Demosthenes' *Against Aristocrates* 196–214; Aeschines' *Against Timarchus* 170–176. Navarre, *Essai sur la rhétorique grecque*, 277ff., recognizes this development and calls it "l'épilogue au sens large"; its elements are identical with Aristotle's complex *epilogos* and the *ethica digressio*: praise of oneself and/or censure of one's adversary, amplification or deprecation of the cause, and appeal to the emotions.

48 "Ipse vero quem ad modum composito et dilibuto capillo passim per forum volitet cum magna caterva togatorum videtis, iudices; videtis ut omnis despiciat, ut hominem prae se neminem putet, ut se solum beatum, solum potentem putet."

49 *De Or.* 2.213–214; cf. Solmsen's comments, "Cicero's First Speeches," 550–551, on the placement of this section of the speech, and the careful arrangement of the speech in general.

50 "Praedia mea tu possides, ego aliena misericordia vivo; concedo, et quod animus aequus est et quia necesse est. Mea domus tibi patet, mihi clausa est; fero. Familia mea maxima tu uteris, ego servum habeo nullum; patior et ferendum puto. Quid vis amplius? quid insequeris, quid oppugnas?"

51 "Dubium est ad quem maleficium pertineat, cum videatis ex altera parte sectorem, inimicum, sicarium eundemque accusatorem hoc tempore, ex altera parte egentem, probatum suis filium, in quo non modo culpa nulla sed ne suscipio quidem potuit consistere?"

52 Kennedy, "Rhetoric of Advocacy," 432.

53 For the Roman practice of assuming the role of prosecutor in order to establish one's own reputation, see *De Off.* 2.49–50. According to Cicero, this should be done only once, or a very few times, and then only in the interest of the state.

54 Cf. Davies, "Cicero, *pro Quinctio* 77," 156–157.

55 Cf. Neumeister, *Grundsätze der forensischen Rhetorik*, 36–41.

56 " 'Quod auri, quod argenti, quod ornamentorum in meis urbibus, sedibus, delubris fuit, quod in una quaque re beneficio senatus populique Romani iuris habui, id mihi tu, C. Verres, eripuisti atque abstulisti; quo nomine abs te sestertium miliens ex lege repeto.' "

57 "In eius modi re quisquam tam impudens reperietur qui ad alienam causam, invitis iis quorum negotium est, accedere aut adspirare audeat? Si tibi, Q. Caecili, hoc Siculi dicerent: 'Te non novimus, nescimus qui sis, numquam te antea vidimus; sine nos per eum nostras fortunas defendere cuius fides est nobis cognita. . . .' "

58 " 'Non enim,' inquit, 'illud peto quod soleo, cum vehementius contendi, impetrare: reus ut absolvatur non peto, sed ut potius ab hoc quam ab illo accusetur, id peto. Da mihi hoc; concede quod facile est, quod honestum, quod non invidiosum; quod cum dederis, sine ullo tuo periculo, sine infamia

illud dederis, ut is absolvatur cuius ego causa laboro.' "

59 Cicero's later estimation of Hortensius (*Brutus* 320) seems to confirm this picture.

60 "Atque is non tam propter Verrem laborat quam quod eum minime res tota delectat; videt enim, si a pueris nobilibus, quos adhuc elusit, si a quadruplatoribus, quos non sine causa contempsit semper ac pro nihilo putavit, accusandi voluntas ad viros fortis spectatosque homines translata sit, sese in iudiciis diutius dominari non posse."

61 "Cognosce ex me, quoniam hoc primum tempus discendi nactus es, quam multa esse opporteat in eo qui alterum accuset; ex quibus si unum aliquod in te cognoveris, ego iam tibi ipse istuc quod expetis mea voluntate concedam."

62 "Aliqua facultas agendi, aliqua dicendi consuetudo, aliqua in foro, iudiciis, legibus aut ratio aut exercitatio."

63 Portraying his adversary as an *amicus* is a favorite tactic that Cicero employs in several speeches. It probably represents an original technique of ethical argumentation. See Craig, "*Accusator as Amicus,*" 31–37.

64 "Tu ipse quem ad modum existimes vide etiam atque etiam, et tu te collige, et qui sis et quid facere possis considera."

65 "Ego qui, sicut omnes sciunt, in foro iudiciisque ita verser ut eiusdem aetatis aut nemo aut pauci pluris causas defenderint, et qui omne tempus quod mihi ab amicorum negotiis datur in his studiis laboribusque consumam, quo paratior ad usum forensem promptiorque esse possim."

66 Cf. Davies, "Cicero, *pro Quinctio* 77," 157.

67 "Cuius ego ingenium ita laudo ut non pertimescam, ita probo ut me ab eo delectari facilius quam decipi putem posse."

68 "Numquam ille me opprimet consilio, numquam ullo artificio pervertet, numquam ingenio me suo labefactare atque infirmare conabitur; novi omnis hominis petitiones rationesque dicendi. . . . Ita contra me ille dicet, quamvis sit ingeniosus, ut non nullum etiam de suo ingenio iudicium fieri arbitretur." Cf. 24.

69 Davies, "Cicero, *pro Quinctio* 77," 157.

70 "Te vero, Caecili, quem ad modum sit elusurus, quam omni ratione iacturus, videre iam videor; quotiens ille tibi potestatem optionemque facturus sit ut eligas utrum velis—factum esse necne, verum esse an falsum—utrum dixeris, id contra te futurum. Qui tibi aestus, qui error, quae tenebrae, di immortales, erunt, homini minime malo! Quid? Cum accusationis tuae membra dividere coeperit et in digitis suis singulas partis causae constituere? Quid? Cum unum quidque transigere, expedire, absolvere? Ipse profecto metuere incipies ne innocenti periculum facessieris."

71 "Itaque semper ii diligentissime laboriosissimeque accusarunt qui se ipsos in discrimen existimationis venire arbitrati sunt."

72 "Habet enim nihil quod in offensione deperdat; ut turpissime flagitiosissimeque discedat, nihil de suis veteribus ornamentis requiret."

73 "Habet honorem quem petimus, habet spem quam propositam nobis habemus, habet existimationem multo sudore labore vigiliisque collectam, ut, si in hac causa nostrum officium ac diligentiam probaverimus, haec quae dixi retinere per populum Romanum incolumia ac salva possimus; si tantulum offensum titubatumque sit, ut ea quae singillatim ac diu collecta sunt uno tempore universa perdamus."

74 A major setback for an orator at this point in his career often ended his

aspirations. Cf. Douglas, "Intellectual Background," 129; also his note on *Brutus* 271, concerning P. Cominius and T. Accius, in *M. Tulli Ciceronis Brutus*, 197.

75 Cf. Kennedy, *Art of Rhetoric*, 159.

76 Ibid., 160–162; cf. Neumeister, *Grundsätze der forensischen Rhetorik*, 41–42.

77 "Neque enim mihi videtur haec multitudo, quae ad audiendum convenit, cognoscere ex me causam voluisse, sed ea quae scit mecum recognoscere."

78 Cf. McClintock, "Cicero's Narrative Technique," 80–81.

79 "Homo vita atque factis omnium iam opinione damnatus, pecuniae magnitudine sua spe et praedicatione absolutus."

80 McClintock, "Cicero's Narrative Technique," 80–81.

81 "Hominem esse arbitror neminem, qui nomen istius audierit, quin facta quoque eius nefaria commemorare possit."

82 "Quae cum ita sint, iste homo amens ac perditus alia mecum ratione pugnat. Non id agit ut alicuius eloquentiam mihi opponat; non gratia, non auctoritate cuiusquam, non potentia nititur. Simulat his se rebus confidere; sed video quid agat; neque enim agit occultissime. Proponit inania mihi nobilitatis, hoc est hominum adrogantium nomina, qui non tam me impediunt quod nobiles sunt, quam adiuvant quod noti sunt: simulat se eorum praesidio confidere, cum interea aliud quiddam iam diu machinetur."

83 Cf. also *In Ver.* 2.3.5–7; 2.4.79–82. Recall Sallust's words about the consulship, *Iug.* 63.6–7: "etiam tum alios magistratus plebs, consulatum nobilitas inter se per manus tradebat. novos nemo tam clarus neque tam egregiis factis erat, quin indignus illo honore et ⟨is⟩ quasi pollutus haberetur." Cf. Wiseman, *New Men*, 101–107, esp. 102–103. The citation of passages from the undelivered second action is justified here, I think, because of the valuable insight it lends into Cicero's ethos at this point in his career. For further discussion of Cicero's published versions of his speeches see chapter 5, n. 11.

84 "Sed non idem licet mihi quod iis qui nobili genere nati sunt, quibus omnia populi Romani beneficia dormientibus deferentur; longe alia mihi lege in hac civitate et condicione vivendum est. . . . Videmus quanta sit in invidia quantoque in odio apud quosdam nobilis homines novorum hominum virtus et industria; si tantulum oculos deiecerimus, praesto esse insidias; si ullum locum aperuerimus suspicioni aut crimini, accipiendum statim vulnus esse; semper nobis vigilandum, semper laborandum videmus. . . . Hominum nobilium non fere quisquam nostrae industriae favet; nullis nostris officiis benevolentiam illorum adlicere possumus; quasi natura et genere diiuncti sint, ita dissident a nobis animo ac voluntate."

85 "Quod ad tuam ipsius amicitiam ceterorumque hominum magnorum atque nobilium faciliorem aditum istius [i.e. Verres] habet nequitia et audacia quam cuiusquam nostrum virtus et integritas? Odistis hominum novorum industriam, despicitis eorum frugalitatem, pudorem contemnitis, ingenium vero et virtutem depressam exstinctamque cupitis: Verrem amatis!"

86 The other great *novus homo* of the first century B.C., C. Marius, is made by Sallust (*Iug.* 85) to express these sentiments even more vociferously in his speech to the people after his election to the consulship. Although too long to quote here, the entire speech is important and very instructive for our understanding and appreciation of the position of a "new man" in Roman society and politics.

87 Cicero's egotism, often offensive to a modern audience, is at least partially explained by these considerations. Roman Republican politics made no room

for shy, retiring, self-effacing men. The Roman reliance upon character as a measure of worth, and the importance of possessing adequate reputation, rank, influence, authority, and even heritage in order to be effective in political circles demanded a kind of ambition and projection of ethos from a Roman statesman to which we are unaccustomed. A certain measure (more perhaps than modern Judeo-Christians are willing to concede) of vanity and braggadocio was expected, even required of a Roman. For a *novus homo*, insecure as Cicero was about his lack of noble ancestry, the requirement seemed even more essential. See Allen, "Cicero's Conceit," 121–144. Cf. Kennedy, *Art of Rhetoric*, 101; also Theodore H. White's discussion of the politician's need for many personae in *The Making of the President, 1964* (New York 1964), 357 ff.; Johnson, "Varieties of Narrative," 68, n. 16, calls White's, analysis "far more relevant to the problem than the observations of scholars who gleefully address themselves to the question of Cicero's vanity in the belief that vanity is a kind of rare disease of which scholars have no first-hand knowledge."

88  " 'Renuntio tibi te hodiernis comitiis esse absolutum.' "

89  "Quid igitur? Quod tota Sicilia, quod omnes Siculi, omnes negotiatores, omnes publicae privataeque litterae Romae sunt, nihilne id valebit? Nihil invito consule designato. Quid? iudices non crimina, non testis, non existimationem populi Romani sequentur? Non; omnia in unius potestate ac moderatione vertentur."

90  "Cupiebam dissimilare me id moleste ferre, cupiebam animi dolorem vultu tegere et taciturnitate celare."

91  Cf. Johnson, "Varieties of Narrative," 67–68.

92  "Sollicitabar rebus maximis uno atque eo perexiguo tempore. Urgebant comitia, et in his ipsis oppugnabar grandi pecunia; instabat iudicium, ei quoque negotio fisci Sicilienses minabantur. Agere quae ad iudicium pertinebant libere comitiorum metu deterrebar; petitioni toto animo servire propter iudicium non licebat; minari denique divisioribus ratio non erat, propterea quod eos intellegere videbam me hoc iudicio districtum atque obligatum futurum."

93  Cf. Kennedy *Art of Rhetoric*, 159–163.

94  Ibid., 160.

95  "Si utar ad dicendum meo legitimo tempore, mei laboris industriae diligentiaeque capiam fructum, et hac accusatione perficiam ut nemo umquam post hominum memoriam paratior, vigilantior, compositior ad iudicium venisse videatur. Sed in hac laude industriae meae reus ne elabatur summum periculum est. . . . Fructum istum laudis, qui ex perpetua oratione percipi potuit, in alia tempore reservemus: nunc hominem tabulis, testibus, privatis publicisque litteris auctoritatibusque accusemus."

96  "Nunc vero, quoniam haec te [Hortensius] omnis dominatio regnumque iudiciorum tanto opere delectat, et sunt homines quos libidinis infamiaeque suae neque pudeat neque taedeat, qui quasi de industria in odium offensionemque populi Romani inruere videantur, hoc me profiteor suscepisse magnum fortasse onus et mihi periculosum, verum tamen dignum in quo omnis nervos aetatis industriaeque meae contenderem. Quoniam totus ordo paucorum improbitate et audacia premitur et urgetur infamia iudiciorum, profiteor huic generi hominem me inimicum accusatorem, odiosum, adsiduum, acerbum adversarium. Hoc mihi sumo, hoc mihi deposco."

97  "Erit tum consul Hortensius cum summo imperio et potestate, ego autem aedilis, hoc est paulo amplius quam privatus; tamen haec huius modi res est quam me acturum esse polliceor, ita populo Romano grata atque iucunda, ut

ipse consul in hac causa prae me minus etiam, si fieri possit, quam privatus esse videatur."

98 "Deinde, si plures improbi fuerint, hoc vobis, hoc populo Romano, iudices, confirmo, vitam mehercule mihi prius quam vim perseverantiamque ad illorum improbitatem persequendam defuturam."

99 *Pro Font.*, e.g., 12–15, 21–40, esp. 27–35, 37–40.

100 *Pro Cluent.*, passim, e.g., 11–16, 23, 26–27, 30, 42, 125, 133–134, 175–177, 188, 192–194, 196, 199.

101 *De Imp. Cn. Pomp.* 1–3, 27–50.

102 Cf. *De Or.* 2.202.

103 Cf. Neumeister, *Grundsätze der forensischen Rhetorik*, 45.

# CHAPTER III

1 Other *novi homines* who reached the consulship in the first century were C. Marius (107, 104, 103, 102, 101, 100, 86 B.C.), T. Didius (98 B.C.), and C. Coelius Caldus (94 B.C.).

2 Cicero's pride in his election was certainly justified. Cf. Wiseman, *New Men,* 163–167: "The orator's achievement was indeed remarkable" (167).

3 *De Leg. Ag.* 2.100. The speech Sallust gives to Marius at his accession to the consulship (*Jug.* 85) expresses similar sentiments.

4 "Versantur enim, Quirites, in animo meo multae et graves cogitationes quae mihi nullam partem neque diurnae neque nocturnae quietis impertiunt, primum tuendi consulatus, quae cum omnibus est difficilis et magna ratio, tum vero mihi praeter ceteros cuius errato nulla venia, recte facto exigua laus et ab invitis expressa proponitur; non dubitanti fidele consilium, non laboranti certum subsidium nobilitatis ostenditur."

5 By the term "consular" I wish to designate the speeches delivered by Cicero while consul and also those delivered as a *consularis* up to his exile in 58.

6 Cf. Kennedy, *Art of Rhetoric*, 188.

7 Cf. Arist. *Rhet.* 2.1.1377b24–28.

8 "Tandem aliquando, Quirites, L. Catilinam, furentem audacia, scelus anhelantem, pestem patriae nefarie molientem, vobis atque huic urbi ferro flammaque minantem ex urbe vel eiecimus vel emisimus vel ipsum egredientem verbis prosecuti sumus."

9 "Quid enim mali aut sceleris fingi aut cogitari potest quod non ille conceperit? Quis tota Italia veneficus, quis gladiator, quis latro, quis sicarius, quis parricida, quis testamentorum subiector, quis circumscriptor, quis ganeo, quis nepos, quis adulter, quae mulier infamis, quis corruptor iuventutis, quis corruptus, quis perditus invenire potest qui se cum Catilina non familiarissime vixisse fateatur?"

10 Cf. *In Cat.* 1.26; *Pro Cael.* 13; Sallust *Cat.* 5.1–5.

11 "Hoc vero quis ferre possit, inertis homines fortissimis viris insidiari, stultissimos prudentissimis, ebrios sobriis, dormientis vigilantibus? qui mihi accubantes in conviviis, complexi mulieres impudicas, vino languidi, conferti cibo, sertis redimiti, unguentis obliti, debilitati stupris eructant sermonibus suis caedem bonorum atque urbis incendia."

12 "Nulla enim est natio quam pertimescamus, nullus rex qui bellum populo Romano facere possit. Omnia sunt externa unius virtute terra marique pacata:

domesticum bellum manet, intus insidiae sunt, intus inclusum periculum est, intus est hostis. Cum luxuria nobis, cum amentia, cum scelere certandum est. Huic ego me bello ducem profiteor, Quirites; suscipio inimicitias hominum perditorum; quae sanari poterunt quacumque ratione sanabo, quae resecanda erunt non patiar ad perniciem civitatis manere. Proinde aut exeant aut quiescant aut, si in urbe et in eadem mente permanent, ea quae merentur expectent."

13  "O condicionem miseram non modo administrandae verum etiam conservandae rei publicae!"

14  "Est mihi tanti, Quirites, huius invidiae falsae atque iniquae tempestatem subire, dum modo a vobis huius horribilis belli ac nefarii periculum depellatur."

15  "Quos pexo capillo, nitidos, aut imberbis aut bene barbatis videtis, manicetis et talaribus tunicis, velis amictos, non togis; quorum omnis industria vitae et vigilandi labor in antelucanis cenis expromitur. In his gregibus omnes aleatores, omnes adulteri, omnes impuri impudique versantur. Hi pueri tam lepidi ac delicati non solum amare et amari neque saltare et cantare sed etiam sicas vibrare et spargere venena didicerunt."

16  Cf. Virgil's description of the Romans, *Aen.* 1.282: "Romanos, rerum dominos gentemque togatam."

17  Cf., e.g., the characters of Quinctius and Naevius in the *Pro Quinctio.*

18  "Ex hac enim parte pudor pugnat, illinc petulantia; hinc pudicitia, illinc stuprum; hinc fides, illinc fraudatio; hinc pietas, illinc scelus; hinc constantia, illinc furor; hinc honestas, illinc turpitudo; hinc continentia, illinc libido; hinc denique aequitas, temperantia, fortitudo, prudentia, virtutes omnes certant cum iniquitate, luxuria, ignavia, temeritate, cum vitiis omnibus; postremo copia cum egestate, bona ratio cum perdita, mens sana cum amentia, bona denique spes cum omnium rerum desperatione confligit."

19  "Atque haec omnia sic agentur ut maximae res minime motu, pericula summa nullo tumultu, bellum intestinum ac domesticum post hominum memoriam crudelissimum et maximum me uno togato duce et imperatore sedetur."

20  Cf. *In Cat.* 3.24–25.

21  Cf. *De Off.* 2.44–48. Generally, oratory is granted the second place to soldiering; cf. also *Pro Mur.* 19–30; *De Or.* 1.2.7; Livy's assessment of Cato, 39.40.4–5; Ovid *Am.* 1.15.3–6.

22  Consider his persistent hope for a triumph following his victory over the Pindenissitae during his governorship of Cilicia (*Ad Att.* 5.20). Perhaps this sentiment reveals a tacit admission on Cicero's part that the real power at this time in the Republic lay with men who were backed by armies, not eloquence.

23  Cicero's famous verse "Cedant arma togae, concedat laurea laudi" (Let arms yield to the toga, let the laurel yield to praise) is certainly indicative of this sentiment. See *In Pisonem* 72–75 for Cicero's explanation of this line. Cf. also Nicolet, "Consul togatus," 241–252, and Macdonald, *Cicero,* 97 n. b, 130 n. a.

24  Cf., e.g., *In Cat.* 3.15, 23, 26; 4.5, 21, 23; *Pro Mur.* 84; *Pro Sulla* 85.

25  "Quibus pro tantis rebus, Quirites, nullum ego a vobis praemium virtutis, nullum insigne honoris, nullum monumentum laudis postulabo praeterquam huius diei memoriam sempiternam. In animis ego vestris omnis triumphos meos, omnia ornamenta honoris, monumenta gloriae, laudis insignia condi et conlocari volo. . . . eandemque diem intellego, quam spero aeternam fore,

propagatam esse et ad salutem urbis et ad memoriam consulatus mei, unoque tempore in hac re publica duos civis exstitisse quorum alter finis vestri imperi non terrae sed caeli regionibus terminaret, alter huius imperi domicilium sedisque servaret."

26 Cf. Macdonald, *Cicero*, 130 n. a; Nicolet, "*Consul Togatus*," 245–252.

27 "Sit Scipio clarus ille cuius consilio atque virtute Hannibal in Africam redire atque Italia decedere coactus est, ornetur alter eximia laude Africanus qui duas urbis huic imperio infestissimas Karthaginem Numantiamque delevit, habeatur vir egregius Paulus ille cuius currum rex potentissimus quondam et nobilissimus Perses honestavit, sit aeterna gloria Marius qui bis Italiam obsidione et metu servitutis liberavit, anteponatur omnibus Pompeius cuius res gestae atque virtutes isdem quibus solis cursus regionibus ac terminis continentur: erit profecto inter horum laudes aliquid loci nostrae gloriae, nisi forte maius est patefacere nobis provincias quo exire possimus quam curare ut etiam illi qui absunt habeant quo victores reverantur."

28 Cicero himself proposed such an alliance to Pompey, *Ad Fam.* 5.7.3. Cf. Nicolet, "*Consul togatus*," 245–252, and Martin, "*Cicéron princeps*," 850–878, esp. 850–858.

29 Cf. H. H. Scullard, "The Political Career of a 'Novus Homo'," 13: "Pompey had not shown sufficient appreciation of Cicero's greatness in saving his country from Catiline. The reason for Pompey's coldness was in fact quite clear: he had hoped to return from the East to Rome in time to win the glory of having suppressed the Catilinarian conspiracy, and had been forestalled by Cicero." Cf. Nicolet, "*Consul togatus*," 245–252.

30 For an explanation of the difference in moods between this speech and the *Catilinarians* see Kennedy, *Art of Rhetoric*, 186–187; Leeman, "Technique of Persuasion," 194–197.

31 The speech was probably delivered during the last two weeks of November in 63, after Catiline and Manlius had taken the field but before the conspirators in Rome had been arrested; see Macdonald, *Cicero*, 183, and Leeman, "Technique of Persuasion," 200.

32 Cf. McClintock, "Narrative Technique," 110, 117.

33 "Ego autem has partis lenitatis et misericordiae quas me natura ipsa docuit semper egi libenter, illam vero gravitatis severitatisque personam non appetivi, sed ab re publica mihi impositam sustinui, sicut huius imperi dignitas in summo periculo civium postulabat."

34 Cf. Leeman, "Technique of Persuasion," 204.

35 The moral obligation to defend one in need is a sincere and important principle of action for Cicero; cf. *De Off.* 2.49–51; *Div. in Caec.* 4–5; *Pro Cluent.* 157; *Phil.* 7.7; *De Inv.* 1.5; *De Or.* 1.169, 202; *Tusc. Disp.* 1.1.

36 Cf. Kennedy, *Art of Rhetoric*, 101.

37 "Atque harum trium partium prima illa quae gravissima debebat esse ita fuit infirma et levis ut illos lex magis quaedam accusatoria quam vera male dicendi facultas de vita L. Murenae dicere aliquid coegerit."

38 In the *Pro Roscio Amerino* Cicero repeatedly (cf. sections 38, 68, 75) stressed the pivotal importance of character in determining a charge of parricide.

39 Leeman, "Technique of Persuasion," 206–207.

40 "Nihil igitur in vitam L. Murenae dici potest, nihil, inquam, omnino, iudices. Sic a me consul designatus defenditur ut eius nulla fraus, nulla avaritia, nulla perfidia, nulla crudelitas, nullum petulans dictum in vita proferatur. Bene

habet; iacta sunt fundamenta defensionis. Nondum enim nostris laudibus quibus utar postea, sed prope inimicorum confessione virum bonum atque integrum hominem defendimus."

41 It should be noted that Murena was a *novus homo*, but only in the sense that his ancestors, despite holding senatorial status (cf. *Pro Mur.* 15), had not attained the consulship, unlike the *novus homo*, Cicero, "whose forebears had been of equestrian status and had not entered the Senate at all" (Wiseman, *New Men*, 1).

42 Cf. Badian, *Roman Imperialism*, 61: "The most interesting feature of his remarkable and instructive speech on that occasion is the fact that this argument could not be simply laughed out of court: the immense seriousness with which the orator treats it—devoting a large part of his speech to its thorough refutation—shows as nothing else can the enduring and even increasing right to high office of the old *nobilitas*." See also Macdonald, *Cicero*, 178–179.

43 Leeman, "Technique of Persuasion," 207.

44 "Qua re ego te semper in nostrum numerum adgregare soleo, quod virtute industriaque perfecisti ut, cum equitis Romani esses filius, summa tamen amplitudine dignus putarere."

45 Craig, "Role of Rational Argumentation," 112.

46 "Technique of Persuasion," 208.

47 Cf. Cicero's pride and elation at his election for praetor, having been chosen first (*De Imp. Cn. Pomp.* 2).

48 "Vigilas tu de nocte ut tuis consultoribus respondeas, ille ut eo quo intendit mature cum exercitu perveniat; te gallorum, illum bucinarum cantus exsuscitat; tu actionem instituis, ille aciem instruit; tu caves ne tui consultores, ille ne urbes aut castra capiantur; ille tenet et scit ut hostium copiae, tu ut aquae pluviae arceantur; ille exercitatus est in propagandis finibus, tuque in regendis."

49 "Non mirum, si ob hanc facultatem homines saepe etiam non nobiles consulatum consecuti sunt."

50 "Cedat, opinor, Sulpici, forum castris, otium militiae, stilus gladio, umbra soli; sit denique in civitate ea prima res propter quam ipsa est civitas omnium princeps."

51 See Craig, "*Accusator* as *Amicus*," 31–37.

52 Ibid., 31.

53 "Dignitas in ista scientia consularis numquam fuit, quae tota ex rebus fictis commenticiisque constaret, gratiae vero multo etiam minus."

54 Craig, "*Accusator* as *Amicus*," 33.

55 "Petere consulatum nescire te, Servi, persaepe tibi dixi; et in eis rebus ipsis quas te magno et forti animo et agere et dicere videbam tibi solitus sum dicere magis te fortem accusatorem mihi videri quam sapientem candidatum."

56 "Sed tamen, Servi, quam te securim putas iniecisse petitioni tuae, cum populum Romanum in eum metum adduxisti ut pertimesceret ne consul Catilina fieret, dum tu accusationem comparares deposita atque abiecta petitione?"

57 "Nolo accusator in iudicium potentiam adferat, non vim maiorem aliquam, non auctoritatem excellentem, non nimiam gratiam. Valeant haec omnia ad salutem innocentium, ad auxilium calamitosorum, in periculo vero et in pernicie civium repudientur."

58 "Quemquamne existimas Catone, proavo tuo, commodiorem, communiorem, moderatiorem fuisse ad omnem rationem humanitatis? De cuius praestanti virtute cum vere graviterque diceres, domesticum te habere dixisti exemplum ad imitandum." For an instructive interpretation of this passage and of Cicero's treatment of Cato's stoicism in general, see Craig, "Cato's Stoicism," 229–239.

59 Plut. *Cato Min.* 21; cf. Leeman, "Technique of Persuasion," 216–217, for a discussion of this comment.

60 On procedures in cases of *ambitus* see *De Or.* 2.105.

61 The latter tactic is actually a subheading of *iuridicialis* called *comparatio*: "Comparatio est cum aliud aliquid factum rectum aut utile contenditur, quod ut fieret, illud quod arguitur dicitur esse commissum" (*Comparatio* is used when it is argued that some other action was lawful and advantageous, and then it is pleaded that the act that is charged was committed in order to make possible this advantageous act) (*De Inv.* 1.15). In other words, the bribery committed by Murena—if committed by Murena—is now unimportant; what is important, as well as lawful (*rectum*) and advantageous (*utile*), is that two consuls take office at the beginning of the year.

62 "Ego quod facio, iudices, cum amicitiae dignitatisque L. Murenae gratia facio, tum me pacis, oti, concordiae, libertatis, salutis, vitae denique omnium nostrum causa facere clamo atque testor. Audite, audite consulem, iudices, nihil dicam adrogantius, tantum dicam totos dies atque noctes de re publica cogitantem!"

63 Cf., e.g., *In Cat.* 1.33; 2.11, 29.

64 "Intus, intus, inquam, est equus Troianus; a quo numquam me consule dormientes opprimemini."

65 "His tantis in rebus tantisque in periculis est tuum, M. Cato, qui mihi non tibi, sed patriae natus esse videris, videre quid agatur, retinere adiutorem, defensorem, socium in re publica, consulem non cupidum, consulem, quod maxime tempus hoc postulat, fortuna constitutum ad amplexandum otium, scientia ad bellum gerendum, animo et usu ad quod velis negotium sustinendum."

66 "Hostis est enim non apud Anienem, quod bello Punico gravissimum visum est, sed in urbe, in foro—di immortales! sine gemitu hoc dici non potest—non nemo etiam in illo sacrario rei publicae, in ipsa, inquam, curia non nemo hostis est."

67 "Quem ego vobis, si quid habet aut momenti commendatio aut auctoritatis confirmatio mea, consul consulem, iudices, ita commendo ut cupidissimum oti, studiosissimum bonorum, acerrimum contra seditionem, fortissimum in bello, inimicissimum huic coniurationi quae nunc rem publicam labefactat futurum esse promittam et spondeam."

68 *Ad Fam.* 5.2.7.

69 Cf. Kennedy, *Art of Rhetoric*, 188.

70 "Sed, ut ille [Torquatus] vidit, quantum de mea auctoritate deripuisset, tantum se de huius praesidiis deminuturum, sic hoc ego sentio, si mei facti rationem vobis constantiamque huius offici ac defensionis probaro, causam quoque me P. Sullae probaturum."

71 See Macdonald, *Cicero*, 307–308.

72 "Hanc mihi tu si propter meas res gestas imponis in omni vita mea, Torquate, personam, vehementer erras. Me natura misericordem, patria severum, cru-

delem nec patria nec natura esse voluit; denique istam ipsam personam vehementem et acrem quam mihi tum tempus et res publica imposuit iam voluntas et natura ipsa detraxit. Illa enim ad breve tempus severitatem postulavit, haec in omni vita misericordiam lenitatemque desiderat."

73 "Multum haec vox fortasse valere deberet eius hominis qui consul insidias rei publicae consilio investigasset, veritate aperuisset, magnitudine animi vindicasset, cum is se nihil audisse de P. Sulla, nihil suspicatum esse diceret. Sed ego nondum utor hac voce ad hunc defendendum; ad purgandum me potius utar." Cf. 10.

74 "Itaque attende, Torquate, quam ego defugiam auctoritatem consulatus mei! Maxima voce ut omnes exaudire possint dico semperque dicam."

75 "Ego consul, cum exercitus perditorum civium clandestino scelere conflatus crudelissimum et luctuosissimum exitium patriae comparasset, cum ad occasum interitumque rei publicae Catilina in castris, in his autem templis atque tectis dux Lentulus esset constitutus, meis consiliis, meis laboribus, mei capitis periculis, sine tumultu, sine dilectu, sine armis, sine exercitu, quinque hominibus comprehensis atque confessis, incensione urbem, internicione civis, vastitate Italiam, interitu rem publicam liberavi; ego vitam omnium civium, statum orbis terrae, urbem hanc denique, sedem omnium nostrum, arcem regum ac nationum exterarum, lumen gentium, domicilium imperi, quinque hominum amentium ac perditorum poena redemi."

76 Cf. Craig, "Accusator as Amicus," 33–34.

77 "Atque etiam illud addam, ne qui forte incipiat improbus subito te amare, Torquate, et aliquid sperare de te, atque ut idem omnes exaudiant clarissima voce dicam. Harum omnium rerum quas ego in consulatu pro salute rei publicae suscepi atque gessi L. ille Torquatus, cum esset meus contubernalis in consulatu atque etiam in praetura fuisset, cum princeps, cum auctor, cum signifer esset iuventutis, actor, adiutor, particeps exstitit. . . . Videsne ut eripiam te ex improborum subita gratia et reconciliem bonis omnibus? Qui te et diligunt et retinent retinebuntque semper nec, si a me forte desciveris, idcirco te a se et a re publica et a tua dignitate deficere patientur."

78 Cf. In Cat. 2.29; 3.1, 18–23.

79 "Cum illae valent apud me excusationes iniuriae tuae, iratus animus tuus, aetas, amicitia nostra, tum nondum statuo te virium satis habere ut ego tecum luctari et congredi debeam. Quod si esses usu atque aetate robustior, essem idem qui soleo cum sum lacessitus; nunc tecum sic agam tulisse ut potius iniuriam quam rettulisse gratiam videar."

80 "Neque enim istorum facinorum tantorum, tam atrocium crimen, iudices, P. Sullae persona suscepit."

81 "Omnibus in rebus, iudices, quae graviores maioresque sunt, quid quisque voluerit, cogitarit, admiserit, non ex crimine, sed ex moribus eius qui arguitur est ponderandum. Neque enim potest quisquam nostrum subito fingi neque cuiusquam repente vita mutari aut natura converti." We have seen the importance Cicero attached to character in other cases; cf., e.g., Pro Quinct. 93; Pro Rosc. Am. 38, 68, 75; Pro Mur. 11.

82 "Intellegetis unum quemque eorum prius ab sua vita quam vestra suspicione esse damnatum." Cf. 71; speaking specifically of Autronius: "Huius si causa non manifestissimis rebus teneretur, tamen eum mores ipsius ac vita convinceret."

83 "Quid reliquae constantiam vitae commemorem, dignitatem, liberalitatem,

moderationem in privatis rebus, splendorem in publicis? . . . Quae domus, quae celebratio cotidiana, quae familiarum dignitas, quae studia amicorum, quae ex quoque ordine multitudo!"

84 "Non, inquam, cadit in hos mores, non in hunc pudorem, non in hanc vitam, non in hunc hominem ista suspicio."

85 "Beluae quaedam illae ex portentis immanes ac ferae forma hominum indutae exstiterunt!"

86 "Penitus introspicite Catilinae, Autroni, Cethegi, Lentuli ceterorumque mentis; quos vos in his libidines, quae flagitia, quas turpitudines, quantas audacias, quam incredibilis furores, quas notas facinorum, quae indicia parricidiorum, quantos acervos scelerum reperietis!"

87 "Valeat ad poenam et ad salutem vita plurimum, quam solam videtis per se ex sua natura facillime perspici, subito flecti fingique non posse."

88 "Quid vero? haec auctoritas—semper enim est de ea dicendum, quamquam a me timide modiceque dicetur—quid? inquam, haec auctoritas nostra, qui a ceteris coniurationis causis abstinuimus, P. Sullam defendimus, nihil hunc tandem iuvabit?" Although Clark (Oxford Classical Text), following Spengel's suggestion, prints *saepe*, I have followed the manuscripts and retained *semper*. Considering the number of references, both veiled and explicit, to Cicero's *auctoritas* throughout the speech, and its undeniable role as a major, if not the major argument for Sulla's defense, *semper* does not seem to overstate the situation.

89 "Sed cum agatur honos meus amplissimus, gloria rerum gestarum singularis, cum, quotiens quisque est in hoc scelere convictus, totiens renovetur memoria per me inventae salutis, ego sim tam demens, ego committam ut ea quae pro salute omnium gessi, casu magis et felicitate a me quam virtute et consilio gesta esse videantur?" Cf. also 84–85.

90 "Grave esse videtur eum qui investigarit coniurationem, qui patefecerit, qui oppresserit, cui senatus singularibus verbis gratias egerit, cui uni togato supplicationem decreverit, dicere in iudicio: 'Non defenderem, si coniurasset.' "

91 Cf. Boulanger, *Cicéron: discours XI*, 92–95; Kennedy, *Art of Rhetoric*, 188.

92 E.g., *Pro Quinct.* 1–2, 8–9, 47, 53, 59, 71–73, 77, 84–87. *In Ver.* 1.35.

93 Cf. the story of Cotta's acquittal as a reaction against the overwhelming authority of Scipio, *Pro Mur.* 58.

94 Cf. Macrobius *Sat.* 2.1.13; see also Macdonald, *Cicero*, 431.

95 "Forte quae res hoc iudicio temptetur, quid agatur, cui causae fundamenta iaciantur, iudices, non videtis. Condemnatus est is qui Catilinam signa patriae inferentem interemit; quid est causae cur non is qui Catilinam ex urbe expulit pertimescat? Rapitur ad poenam qui indicia communis exiti cepit; cur sibi confidat is qui ea proferenda et patefacienda curavit? Socii consiliorum, ministri comitesque vexantur; quid auctores, quid duces, quid principes sibi exspectent?"

96 " . . . qui mihi videtur quasi quoddam exemplar pristinae gravitatis et monimentum antiquitatis in re publica divinitus reservari." This fragment is from the manuscript of Nicolas of Cusa, printed with others by Webster in his edition, *Pro L. Flacco Oratio*, but not given by Clark in the Oxford Classical Texts edition.

97 Such attacks on the character of the provincials seem to have been a stock element in extortion trials; cf., e.g., *Pro Scaur.* 17–21, 42–45; *Pro Font.* 16, 21–35; Cicero, of course, is careful to draw a different picture of the Sicilians in the *Verrines*.

98 Macdonald, *Cicero*, 428, reminds us of the letter Cicero had written to his brother (intended, however, for public consumption) during the year previous to this case (*Ad Quint. Fr.* 1.1), in which he instructs Quintus on the problems and responsibilities of provincial governorship. There he makes a special point of the great debt which he and the Romans in general owed to the Greeks (1.1.28), a line that "made it difficult for Cicero to undermine their credit as bluntly as he would have liked."

99 "Tribuo illis litteras, do multarum artium disciplinam, non adimo sermonis leporem, ingeniorum acumen, dicendi copiam, denique etiam, si qua sibi alia sumunt, non repugno; testimoniorum religionem et fidem numquam ista natio coluit, totiusque huiusce rei quae sit vis, quae auctoritas, quod pondus, ignorant."

100 Cf. Cicero's description of the Gallic witnesses in the *Pro Fonteio*, 27–32.

101 "Hisce utitur laudatoribus Flaccus, his innocentiae testibus, ut Graecorum cupiditati Graecorum auxilio resistamus."

102 "Sed quid ego de epistulis Falcidi aut de Androne Sextilio aut Deciani censu tam diu disputo, de salute omnium nostrum, de fortunis civitatis, de summa re publica taceo?"

103 "Nos iam ab indicibus nominamur, in nos crimina finguntur, nobis pericula comparantur."

104 "Qua re, si quis illuc me vocat, venio; populum Romanum disceptatorem non modo non recuso sed etiam deposco. Vis absit, ferrum ac lapides removeantur, operae facessant, servitia sileant; nemo erit tam iniustus qui me audierit, sit modo liber et civis, quin potius de praemiis meis quam de poena cogitandum putet."

105 "Consul ego nuper defendi C. Pisonem; qui, quia consul fortis constansque fuerat, incolumis est rei publicae conservatus. Defendi item consul L. Murenam, consulem designatum" (98).

106 "Graecis autem Lydis et Phrygibus et Mysis obsistent Massilienses, Rhodii, Lacedaemonii, Athenienses, cuncta Achaia, Thessalia, Boeotia."

107 "Prosit quod hic vobis videntibus in periculis communibus omnium nostrum sua pericula cum meis coniunxit."

108 "O nox illa"; "O Nonae illae Decembres quae me consule fuistis!"; "O nox illa"; "O mea dextera illa, mea fides, mea promissa."

109 "Ego te" (102); "flens flentem" (102); "ego te . . . ego te" (103).

110 "Ac L. Flaccum quidem, iudices, si, quod di immortales omen avertant, gravis iniuria adflixerit, numquam tamen prospexisse vestrae saluti, consuluisse vobis, liberis, coniugibus, fortunis vestris paenitebit; semper ita sentiet, talem se animum et generis dignitati et pietati suae et patriae debuisse."

111 "Huic, huic misero puero vestro ac liberorum vestrorum supplici, iudices, hoc iudicio vivendi praecepta dabitis. Cui si patrem conservatis, qualis ipse debeat esse civis praescribetis; si eripitis, ostendetis bonae rationi et constanti et gravi nullum a vobis fructum esse propositum."

112 "Nomen clarissimum et fortissimum vel generis vel vetustatis vel hominis causa rei publicae reservate."

113 *Cicero: The Speeches*, 358–359.

114 Gotoff, *Cicero's Elegant Style*, 8–9. See also his comment in "Cicero's Analysis of Prosecution Speeches," 124: "I also maintain that nothing in a speech by Cicero is wasted on egotistic self-indulgence or obviously gratuitous stroking of the audience. Neither strategy would be likely to lead to a forensic victory; and victory was what Cicero's profession was all about."

# CHAPTER IV

1 Cf. *Ad Att.* 3.3; 3.4; 3.7.2; 3.9.1; 3.19.1; *Ad Quint. Fr.* 1.3.
2 See *Ad Att.* 3, passim.
3 Cf., e.g., *Ad Att.* 3.10.2; 3.15.2, 8; 3.19.3; 3.20.1.
4 *Ad Att.* 4.1. Cf. also *Pro Sest.* 131.
5 Madvig, *Adversaria Critica* 2.211 as quoted by N. H. Watts, *Cicero: The Speeches,* 47: "Sunt hae orationes tumidae . . . sed Ciceronis sunt, de statu deiecti, pristinum dignitatis et auctoritatis fastigium neque firmis viribus neque constanti et gravi animo repetentis."
6 "De genere vitae, de natura, de moribus, de incredibili amore in bonos, de studio conservandae salutis communis atque oti."
7 Cf. McClintock, "Cicero's Narrative Technique," 122.
8 " . . . totum superioris anni rei publicae naufragium . . . in quo conligendo ac reficienda salute communi omnia reperientur P. Sesti facta, dicta, consilia versata."

9 Cf. May, "Image of the Ship of State," 259–264.
10 "Alter unguentis adfluens, calamistrata coma, despiciens conscios stuprorum ac veteres vexatores aetatulae suae, puteali et faeneratorum gregibus inflatus."
11 "Alter, o di boni, quam taeter incedebat, quam truculentus, quam terribilis aspectu!"
12 McClintock, "Cicero's Narrative Technique," 132.
13 "Unum aliquem te ex barbatis illis, exemplum imperi veteris, imaginem antiquitatis, columen rei publicae diceres intueri."
14 "Quis enim clavum tanti imperi tenere et gubernacula rei publicae tractare in maximo cursu ac fluctibus posse arbitraretur hominem emersum subito ex diuturnis tenebris lustrorum ac stuprorum, vino, ganeis, lenociniis adulteriisque confectum? cum is praeter spem in altissimo gradu alienis opibus positus esset, qui non modo tempestatem impendentem intueri temulentus, sed ne lucem quidem insolitam aspicere posset."
15 "Mihi autem hoc propositum est ostendere, omnia consilia P. Sesti mentemque totius tribunatus hanc fuisse, ut adflictae et perditae rei publicae quantum posset mederetur. Ac si in exponendis vulneribus illis de me ipso plura dicere videbor, ignoscite; nam et illam meam cladem vos et omnes boni maximum esse rei publicae vulnus iudicastis, et P. Sestius est reus non suo, sed meo nomine: qui cum omnem vim sui tribunatus in mea salute consumpserit, necesse est meam causam praeteriti temporis cum huius praesenti defensione esse coniunctam."
16 See May, "Rhetoric of Advocacy," 308–315.
17 "Sed cum viderem me non diutius quam ipsam rem publicam ex hac urbe afuturum, neque ego illa exterminata mihi remanendum putavi, et illa, simul atque revocata est, me secum pariter reportavit. Mecum leges, mecum quaestiones, mecum iura magistratuum, mecum senatus auctoritas, mecum libertas, mecum etiam frugum ubertas, mecum deorum et hominum sanctitates omnes et religiones afuerunt. Quae si semper abessent, magis vestras fortunas lugerem quam desiderarem meas; sin aliquando revocarentur, intellegebam mihi cum illis una esse redeundum."
18 Cf., e.g., *Post Red. in Sen.* 4, 16, 17–18, 25, 34, 36; *Post Red. ad Quir.* 14, 16–17; *De Dom. Sua* 17, 63, 73, 99, 137, 141, 146; *De Har. Resp.* 15, 17, 45; *De Prov. Cons.* 45; *In Vat.* 8; *In Pis.* 21, 25, 77; *Pro Balb.* 58.

19 Cf. other points in the speech for the use of this metaphor; e.g., 1, 5, 17, 24, 31, 81, 135.

20 "Statim me perculso ad meum sanguinem hauriendum, et spirante etiam re publica ad eius spolia detrahenda advolaverunt."

21 "Furiae concitatae tamquam ad funus rei publicae convolant."

22 Cf., e.g., 33, 78, 53 (in reference to the day of Clodius' bill), 65. These examples both illustrate Cicero's identification with the Republic and characterize his enemies as the pestilence which has afflicted it (him).

23 For other instances of identification with the Republic see, e.g., 33, 43, 44, 49, 50, 52, 53, 54.

24 "Etenim si mihi in aliqua nave cum meis amicis naviganti hoc, iudices, accidisset, ut multi ex multis locis praedones classibus eam navem se oppressuros minitarentur nisi me unum sibi dedidissent, si id vectores negarent ac mecum simul interire quam me tradere hostibus mallent, iecissem ipse me potius in profundum, ut ceteros conservarem, quam illos mei tam cupidos non modo ad certam mortem, sed in magnum vitae discrimen adducerem. Cum vero in hanc rei publicae navem, ereptis senatui gubernaculis fluitantem in alto tempestatibus seditionum ac discordiarum, armatae tot classes, nisi ego essem unus deditus, incursurae viderentur, cum proscriptio, caedes, direptio denuntiaretur, cum alii me suspicione periculi sui non defenderent, alii vetere odio bonorum incitarentur, alii inviderent, alii obstare sibi me arbitrarentur, alii ulcisci dolorem aliquem suum vellent, alii rem ipsam publicam atque hunc bonorum statum otiumque odissent et ob hasce causas tot tamque varias me unum deposcerent, depugnarem potius cum summo non dicam exitio, sed periculo certe vestro liberorumque vestrorum, quam id quod omnibus impendebat unus pro omnibus susciperem ac subirem?"

25 See Fantham, *Comparative Studies*, 127; cf. *De Dom. Sua* 24.

26 See *De Or.* 3.166; Quint. 8.6.44.

27 See *Oxford Classical Dictionary*, 333, s.v. *devotio*. Cf. Livy 8.9.4–10; for other literary uses of the *devotio* theme, see, e.g., Virgil *Aen.* 11.440–444; 12.229–237, 646–695; Lucan *Bel. Civ.* 6.144–262; Statius *Theb.* 10.756–782. For these references, I am indebted to an unpublished paper by Richard C. McClintock delivered at the American Philological Association meeting, December 1975, entitled "*Thebaid* 10.756ff.: The Death of Menoeccus as *Devotio*."

28 Cf. Livy 8.9 and 10.28.

29 "Quod precatus a Iove Optimo Maximo ceterisque dis immortalibus sum, Quirites, eo tempore cum me fortunasque meas pro vestra incolumitate otio concordiaque devovi, . . . sin et ea quae ante gesseram conservandae civitatis causa gessissem et illam miseram profectionem vestrae salutis gratia suscepissem, ut quod odium scelerati homines et audaces in rem publicam et in omnis bonos conceptum iam diu continerent, id in me uno potius quam in optimo quoque et universa civitate defigerent."

30 Cf. *Pro Sest.* 45–46; *De Har. Resp.* 44; *De Prov. Cons.* 23; *In Pis.* 21; *Pro Balb.* 58.

31 Cf. *Post Red. in Sen.* 32–34; *Post Red. ad Quir.* 13–16; *Pro Sest.* 36–50; *In Vat.* 6–9.

32 Cf. also *De Domo Sua* 145 for yet another use of the words *devoveo* and *devotio*.

33 "Audieram et legeram clarissimos nostrae civitatis viros se in medios hostis ad perspicuam mortem pro salute exercitus iniecisse: ego pro salute universae rei publicae dubitarem hoc meliore condicione esse quam Decii, quod illi ne auditores quidem suae gloriae, ego etiam spectator meae laudis esse potuissem?"

34 "Bis servavi rem publicam, qui consul togatus armatos vicerim, privatus con- sulibus armatis cesserim."

35 "Servavi igitur rem publicam discessu meo, iudices: caedem a vobis liberisque vestris, vastitatem, incendia, rapinas meo dolore luctuque depuli, et unus rem publicam bis servavi, semel gloria, iterum aerumna mea."

36 "Respirasse homines videbantur nondum re, sed spe rei publicae reciperan- dae."

37 "Tum princeps rogatus sententiam L. Cotta dixit . . . iure iudiciisque sub- latis, magna rerum permutatione impendente, declinasse me paulum et spe reliquae tranquillitatis praesentis fluctus tempestatemque fugisse; qua re, cum absens rem publicam non minus magnis periculis quam quodam tem- pore praesens liberassem, non restitui me solum sed etiam ornari a senatu decere."

38 *On the Crown* 110–125. Cf. Kennedy's statement, *Art of Persuasion*, 231: "What Aeschines wished to be the main issue of the trial becomes a kind of over- looked valley of detail, lost between the enormous cliffs of Demosthenes' statesmanship and Aeschines' crimes."

39 Kennedy, *Art of Rhetoric*, 196.

40 Cf. *In Cat.* 4.15, 18, 22; *Ad Att.* 1.16.6, 1.14.4.

41 Gardner, *Cicero: Pro Sestio and In Vatinium*, 301.

42 "Quid est igitur propositum his rei publicae gubernatoribus quod intueri et quo cursum suum derigere debeant? Id quod est praestantissimum maxime- que optabile omnibus sanis et bonis et beatis, cum dignitate otium."

43 Wirszubski, "Cicero's *cum dignitate otium*," 13; see also Balsdon, "*Auctoritas, dignitas, otium*," 43–50; Lacey, "Cicero, *Pro Sestio* 96–143," 67–71; Gardner, *Cicero: Pro Sestio and In Vatinium*, 302–305; Fuhrmann, "*Cum dignitate otium*," 481–500.

44 " . . . in re publica fluctus excitantur . . . ut vigilandum sit iis qui sibi guber- nacula patriae depoposcerunt, enitendumque omni scientia ac diligentia ut, conservatis iis quae ego paulo ante fundamenta ac membra esse dixi, tenere cursum possint et capere oti illum portum et dignitatis."

45 "Ipse ille maxime ludius, non solum spectator sed actor et acroama, qui omnia sororis embolia novit, qui in coetum mulierum pro psaltria adducitur, nec tuos ludos aspexit in illo ardenti tribunatu suo nec ullos alios nisi eos a quibus vix vivus effugit."

46 "At cum de dignitate mea ferebatur, nemo sibi nec valetudinis excusationem nec senectutis satis iustam putavit; nemo fuit qui se non rem publicam mec- um simul revocare in suas sedis arbitraretur."

47 "Quae tum significatio fuerit omnium, quae declaratio voluntatis ab universo populo Romano in causa hominis non popularis, equidem audiebam: existi- mare facilius possunt qui adfuerunt."

48 "Quem curia magis requisivit, quem forum luxit? Quem aeque ipsa tribunalia desideraverunt? Omnia discessu meo deserta, horrida, muta, plena luctus et maeroris fuerunt. Quis est Italiae locus in quo non fixum sit in publicis monumentis studium salutis meae, testimonium dignitatis?"

49 "Haec est una via, mihi credite, et laudis et dignitatis et honoris, a bonis viris sapientibus et bene natura constitutis laudari et diligi; nosse discriptionem civitatis a maioribus nostris sapientissime constitutam."

50 "Sed mihi omnis oratio est cum virtute non cum desidia, cum dignitate non cum voluptate, cum iis qui se patriae, qui suis civibus, qui laudi, qui gloriae, non qui somno et conviviis et delectationi natos arbitrantur. Nam si qui

voluptatibus ducuntur et se vitiorum inlecebris et cupiditatium lenociniis de-
diderunt, missos faciant honores, ne attingant rem publicam, patiantur viro-
rum fortium labore se otio suo perfrui."

51  "Qua re vos obtestor atque obsecro ut, si me salvum esse voluistis, eos con-
servetis per quos me reciperavistis."

52  Kennedy, *Art of Rhetoric*, 198. For a discussion of the problems confronting
Cicero in this defense see Geffcken, *Comedy in the Pro Caelio*, 8–10; other
helpful studies of this speech include Stroh, *Taxis und Taktik*, 241–298; Classen, "Ciceros Rede für Caelius"; Gotoff, "Cicero's Analysis of the Prosecution
Speeches"; and, of course, Austin's commentary on the *Pro Caelio*.

53  This thesis is set forth and corroborated convincingly by Geffcken, *Comedy in
the Pro Caelio*, whose penetrating analysis leaves little room for addition or
correction. Subsequent comments here are indebted to Geffcken's study and
follow its line of argument, although the tack of my analysis proves slightly
different, having specifically as its focal point the examination of Cicero's use
of ethos within this scheme.

54  For a detailed discussion of the formal charges against Caelius see Austin, *Pro
Caelio*, 152–154 and Stroh, *Taxis und Taktik*, 244–249. Cf. Gotoff, "Cicero's
Analysis of Prosecution Speeches," 124: "When we read the *Pro Caelio*, we are
aware more of a defense of Caelius' character than an argument against the
specific charges."

55  Austin, *Pro Caelio*, 45.

56  Geffcken, *Comedy in the Pro Caelio*, 43–47.

57  Cf. his treatment of Caecilius in the *Divinatio*, and of Torquatus in the *Pro
Sulla*.

58  Craig, "*Accusator* as *Amicus*," 35.

59  "Tecum, Atratine, agam lenius, quod et pudor tuus moderatur orationi meae
et meum erga te parentemque tuum beneficium tueri debeo. Illud tamen te
esse admonitum volo, primum ut qualis es talem te omnes esse existiment, ut
quantum a rerum turpitudine abes tantum te a verborum libertate seiungas;
deinde ut ea in alterum ne dicas quae, cum tibi falso responsa sint, erubescas.
Quis est enim cui via ista non pateat, quis est qui huic aetati atque isti
dignitati non possit quam velit petulanter, etiam si sine ulla suspicione, at
non sine argumento male dicere? Sed istarum partium culpa est eorum qui te
agere voluerunt; laus pudoris tui, quod ea te invitum dicere videbamus,
ingeni, quod ornate politeque dixisti."

60  Cf. Geffcken, *Comedy in the Pro Caelio*, 43–47. See Gotoff, "Cicero's Analysis
of Prosecution Speeches," for a detailed analysis.

61  "Egone quid dicam, quid velim? quae tu omnia / Tuis foedis factis facis ut
nequiquam velim."

62  Cf. Gotoff, "Cicero's Analysis of Prosecution Speeches," 126, and 128, n. 31:
"Cicero's humane persona is an attractive alternative to Herennius' censo-
riousness."

63  "Fores ecfregit, restituentur; discidit / Vestem, resarcietur."

64  "Detur aliqui ludus aetate; sit adulescentia liberior; non omnia voluptatibus
denegentur; non semper superet vera illa et derecta ratio; vincat aliquando
cupiditas voluptasque rationem, dum modo illa in hoc genere praescriptio
moderatioque teneatur. Parcat iuventus pudicitiae suae, ne spoliet alienam. . . . Postremo cum paruerit voluptatibus, dederit aliquid temporis ad
ludum aetatis atque ad inanis hasce adulescentiae cupiditates, revocet se
aliquando ad curam rei domesticae, rei forensis reique publicae, ut ea quae

ratione antea non perspexerat satietate abiecisse et experiendo contempsisse videatur." Cf. Gotoff, "Cicero's Analysis of Prosecution Speeches," 130.

65 "Verum si quis est qui etiam meretriciis amoribus interdictum iuventuti putet, est ille quidem valde severus . . . sed abhorret non modo ab huius saeculi licentia verum etiam a maiorum consuetudine atque concessis."

66 Geffcken, *Comedy in the Pro Caelio*, 46.

67 "Qui ut huic togam virilem dedit—nihil dicam hoc loco de me; tantum sit quantum vos existimatis; hoc dicam, hunc a patre continuo ad me esse deductum—nemo hunc M. Caelium in illo aetatis flore vidit nisi aut cum patre aut mecum aut in M. Crassi castissima domo cum artibus honestissimis erudiretur."

68 Cf. Stroh, *Taxis und Taktik*, 259.

69 "Neque ego umquam fuisse tale monstrum in terris ullum puto, tam ex contrariis diversisque atque inter se pugnantibus naturae studiis cupiditatibusque conflatam."

70 "Me ipsum, me inquam, quondam paene ille decepit, cum et civis mihi bonus et opimi cuiusque cupidus et firmus amicus ac fidelis videretur; cuius ego facinora oculis prius quam opinione, manibus ante quam suspicione deprendi. Cuius in magnis catervis amicorum si fuit etiam Caelius, magis est ut ipse moleste ferat errasse se, sicuti non numquam in eodem homine me quoque erroris mei paenitet, quam ut istius amicitiae crimen reformidet."

71 Cf., e.g., Naevius' portrait in the *Pro Quinctio* in terms of a *praeco* and a *scurra*.

72 For a detailed examination of these themes see Geffcken, *Comedy in the Pro Caelio*, 33–41.

73 Austin, *Pro Caelio*, 89, notes that "Cicero's audience would find another sense present in *nobilis* (cf. Donatus on Ter. *Hec.* 797, 'et meretrix et gladiator nobiles dici solent', Ter. *Heaut.* 227, 'procax, magnifica, sumptuosa, nobilis', also of a *meretrix*)."

74 "Quod quidem facerem vehementius, nisi intercederent mihi inimicitiae cum istius mulieris viro—fratrem volui dicere; semper hic erro. Nunc agam modice . . . nec enim muliebris umquam inimicitias mihi gerendas putavi, praesertim cum ea quam omnes semper amicam omnium potius quam cuiusquam inimicam putaverunt."

75 Cf. Stroh's analysis of this part of the speech, *Taxis und Taktik*, 280–288.

76 " 'Ideone ego pacem Pyrrhi diremi ut tu amorum turpissimorum cotidie foedera ferires, ideo aquam adduxi ut ea tu inceste uterere, ideo viam munivi ut eam tu alienis viris comitata celebrares?' "

77 Cf. Geffcken, *Comedy in the Pro Caelio*, 21.

78 "Ex his igitur sumam aliquem ac potissimum minimum fratrem . . . qui te amat plurimum, qui propter nescio quam, credo, timiditatem et nocturnos quosdam inanis metus tecum semper pusio cum maiore sorore cubitabat."

79 E.g., "Confer te alio" (take yourself to another). Geffcken, *Comedy in the Pro Caelio*, 21.

80 Cf. Quint. 3.8.54.

81 "Nihil iam in istam mulierem dico; sed, si esset aliqua dissimilis istius quae se omnibus pervolgaret, quae haberet palam decretum semper aliquem, cuius in hortos, domum, Baias iure suo libidines omnium commearent, quae etiam aleret adulescentis et parsimoniam patrum suis sumptibus sustineret; si vidua libere, proterva petulanter, dives effuse, libidinosa meretricio more viveret, adulterum ego putarem si quis hanc paulo liberius salutasset?"

82 *Pace* Norden, "Aus Ciceros Werksatt," and Heinze, "Ciceros Rede *Pro Caelio*,"

who interpret the repetition of these and other passages quite differently. Cf. Stroh, *Taxis und Taktik*, 269, 289–290 and Gotoff, "Cicero's Analysis of Prosecution Speeches," 122.

83　"Sed quoniam emersisse iam e vadis et scopulos praetervecta videtur esse oratio mea, perfacilis mihi reliquus cursus ostenditur."

84　For the use of the related words *familiaritas, familiaris, familiter* in the speech see Geffcken, *Comedy in the Pro Caelio*, 34–35.

85　Cf. Plut. *Cic.* 29; Caelius called Clodia *quadrantaria Clytaemnestra* (Quint. 8.6.53), likening her to the tragic queen who killed her husband and a woman who sells herself for the price of a *quadrans*.

86　"Totum crimen proferetur ex inimica, ex infami, ex crudeli, ex facinerosa, ex libidinosa domo."

87　"Ut res minime dubitanda in contentione ponatur, utrum temeraria, procax, irata mulier finxisse crimen, an gravis sapiens moderatusque vir religiose testimonium dixisse videatur."

88　That Cicero viewed this episode as a *fabula* or a *mimus* and Clodia as its author is made clear in 64 and 65. For Clodia as a *miles gloriosa* see Geffcken, *Comedy in the Pro Caelio*, 37–40.

89　"Praegestit animus iam videre, primum lautos iuvenes mulieris beatae ac nobilis familiaris, deinde fortis viros ab imperatrice in insidiis atque in praesidio balnearum conlocatos. Ex quibus requiram quem ad modum latuerint aut ubi, alveusne ille an equus Troianus fuerit qui tot invictos viros muliebre bellum gerentis tulerit ac texerit."

90　"Mimi ergo iam exitus, non fabulae; in quo cum clausula non invenitur, fugit aliquis e manibus, dein scabilla concrepant, aulaeum tollitur."

91　"Quem si nobis, si suis, si rei publicae conservatis, addictum, deditum, obstrictum vobis ac liberis vestris habebitis omniumque huius nervorum ac laborum vos potissimum, iudices, fructus uberes diuturnosque capietis."

92　See Kennedy, *Art of Rhetoric*, 204.

93　"Equidem ad reliquos labores, quos in hac causa maiores suscipio quam in ceteris, etiam hanc molestiam adsumo, quod mihi non solum pro Cn. Plancio dicendum est, cuius ego salutem non secus ac meam tueri debeo, sed etiam pro me ipso, de quo accusatores plura paene quam de re reoque dixerunt."

94　See, e.g., *Pro Sull.* 2; *Pro Sest.* 31.

95　"Quamquam mihi non sumo tantum neque adrogo, iudices, ut Cn. Plancium suis erga me meritis impunitatem consecutum putem." Cf. 4.

96　" 'Ego tibi, Laterensis, Plancium non anteposui sed, cum essetis aeque boni viri, meum beneficium ad eum potius detuli qui a me contenderat quam ad eum qui mihi non nimis submisse supplicarat . . . sed amplissimos honores ut pro dignitate tua consequare, condiscas censeo mihi paulo diligentius supplicare.' "

97　"Nostrum est autem, nostrum qui in hac tempestate populi iactemur et fluctibus ferre modice populi voluntates, adlicere alienas, retinere partas, placare turbatas; honores si magni non putemus, non servire populo; sin eos expetamus, non defetigari supplicando."

98　The defeat of a candidate boasting *nobilitas* by another not in possession of such standing appears to have been sufficient grounds for initiating a charge of *ambitus*; cf. *Pro Mur.* 15–18. This in itself is an extraordinary statement of the weight that such *dignitas* and *auctoritas* carried in Roman society, even in Cicero's time. Cf. Badian, *Roman Imperialism*, 61.

99　"Neque enim ego sic rogabam ut petere viderer, quia familiaris esset meus, quia vicinus, quia huius parente semper plurimum essem usus, sed ut quasi parenti et custodi salutis meae. Non potentia mea sed causa rogationis fuit gratiosa. Nemo mea restitutione laetatus est, nemo iniuria doluit, cui non huius in me misericordia grata fuerit. Etenim si ante reditum meum Cn. Plancio se volgo viri boni, cum hic tribunatum peteret, ultro offerebant, cui nomen meum absentis honori fuisset, ei meas praesentis preces non putas profuisse?"

100 "Atque haec sunt indicia, iudices, solida et expressa, haec signa probitatis non fucata forensi specie, sed domesticis inusta notis veritatis. . . . Omnibus igitur rebus ornatum hominem tam externis quam domesticis, non nullis rebus inferiorem quam te, genere dico et nomine, superiorem aliis, municipum vicinorum, societatum studio, meorum temporum memoria, parem virtute, integritate, modestia aedilem factum esse miraris?"

101 Recall that Cicero, writing in the *De Oratore* (2.105) about a year before the delivery of this speech, recommends denial of the charge as the chief line of defense in a trial involving *ambitus*.

102 See Watts, *Cicero: The Speeches*, 402–405, for a discussion of the jury selection and the *Lex Licinia de Sodaliciis*.

103 "Non dubito quin omnis ad te conversura se fuerit multitudo. Numquam enim fere nobilitas, integra praesertim atque innocens, a populo Romano supplex repudiata est."

104 See Craig, "*Accusator* as *Amicus*, 35–36 n. 15.

105 It is interesting to note that Cicero, the master of irrelevancy—particularly of irrelevant arguments based on character—here, in a kind of *remotio criminis*, shifts the charge to his adversaries. Arguments strictly irrelevant to the main charge are used by Cicero not only in this speech but in all those studied in this book.

106 For a different view of such professions as stepping stones to office see *Pro Mur.* 22–30.

107 "Non valuit rebus isdem quibus fortasse non nulli, at valuit adsiduitate, valuit observandis amicis, valuit liberalitate; fuit in oculis, petivit, ea est usus ratione vitae qua minima invidia novi homines plurimi sunt eosdem honores consecuti."

108 Cf. Craig, "*Accusator* as *Amicus*," 35.

109 "Qui cum mihi esses amicissimus, cum vel periculum vitae tuae mecum sociare voluisses, cum me in illo tristi et acerbo luctu atque discessu non lacrimis solum tuis sed animo, corpore, copiis prosecutus esses, cum meos liberos et uxorem me absente tuis opibus auxilioque defendisses, sic mecum semper egisti, te mihi remittere atque concedere ut omne studium meum in Cn. Planci honore consumerem, quod eius in me meritum tibi etiam ipsi gratum esse dicebas."

110 Q. Metellus Numidicus, who without recourse to arms withdrew from the city in 100 to avoid swearing allegiance to the legislation of Saturninus and Glaucia, is often mentioned by Cicero when speaking of his own case. Cf. *Post Red. in Sen.* 25, 37; *Post Red. ad Quir.* 6, 9–16; *De Dom. Sua* 87–88; *Pro Sest.* 37–38, 101; *Ad Fam.* 1.9.16. Metellus won everlasting glory for his action, which (according to Cicero) was in defense of his own conduct, not on behalf of the welfare of the Republic, making Cicero, of course, the greater hero.

111 Cf. *Post Red. in Sen.* 32–34; *Post Red. ad Quir.* 13–16; *De Dom. Sua* 96–99; *Pro Sest.* 36–50; *In Vat.* 6–9.

112 "Res vero ipsa publica, si loqui posset, ageret mecum ut, quoniam sibi servis-

sem semper, numquam mihi, fructus autem ex sese non, ut oportuisset, laetos et uberes, sed magna acerbitate permixtos tulissem, ut iam mihi servirem, consulerem meis; se non modo satis habere a me sed etiam vereri ne parum mihi pro eo quantum a me haberet reddidisset."

113 "Statim ad me lictoribus dimissis, insignibus abiectis, veste mutata profectus est."

114 "O excubias tuas, Cn. Planci, miseras, o flebilis vigilias, o noctes acerbas, o custodiam etiam mei capitis infelicem! Si quidem ego tibi vivus non prosum, qui fortasse mortuus profuissem. Memini enim, memini neque umquam obliviscar noctis illius cum tibi vigilanti, adsidenti, maerenti vana quaedam miser atque inania falsa spe inductus pollicebar."

115 "Quid enim possum aliud nisi . . . te cum mea salute complecti? Salutem tibi idem dare possunt qui mihi reddiderunt. Te tamen . . . retinebo et complectar, nec me solum deprecatorem fortunarum tuarum sed comitem sociumque profitebor; atque, ut spero, nemo erit tam crudeli animo tamque inhumano nec tam immemor non dicam meorum in bonos meritorum, sed bonorum in me, qui a me mei servatorem capitis divellat ac distrahat."

# CHAPTER V

1 Johnson, "Varieties of Narrative," 93.

2 Ibid.

3 Cicero claims several times that dictatorship offers no place for *dignitas*; cf., e.g., *De Off.* 2.2; *Brut.* 7; *Ad Fam.* 4.13.2, 6.10.2.

4 See Wooten, *Cicero's Philippics*, esp. 169–175.

5 "Vir magnus, acer, memorabilis," Livy *ex libro* 120 as reported by M. Seneca *Suasor.* 6.16–17, 21–22.

6 *Logios kai philopatris*, Plut. *Cic.* 49.

7 We have seen Cicero set up such character antitheses often in the speeches. Wooten, *Cicero's Philippics*, 58–86, refers to this method as the "disjunctive mode."

8 Kennedy, *Art of Rhetoric*, 233.

9 See Plut. *Cic.* 35.

10 Ascon. *In Milon.* 36.

11 For the debate over the spoken versus the written version of the speech see Humbert, *Les plaidoyers écrits et les plaidoiries réelles de Cicéron*, 262–263; Settle, "The Trial of Milo and the Other *Pro Milone*," 268–280; cf. Kennedy, *Art of Rhetoric*, 232–233. Despite these interesting attempts to address the question of the published versus the spoken version of the orations, the problem remains, except in obvious cases, virtually insoluble. It is tempting to speculate whether and to what degree speeches in the Ciceronian corpus had been altered by Cicero when he prepared them for publication. The evidence in most cases, however, is inconclusive. For oratory, i.e., the art of verbal persuasion, is perhaps the most fluid and, for that reason, mutable literary genre of antiquity. Each occasion demands a specific response, the "discovery of the possible means of persuasion" in reference to each rhetorical challenge. Unfortunately, without the luxury of having had tape- and video-recorders in the Roman Forum, we can never hope to comprehend a Ciceronian oration exactly as the master himself delivered it. Thus it has been my practice to accept, unless incontrovertible evidence proves otherwise, the published

speeches of Cicero as fairly reliable versions of his spoken orations, not pre-
cluding slight alterations and improvements of style and arrangement, much
in the same way those who deliver lectures and speeches are wont to make
adjustments before final publication. Quintilian's comments at 12.10.49–57,
esp., e.g., 51, are important for this discussion: "Mihi unum atque idem
videtur bene dicere ac bene scribere, neque aliud esse oratio scripta quam
monumentum actionis habitae"; and again at 54–55: "An Demosthenes male
sic egisset, ut scripsit, aut Cicero? aut eos praestantissimos oratores alia re
quam scriptis cognoscimus? Melius egerunt igitur an peius? Nam si peius, sic
potius oportuit dici, ut scripserunt; si melius, sic potius oportuit scribi, ut
dixerunt. Quid ergo? Semper sic aget orator, ut scribet? Si licebit, semper."
Stroh, *Taxis und Taktik*, 31–54, refutes Humbert's thesis and concludes his
excursus, "Zur These von Jules Humbert und dem Problem der schriftlichen
Redaktion von Ciceros Gerichtsreden," with these words: "Allein aus dem
Hauptzweck, für den sie geschrieben sich, ergibt sich, daß man sie als ein-
heitliche Werke zu betrachten hat, wobei hier 'Einheit' in dem Sinn zu verste-
hen ist, daß sie auf eine konkrete Situation und ein konkretes Publikum
bezogen sind. Die Übereinstimmung der gesprochenen mit der geschriebe-
nen Rede mag in einem gewissen Mass Fiktion sein; aber wenn wir rhetorisch
richtig interpretieren wollen, dann haben wir—so paradox es klingt—diese
Fiktion als Wirklichkeit zu nehmen."

12  McClintock, "Cicero's Narrative Technique," 145.

13  "Ubi vidit homo ad omne facinus paratissimus fortissimum virum, inimicissimum suum, certissimum consulem, idque intellexit non solum sermonibus,
sed etiam suffragiis populi Romani saepe esse declaratum, palam agere coepit
et aperte dicere occidendum Milonem."

14  Cf. Craig, "Role of Rational Argumentation," 166–167.

15  "Itaque quando illius postea sica illa quam a Catilina acceperat conquievit?
Haec intenta nobis est, huic ego vos obici pro me non sum passus, haec
insidiata Pompeio est, haec viam Appiam, monumentum sui nominis, nece
Papiri cruentavit, haec eadem longo intervallo conversa rursus est in me."

16  "Quid? Comitiis in campo quotiens potestas fuit! Cum ille in saepta inrupis-
set, gladios destringendos, lapides iaciendos curasset, dein subito voltu Mi-
lonis perterritus fugeret ad Tiberim, vos et omnes boni vota faceretis ut Miloni uti virtute sua liberet."

17  "Quae fuerit celeritas reditus eius, qui ingressus in forum ardente curia, quae
magnitudo animi, qui voltus, quae oratio."

18  "Non poteram Cn. Pompeium, praestantissima virtute virum, timidum suspi-
cari; diligentiam pro tota re publica suscepta nimiam nullam putabam."

19  "Quod si locus Miloni datus esset, probasset profecto tibi ipsi, neminem umquam hominem homini cariorem fuisse quam te sibi; nullum se umquam
periculum pro tua dignitate fugisse, cum illa ipsa taeterrima peste se saepis-
sime pro tua gloria contendisse; tribunatum suum ad salutem meam, quae
tibi carissima fuisset, consiliis tuis gubernatum; se a te postea defensum in
periculo capitis, adiutum in petitione praeturae; duos se habere semper
amicissimos sperasse, te tuo beneficio, me suo."

20  " 'Vides quam sit varia vitae commutabilisque ratio, quam vaga volubilisque
fortuna, quantae infidelitates inimicitiis, quam ad tempus aptae simulationes,
quantae in periculis fugae proximorum, quantae timiditates. Erit, erit illud
profecto tempus et inlucescet ille aliquando dies, cum tu . . . et amicissimi

benevolentiam et gravissimi hominis fidem et unius post homines natos for-
tissimi viri magnitudinem animi desideres.' "

21  Ascon. *In Milon.* 36; Quint. 3.6.93.

22  See May, "The *Ethica Digressio* and Cicero's *Pro Milone*," 240–246.

23  ". . . eum qui civem quem senatus, quem populus Romanus, quem omnes
gentes urbis ac vitae civium conservatorem iudicarant servorum armis ex-
terminavit; eum qui regna dedit, ademit, orbem terrarum quibuscum voluit
partitus est; eum qui plurimis caedibus in foro factis singulari virtute et gloria
civem domum vi et armis compulit; eum cui nihil umquam nefas fuit nec in
facinore nec in libidine; . . . eum denique cui iam nulla lex erat, nullum civile
ius, nulli possessionum termini."

24  " 'Adeste, quaeso, atque audite, cives! P. Clodium interfeci, eius furores, quos
nullis iam legibus, nullis iudiciis frenare poteramus, hoc ferro et hac dextera a
cervicibus vestris reppuli, per me ut unum ius aequitas, leges libertas, pudor
pudicitia maneret in civitate.' "

25  "Ea vis igitur ipsa quae saepe incredibilis huic urbi felicitates atque opes
attulit illam perniciem exstinxit ac sustulit, cui primum mentem iniecit ut vi
inritare ferroque lacessere fortissimum virum auderet."

26  "Regiones me hercule ipsae quae illam beluam cadere viderunt, commosse se
videntur et ius in illo suum retinuisse. Vos enim iam, Albani tumuli atque
luci, vos, inquam, imploro atque testor, vosque, Albanorum obrutae arae
. . . quas ille praeceps amentia caesis prostratisque sanctissimis lucis sub-
structionum insanis molibus oppresserat; vestrae tum religiones viguerunt,
vestra vis valuit, quam ille omni scelere polluerat."

27  "Polluerat stupro sanctissimas religiones, senatus gravissima decreta perfre-
gerat, pecunia se a iudicibus palam redemerat, vexarat in tribunatu senatum,
omnium ordinum consensu pro salute rei publicae gesta resciderat, me patria
expulerat, bona diripuerat, domum incenderat, liberos, coniugem meam vexarat, Cn. Pompeio nefarium bellum indixerat. . . . Capere eius amentiam civitas, Italia, provinciae, regna non poterant."

28  "Excitate, excitate ipsum, si potestis, a mortuis: frangetis impetum vivi cuius
vix sustinetis furias insepulti?"

29  " 'Valeant,' inquit 'valeant cives mei; sint incolumes, sint florentes, sint beati;
stet haec urbs praeclara mihique patria carissima, quoquo modo erit merita
de me; tranquilla re publica mei cives, quoniam mihi cum illis non licet, sine
me ipsi, sed propter me tamen perfruantur. Ego cedam atque abibo.' "

30  "Quod tibi, T. Anni, nullum a me amoris, nullum studi, nullum pietatis
officium defuit. Ego inimicitias potentium pro te appetivi; ego meum saepe
corpus et vitam obieci armis inimicorum tuorum; ego me plurimis pro te
supplicem abieci; bona, fortunas meas ac liberorum meorum in communio-
nem tuorum temporum contuli; hoc denique ipso die, si qua vis est parata, si
qua dimicatio capitis futura, deposco."

31  Cf. *Pro Sull.* 92; *Pro Rab. Post.* 48; *Pro Planc.* 104.

32  *Luxuriance and Economy*, 37. The context reads in this way: "It is rather a
question . . . of the *Pro Milone*'s being a lifeless, utterly unreal perfection, a
speech in which brilliance of manner and formal excellence are all the speech
has, its tone operatic, its persona a caricature of itself in its prime, its matter
beyond the persona's capacity to do anything with."

33  Cf. *Pro Reg. Deiot.* 5–7.

34  "Ita mihi pulcher hic dies visus est, ut speciem aliquam viderer videre quasi

reviviscentis rei publicae. . . . ego rogatus mutavi meum consilium. Nam statueram non me hercule inertia, sed desiderio pristinae dignitatis in perpetuum tacere. Fregit hoc meum consilium et Caesaris magnitudo animi et senatus officium; itaque pluribus verbis egi Caesari gratias, meque metuo ne etiam in ceteris rebus honesto otio privarim, quod erat unum solacium in malis. Sed tamen, quoniam effugi eius offensionem, qui fortasse arbitraretur me hanc rem publicam non putare, si perpetuo tacerem, modice hoc faciam aut etiam intra modum, ut et illius voluntati et meis studiis serviam."

35 Most modern scholarship has tended to accept the view of a staged trial for propaganda purposes. For the debate on this question see, e.g., Drumann, *Geschichte Roms*, 6:232ff.; Walser, "Der Prozess gegen Q. Ligarius," 90–96; Kumaniecki, "Der Prozess des Q. Ligarius," 434–457; McDermott, "In Ligarianam," 317–347; Kennedy, *Art of Rhetoric*, 260–264; and Craig, "The Central Argument," 193–199.

36 Craig, "The Central Argument," accepting the scenario of a staged trial for propaganda purposes, deftly outlines the rhetorical challenge facing Cicero, of dealing with the paradoxical image of Caesar as the merciful conqueror yet fair judge, that is, the conflicting demands between public relations and judicial process, and Cicero's response to those demands.

37 Cf. Quint. 5.13.5, 31.

38 "Habes igitur, Tubero, quod est accusatori maxime optandum, confitentem reum, sed tamen hoc confitentem, se in ea parte fuisse qua te, qua virum omni laude dignum, patrem tuum."

39 Harold C. Gotoff, "Towards a Practical Criticism of Cicero's *Pro Ligario*," paper delivered at the 80th Meeting of the Classical Association of the Middle West and South, Williamsburg, Virginia, 26 April 1984, copy in my files, 8.

40 Ibid., 9. Cf. Gotoff's concluding comment, 10: "What is significant about the strategy of *this* particular speech, this example of *deprecatio*, is Cicero's decision to turn it largely into a *vituperatio Tuberonum*. He may be throwing his client and himself upon the mercy of the court; what he is throwing at the Tuberos, *père et fils*, is something quite different."

41 Cf. McClintock, "Cicero's Narrative Technique," 159.

42 "Domo est egressus non modo nullum ad bellum sed ne ad minimam quidem suspicionem belli; legatus in pace profectus in provincia pacatissima ita se gessit ut ei pacem esse expediret."

43 "Nullum igitur habes, Caesar, adhuc in Q. Ligario signum alienae a te voluntatis; cuius ego causam animadverte, quaeso, quo fide defendam: prodo meam. O clementiam admirabilem atque omnium laude, praedicatione, litteris monumentisque decorandam! M. Cicero apud te defendit alium in ea voluntate non fuisse in qua se ipsum confitetur fuisse, nec tuas tacitas cogitationes extimescit nec quid tibi de alio audienti de se occurrat reformidat."

44 "Quid enim, Tubero, tuus ille districtus in acie Pharsalica gladius agebat? Cuius latus ille mucro petebat? Qui sensus erat armorum tuorum? Quae tua mens, oculi, manus, ardor animi? Quid cupiebas, quid optabas? Nimis urgeo; commoveri videtur adulescens. Ad me revertar. Isdem in armis fui."

45 Craig, "*Accusator* as *Amicus*," 36.

46 Ibid. Cf. Quint. 11.1.80.

47 "Hoc egit civis Romanus ante te nemo: externi sunt isti mores aut levium Graecorum aut immanium barbarorum."

48 "Novi enim te, novi patrem, novi domum nomenque vestrum; studia generis

ac familiae vestrae virtutis, humanitatis, doctrinae, . . . Itaque certo scio vos non petere sanguinem."

49  Cf. Neumeister, *Grundsätze der forensischen Rhetorik*, 50–51.

50  "Si, cum hoc domi faceremus, quod et fecimus et, ut spero, non frustra fecimus, tu repente inruisses et clamare coepisses, 'C. Caesar, cave credas, cave ignoscas, cave te fratrum pro fratris salute obsecrantium misereat,' nonne omnem humanitatem exuisses?" The bond between Ligarius and his fate and the sentiments of his pro-Caesarian brothers is an important theme in the speech; cf. 5, 33–36.

51  "Haec nec hominis nec ad hominem vox est. Qua qui apud te, C. Caesar, utetur, suam citius abiciet humanitatem quam extorquebit tuam."

52  Craig, "The Central Argument," 198; Craig points out that this is the central argument of the speech, and he discusses at length its role in the speech. Cf. Neumeister, *Grundsätze der forensischen Rhetorik*, 51–52.

53  "Quae est ergo apud Caesarem querela, cum eum accusetis a quo queramini prohibitos vos contra Caesarem gerere bellum? Atque in hoc quidem vel cum mendacio, si voltis, gloriemini per me licet, vos provinciam fuisse Caesari tradituros. Etiam si a Varo et a quibusdam aliis prohibiti estis, ego tamen confitebor culpam esse Ligari qui vos tantae laudis occasione privarit."

54  "Sed vide, quaeso, Caesar, constantiam ornatissimi viri L. Tuberonis, quam ego, quamvis ipse probarem, ut probo, tamen non commemorarem, nisi a te cognovissem in primis eam virtutem solere laudari. Quae fuit igitur umquam in ullo homine tanta constantia? Constantiam dico; nescio an melius patientiam possim dicere. Quotus enim istud quisque fecisset ut, a quibus partibus in dissensione civili non esset receptus, essetque etiam cum crudelitate reiectus, ad eas ipsas partis rediret? Magni cuiusdam animi atque eius viri quem de suscepta causa propositaque sententia nulla contumelia, nulla vis, nullum periculum posset depellere."

55  "Quicquid dixi, ad unam summam referri volo vel humanitatis vel clementiae vel misericordiae."

56  See above, n. 50.

57  "Quod si penitus perspicere posses concordiam Ligariorum, omnis fratres tecum iudicares fuisse. An potest quisquam dubitare quin, si Q. Ligarius in Italia esse potuisset, in eadem sententia futurus fuerit in qua fratres fuerunt? . . . Voluntate igitur omnes tecum fuerunt: tempestate abreptus est unus qui, si consilio id fecisset, esset eorum similis quos tu tamen salvos esse voluisti."

58  Craig, "Role of Rational Argumentation," 217–218.

59  Wooten, *Cicero's Philippics*, 14. I am indebted to Wooten's fine analysis of the *Philippics* for this part of my study.

60  Ibid., 171.

61  Cf. Kennedy, *Art of Rhetoric*, 272.

62  Wooten, *Cicero's Philippics*, 58–86, applies this term to the Ciceronian juxtaposition of fundamentally opposed systems. "This determines many aspects of the orator's style—sentence patterns, arguments, presentations of character, structure of speeches, and images" (58).

63  Wooten, ibid., 63–68, discusses in some detail this devolution of character and effectively compares it with Demothenes' portrait of Philip.

64  Cf. Johnson, "Varieties of Narrative," 148.

65  Wooten, *Cicero's Philippics*, 60.

66  Ibid.

67  "C. Caesar adulescens, paene potius puer, incredibili ac divina quadam mente atque virtute, cum maxime furor arderet Antoni . . . firmissimum exercitum ex invicto genere veteranorum militum."

68  "Quippe qui in hospitis tectis Brundisi fortissimos viros optimosque civis iugulari iusserit; quorum ante pedes eius morientium sanguine os uxoris respersum esse constabat."

69  Wooten, *Cicero's Philippics*, 60, discerns the pattern in Cicero's mode of characterization: praise–attack–praise–proposal.

70  "O civem natum rei publicae, memorem sui nominis imitatoremque maiorum!"

71  "Atque ille Tarquinius quem maiores nostri non tulerunt non crudelis, non impius, sed superbus est habitus et dictus: quod nos vitium in privatis saepe tulimus, id maiores nostri ne in rege quidem ferre potuerunt. L. Brutus regem superbum non tulit: D. Brutus sceleratum atque impium regnare patietur? Quid Tarquinius tale qualia innumerabilia et facit et fecit Antonius?"

72  "Nec vero M. Antonium consulem post Lupercalia debuistis putare: quo enim ille die, populo Romano inspectante, nudus, unctus, ebrius est contionatus et id egit ut conlegae diadema imponeret, eo die se non modo consulatu sed etiam libertate abdicavit."

73  "Hunc igitur ego consulem, hunc civem Romanum, hunc liberum, hunc denique hominem putem qui foedo illo et flagitioso die et quid pati C. Caesare vivo posset et quid eo mortuo consequi ipse cuperet ostendit?"

74  Wooten, *Cicero's Philippics*, 66–67.

75  See Paul Jal, "Hostis (publicus) dans la littérature latine," 59.

76  Cicero later (*Phil.* 4.15) directly compares Antony to Catiline.

77  "Primum in Caesarem ut maledicta congessit deprompta ex recordatione impudicitiae et stuprorum suorum! Quis enim hoc adulescente castior, quis modestior, quod in iuventute habemus inlustrius exemplum veteris sanctitatis? Quis autem illo qui male dicit impurior?"

78  Wooten, *Cicero's Philippics*, 64; see *De Or.* 1.8.32.

79  "Quis sic loquitur? . . . Nonne satius est mutum esse quam quod nemo intellegat dicere?" Cf. also 22: "En cur magister eius ex oratore arator factus, possideat in agro publico campi Leontini duo milia iugerum immunia, ut hominem stupidum magis etiam infatuet mercede publica!"

80  "Illud quaero, cur tam mansuetus in senatu fuerit, cum in edictis tam fuisset ferus."

81  "Hanc vero taeterrimam beluam quis ferre potest aut quo modo? Quid est in Antonio praeter libidinem, crudelitatem, petulantiam, audaciam? Ex his totus vitiis conglutinatus est. Nihil apparet in eo ingenuum, nihil moderatum, nihil pudens, nihil pudicum."

82  References to Antony and his followers as inhuman beasts are found throughout the *Philippics*; cf., e.g., 4.12; 6.7; 7.27; 12.26; 13.1, 5, 22, 49.

83  "Hodierno die primum, patres conscripti, longo intervallo in possessionem libertatis pedem ponimus: cuius quidem ego quoad potui non modo defensor sed etiam conservator fui."

84  "Quapropter, quoniam res in id discrimen adducta est utrum ille poenas rei publicae luat an nos serviamus, aliquando, per deos immortalis, patres conscripti, patrium animum virtutemque capiamus, ut aut libertatem propriam Romani generis et nominis recuperemus aut mortem servituti anteponamus!"

85 "Ne fortuna quidem fractus minuit audaciam nec ruere demens nec furere desinit."

86 "Haec eadem, quacumque exercitum duxit, fecit M. Antonius."

87 "Nullum tempus, patres conscripti, dimittam neque diurnum neque nocturnum quin de libertate populi Romani et dignitate vestra quod cogitandum sit cogitem, quod agendum atque faciendum, id non modo non recusem sed etiam appetam atque deposcam."

88 Wooten, *Cicero's Philippics*, 68.

89 "Totam rem p. sum complexus egique acerrime senatumque iam languentem et defessum ad pristinam virtutem consuetudinemque revocavi magis animi quam ingeni viribus. Hic dies meaque contentio atque actio spem primum populo R. attulit libertatis reciperandae."

90 Wooten, *Cicero's Philippics*, 162.

91 Ibid., 161.

92 "Quid autem non integrum est sapienti quod restitui potest? Cuiusvis hominis est errare; nullius nisi insipientis perseverare in errore. Posteriores enim cogitationes, ut aiunt, sapientiores solent esse. Discussa est illa caligo quam paulo ante dixi; diluxit, patet, videmus omnia, neque per nos solum, sed admonemur a nostris."

93 Wooten, *Cicero's Philippics*, 159.

94 "In hac ego legatione sim aut ad id consilium admiscear in quo ne si dissensero quidem a ceteris sciturus populus Romanus sit? Ita fiet ut, si quid remissum aut concessum sit, meo semper periculo peccet Antonius, cum ei peccandi potestas a me concessa videatur."

95 Cf. Wooten, *Cicero's Philippics*, 160.

96 "Ego numquam legatos mittendos censui; ego ante reditum legatorum ausus sum dicere, pacem ipsam si adferrent, quoniam sub nomine pacis bellum lateret, repudiandum; ego princeps ⟨sumendorum⟩ sagorum; ego semper illum appellavi hostem, cum alii adversarium; semper hoc bellum, cum alii tumultum. Nec haec in senatu solum: eadem ad populum semper egi; neque solum in ipsum sed in eius socios facinorum et ministros, et praesentis et eos qui una sunt, in totam denique M. Antoni domum sum semper invectus."

97 Here and throughout my analysis of the *Philippics* I have used as the critical text the new edition and translation by D. R. Shackleton Bailey. *Sumendorum* was added by Shackleton Bailey, who points out that "the gerundive construction with *princeps* is common in these speeches; cf. 4.1, 5 44, 7.23, 10.24, 14.20, 26. Cicero says *belli princeps* (fitting in with a string of parallel genitives) in 2.71 and *principem malefici* in *Pro Cluent.* 106, but *princeps sagorum* is surely too much" (388).

98 See Wooten, *Cicero's Philippics*, 98–100, for a fine analysis of this period.

99 "Itaque ego ille qui semper pacis auctor fui cuique pax, praesertim civilis, quamquam omnibus bonis, tamen in primis fuit optabilis—omne enim curriculum industriae nostrae in foro, in curia, in amicorum periculis propulsandis elaboratum est; hinc honores amplissimos, hinc mediocris opes, hinc dignitatem si quam habemus consecuti sumus—ego igitur pacis, ut ita dicam, alumnus qui quantuscumque sum—nihil enim mihi adrogo—sine pace civili certe non fuissem—periculose dico: quem ad modum accepturi, patres conscripti, sitis, horreo, sed pro mea perpetua cupiditatae vestrae dignitatis retinendae et augendae quaeso oroqe vos, patres conscripti, ut primo, etsi erit vel acerbum auditu vel incredibile a M. Cicerone esse dictum, accipiatis

sine offensione quod dixero, neve id prius quam quale sit explicaro repudi-etis—ego ille, dicam saepius, pacis semper laudator, semper auctor, pacem cum M. Antonio esse nolo."

100 "Non possum animo aequo videre tot tam importunos, tam sceleratos hostis; nec id fit fastidio meo, sed caritate rei publicae."

101 Cf. Wooten, *Cicero's Philippics*, 161.

102 "Vobis tamen et populo Romano vilis meus spiritus esse non debet. Is enim sum, nisi me forte fallo, qui vigiliis, curis, sententiis, periculis etiam quae plurima adii propter acerbissimum omnium in me odium impiorum perfe-cerim ut non obstarem rei publicae, ne quid adrogantius videar dicere. Quod cum ita sit, nihilne mihi de periculo meo cogitandum putatis?"

103 "Res declarat. Vicesimus annus est cum omnes scelerati me unum petunt. Itaque ipsi, ne dicam mihi, rei publicae poenas dederunt: me salvum adhuc res publica conservavit sibi. Timide hoc dicam—scio enim quidvis homini accidere posse—verum tamen: ⟨numquam imprudens oppressus sum⟩. Semel circumsessus ⟨col⟩lectis valentissimorum hominum viribus cedidi sciens ut honestissime possem exsurgere." See Shackleton Bailey, *Philippics*, 314, 388, for this emendation.

104 "Ego me vix tuto futurum puto. Novi hominis furorem, novi effrenatam violentiam. Cuius acerbitas morum immanitasque naturae ne vino quidem permixta temperari solet, hic ira dementiaque inflammatus adhibito fratre Lucio, taeterrima belua, numquam profecto a me sacrilegas manus atque impias abstinebit."

105 "Custodiatur igitur vita mea rei publicae eaque, quoad vel dignitas aut natura patietur, patriae reservetur."

106 Cf. Wooten, *Cicero's Philippics*, 161.

107 Plut. *Cic.* 49.

# CHAPTER VI

1 Gotoff, "Cicero's Analysis of Prosecution Speeches," reminds us of the im-portant fact that Cicero was a practicing advocate whose entire speech was aimed at a single goal, securing a forensic victory: "I also maintain that noth-ing in a speech by Cicero is wasted on egotistic self-indulgence or obviously gratuitous stroking of the audience. Neither strategy would be likely to lead to forensic victory; and victory was what Cicero's profession was all about" (124).

2 Cf. Gotoff, "Cicero's Analysis of Prosecution Speeches," 123: "The defense advocate will argue where and what he thinks will be most effective and will treat the opposition arguments in the manner that he thinks he can best control and manipulate. Logical and legal arguments, even when favorable, can get complicated, facts and figures, confusing; and his listeners are neither logicians nor computers. On the other hand, they can be appealed to in a variety of persuasive ways that are barely treated by the abstract reconstruc-tions of theoretical rhetoric. In his judicial speeches the only thing Cicero needs to create in his listeners is a disposition to acquit. Whether they should so vote because the charges against his client are dismissed as irrelevant, disproved as false, or despised as a cover for the character assassination of his client is a secondary matter."

# BIBLIOGRAPHY

Allen, Walter, Jr. "Cicero's Conceit." *Transactions of the American Philological Association* 85 (1954):121–144.

Austin, R. G., ed. *M. Tulli Ciceronis Pro M. Caelio Oratio.* Oxford: Oxford University Press, 1960.

Ayers, D. M. "Cato's Speech against Murena." *Classical Journal* 49 (1954):245–254.

Badian, E. *Roman Imperialism in the Late Republic.* Ithaca: Cornell University Press, 1968.

Balsdon, J. P. V. D. "*Auctoritas, Dignitas, Otium.*" *Classical Quarterly* 10 (1960):43–50.

Boulanger, André. *Cicéron: discours XI.* Paris: Société d'édition "Les Belles Lettres," 1957.

Canter, H. V. "Irony in the Orations of Cicero." *American Journal of Philology* 57 (1936):354–361.

Carpino, T. Piscitelli. "Dignitas in Cicerone: tre semantica e semiologia." *Bolletino di studi latini* 9 (1979):253–267.

Clarke, M. L. "Ciceronian Oratory." *Greece and Rome* 14 (1945):72–81.

Classen, C. Joachim. "Ciceros Rede für Caelius." In *Aufstieg und Niedergang der römischen Welt,* edited by H. Temporini, I.3:60–94. Berlin and New York: de Gruyter, 1973.

Cope, E. M. *Aristotle's Rhetoric with a Commentary.* 3 vols. Edited by J. E. Sandys. Cambridge: Cambridge University Press, 1877.

————. *An Introduction to Aristotle's Rhetoric with Analysis, Notes, and Appendices.* London and Cambridge: Macmillan, 1867; reprinted New York: G. Olms, 1970.

Craig, Christopher P. "The *Accusator* as *Amicus*: An Original Roman Tactic of Ethical Argumentation." *Transactions of the American Philological Association* 111 (1981): 31–37.

————. "Cato's Stoicism and the Understanding of Cicero's Speech for Murena." *Transactions of the American Philological Association* 116 (1986):229–239.

————. "The Central Argument of Cicero's Speech for Ligarius." *Classical Journal* 79 (1984):193–199.

————. "The Role of Rational Argumentation in Selected Judicial Speeches of Cicero." Ph.D. dissertation, University of North Carolina at Chapel Hill, 1979.

Davies, J. C. "Cicero, pro Quinctio 77." *Latomus* 28 (1969):156–157.

Dorey, T. A. "Honesty in Roman Politics." In *Cicero,* edited by T. A. Dorey, 27–45. London: Routledge & Kegan Paul, 1964.

————, ed. *Cicero.* London: Routledge & Kegan Paul, 1964.

Douglas, A. E. "A Ciceronian Contribution to Rhetorical Theory." *Eranos* 55 (1957): 18–26.

———. "The Intellectual Background of Cicero's *Rhetorica*: A Study in Method." In *Aufstieg und Niedergang der römischen Welt*, edited by H. Temporini, I.3:96–138. Berlin and New York: de Gruyter, 1973.

———. , ed. *M. Tulli Ciceronis Brutus*. Oxford: Oxford University Press, 1966.

Drumann, W. *Geschichte Roms*. Rev. by F. Groebe. 6 vols. Leipzig, 1901-1929.

Fantham, Elaine. "Ciceronian *Conciliare* and Aristotelian *Ethos*." *Phoenix* 27 (1973): 262–275.

———. *Comparative Studies in Republican Latin Imagery*. Toronto: University of Toronto Press, 1972.

Freese, J. H., ed. *Cicero: The Speeches*. Loeb Classical Library. Cambridge: Harvard University Press, 1961.

Fuhrmann, M. "*Cum dignitate otium*: Politische Programm und Staatstheorie bei Cicero." *Gymnasium* 67 (1960):481–500.

Gardner, R., ed. *Cicero: The Speeches Pro Caelio, De Provinciis Consularibus, Pro Balbo*. Loeb Classical Library. Cambridge: Harvard University Press, 1958.

———, ed. *Cicero: The Speeches Pro Sestio and In Vatinium*. Loeb Classical Library. Cambridge: Harvard University Press, 1958.

Geffcken, Katherine A. *Comedy in the Pro Caelio*. Leiden: E. J. Brill, 1973.

Gelzer, M. *The Roman Nobility*. Translated by R. Seager. New York: Barnes & Noble, 1969.

Gotoff, Harold C. "Cicero's Analysis of the Prosecution Speeches in the *Pro Caelio*: An Exercise in Practical Criticism." *Classical Philology* 81 (1986):122–132.

———. *Cicero's Elegant Style: An Analysis of the Pro Archia*. Urbana: University of Illinois Press, 1979.

Greenidge, A. H. J. *The Legal Procedure of Cicero's Time*. Oxford: Oxford University Press, 1901.

Greenwood, L. H. G., ed. *The Verrine Orations*. 2 vols. Loeb Classical Library. Cambridge: Harvard University Press, 1959.

Grimaldi, William M. A., S.J. *Aristotle's Rhetoric I: A Commentary*. New York: Fordham University Press, 1980.

———. "A Note on the πίστεις in Aristotle's Rhetoric." *American Journal of Philology* 78 (1957):188–192.

———. *Studies in the Philosophy of Aristotle's Rhetoric*. Wiesbaden: F. Steiner, 1972.

Heinze, R. "Auctoritas." *Hermes* 60 (1925):348–366.

———. "Ciceros Rede *Pro Caelio*." *Hermes* 60 (1925):193–258.

Hendrickson, G. L. "The Origin and Meaning of the Ancient Characters of Style." *American Journal of Philology* 26 (1905):249–290.

Hodge, H. G., ed. *Cicero: The Speeches*. Loeb Classical Library. Cambridge: Harvard University Press, 1959.

Humbert, Jules. *Les plaidoyers écrits et les plaidoiries réelles de Cicéron*. Paris: Presses Universitaires de France, 1925.

Imholz, A. A. "Gladiatorial Metaphors in Cicero's *Pro Sex. Roscio Amerino*." *Classical World* 65 (1972):228–230.

Jal, Paul. "Hostis (publicus) dans la littérature latine." *Revue des études anciennes* 65 (1963):53–79.

Johnson, W. R. *Luxuriance and Economy: Cicero and the Alien Style*. Berkeley: University of California Press, 1971.

———. "Varieties of Narrative in Cicero's Speeches." Ph.D. dissertation, University of California at Berkeley, 1967.

Jones, R. E. "The Accuracy of Cicero's Characterizations." *American Journal of Philology* 60 (1939):307–325.

Kennedy, George A. *The Art of Persuasion in Greece*. Princeton: Princeton University Press, 1963.

———. *The Art of Rhetoric in the Roman World*. Princeton: Princeton University Press, 1972.

———. *Classical Rhetoric and Its Christian and Secular Tradition from Ancient to Modern Times*. Chapel Hill: University of North Carolina Press, 1980.

———. "The Rhetoric of Advocacy in Greece and Rome." *American Journal of Philology* 89 (1968):419–436.

Ker, Walter C. A., ed. *Cicero: Philippics*. Loeb Classical Library. London: William Heinemann, 1926.

Kinsey, T. E. "Cicero, Hortensius and Philippus in the *Pro Quinctio*." *Latomus* 29 (1970):737–738.

———. , ed. *M. Tulli Ciceronis Pro Quinctio Oratio*. Sydney: Sydney University Press, 1971.

Kumaniecki, K. "Der Prozess des Q. Ligarius." *Hermes* 95 (1967):434–457.

Lacey, W. K. "Cicero, Pro Sestio 96–143." *Classical Quarterly* 12 (1962):67–71.

Leeman, A. D. "The Technique of Persuasion in Cicero's *Pro Murena*." In *Eloquence et rhétorique chez Cicéron*, 193–236. Fondation Hardt pour l'étude de l'antiquité classique, Entretiens 28. Geneva: Fondation Hardt, 1982.

Lord, Louis F., ed. *Cicero: The Speeches*. Loeb Classical Library. Cambridge: Harvard University Press, 1937.

Macdonald, C., ed. *Cicero: The Speeches*. Loeb Classical Library. Cambridge: Harvard University Press, 1977.

Malcovati, Henrica, ed. *Oratorum Romanorum Fragmenta Liberae Rei Publicae*. 3rd ed. Turin: In aedibus Io. Bapt. Paraviae et Sociorum, 1967.

Martin, Paul M. "Cicéron *princeps*." *Latomus* 39 (1980):850–878.

May, James M. "The *Ethica Digressio* and Cicero's *Pro Milone*: A Progression of Intensity from *Logos* to *Ethos* to *Pathos*." *Classical Journal* 74 (1979):240–246.

———. *Ethica Digressio* as a Transition from Proof to Peroration in Cicero's Judicial Speeches." Ph.D. dissertation, University of North Carolina at Chapel Hill, 1977.

———. "The Image of the Ship of State in Cicero's *Pro Sestio*." *Maia: Rivista di letterature classiche*, September–December 1980, fasc. 3:259–264.

———. "The Rhetoric of Advocacy and Patron–Client Identification: Variation on a Theme." *American Journal of Philology* 102 (1981):308–315.

McClintock, Richard C. "Cicero's Narrative Technique in the Judicial Speeches." Ph.D. dissertation, University of North Carolina at Chapel Hill, 1975.

McDermott, W. C. "In Ligarianam." *Transactions of the American Philological Association* 101 (1970):317–347.

Mitchell, Thomas N. *Cicero: The Ascending Years*. New Haven: Yale University Press, 1979.

Navarre, Octave. *Essai sur la rhétorique grecque avant Aristote*. Paris: Librairie Hachette, 1900.

Neumeister, Christoff. *Grundsätze der forensischen Rhetorik gezeigt an Gerichtsreden Ciceros*. Langue et parole, Sprach- und Literaturstrukturelle Studien 3. Munich: M. Hueber, 1964.

Nicolet, Cl. "*Consul togatus*." *Revue des études latines* 38 (1960):236–263.

Nisbet, R. G. M. "The Speeches." In *Cicero*, edited by T. A. Dorey, 47–79. London: Routledge & Kegan Paul, 1964.

*Bibliography*

Norden, E. "Aus Ciceros Werkstatt." *Sitzungsberichte der Preussischen Akademie der Wissenschaft* (1913):2–32.

*The Oxford Classical Dictionary.* 2nd ed. Edited by N. G. L. Hammond and H. H. Scullard. Oxford: Oxford University Press, 1970.

Radermacher, Ludwig. *Artium Scriptores (Reste der voraristotelischen Rhetorik).* Akademie der Wissenschaften, Wien, philosophisch-historische Klasse, Sitzungsberichte, 217, no. 3. Vienna: Rudolph M. Rohrer, 1951.

Ruebel, James S. "The Trial of Milo in 52 B.C.: A Chronological Study." *Transactions of the American Philological Association* 109 (1979):231–249.

Sattler, William M. "Conceptions of Ethos in Ancient Rhetoric." *Speech Monographs* 14 (1947):55–65.

Scullard, H. H. "The Political Career of a 'Novus Homo'." In *Cicero*, edited by T. A. Dorey, 1–25. London: Routledge & Kegan Paul, 1964.

Settle. J. N. "The Publication of Cicero's Orations." Ph.D. dissertation, University of North Carolina at Chapel Hill, 1962.

———. "The Trial of Milo and the Other *Pro Milone.*" *Transactions of the American Philological Association* 94 (1963):268–280.

Shackleton Bailey, D. R., ed. *Cicero: Philippics.* Chapel Hill: University of North Carolina Press, 1986.

Solmsen, Friedrich. "The Aristotelian Tradition in Ancient Rhetoric." *American Journal of Philology* 62 (1941):35–50, 169–190.

———. "Aristotle and Cicero on the Orator's Playing upon the Feelings." *Classical Philology* 33 (1938):390–404.

———. "Cicero's First Speeches: A Rhetorical Analysis." *Transactions of the American Philological Association* 69 (1938):542–556.

Stroh, Wilfried. *Taxis und Taktik: Die advokatische Dispositionskunst in Ciceros Gerichtsreden.* Stuttgart: B. G. Teubner, 1975.

Süss, Wilhelm. *Ethos: Studien zur älteren griechischen Rhetorik.* Leipzig and Berlin: B. G. Teubner, 1910.

Taylor, Lily Ross. *Party Politics in the Age of Caesar.* Berkeley: University of California Press, 1949.

Voit, Ludwig. *Δεινότης: Eine antiker Stilbegriff.* Leipzig: B. G. Teubner, 1934.

Walser, G. "Der Prozess gegen Q. Ligarius im Jahre 46 v. Chr." *Historia* 8 (1959):90–96.

Watts, N. H., ed. *Cicero: The Speeches.* Cambridge: Harvard University Press, 1965.

Webster, T. B. L., ed. *Pro L. Flacco Oratio.* Oxford: Oxford University Press, 1931.

Wirszubski, Ch. "Cicero's *cum dignitate otium*: A Reconsideration." *Journal of Roman Studies* 44 (1954):1–13.

Wiseman, T. P. *New Men in the Roman Senate.* Oxford: Oxford University Press, 1971.

Wooten, Cecil. *Cicero's Philippics and Their Demosthenic Model.* Chapel Hill: University of North Carolina Press, 1983.

# INDEX

Client, 10, 59, 94, 118, 141, 174 (n. 44)
Clodia, 106, 108, 110–116; as prostitute, 106, 110, 112–115; as *miles gloriosa (dux femina)*, 110, 114–115
Clodius Pulcher, P., 80, 88, 90–105 passim, 110–112, 124, 129–139 passim, 153, 158, 161, 168; madness (*furor*) of, 91, 95, 99, 130–131, 134–137, 139; as a beast, 92, 131, 134, 135, 139; as pestilence of the Republic, 95, 105, 133–134, 136; as un-Roman, 134, 139
Comitia Centuriata, 88
*Conciliare*, 4, 5. See also *Delectare*
*Concordia Ordinum*, 100
*Constitutio coniecturalis*, 66
*Constitutio definitiva*, 66, 131
*Constitutio iuridicialis*, 66, 134, 186 (n. 61)
Consular speeches: of Cicero, 48, 49–87, 98, 164, 182 (n. 5)
*Contentio dignitatis*, 60–63, 68, 117, 119, 126
Cornelius, C., 73, 74
Cotta, L. Aurelius, 8, 99
Crassus, L., 34
Crassus, M., 109
Curio, C., 42–43
*Cursus honorum*: of Cicero, 38, 48, 49

Decii Mures, 97, 98
Decius Mus, P., 97, 98
*Delectare*, 4, 5, 116. See also *Conciliare*
Demosthenes, 29, 99, 136, 156, 177 (n. 38), 178 (n. 47); *On the Crown*, 99, 136
*Deprecatio*, 142, 146, 147, 168
*Devotio*, 97, 98
*Dignitas*, 7, 13, 31, 38, 62, 63, 64, 69, 79, 103, 128, 141, 173 (n. 34), 195 (n. 98); as contributing to the effectiveness of a speaker's character, 4, 9, 11–12, 47, 50, 163, 169; of Cicero, 12, 13, 42, 45, 48, 49, 50, 51, 69, 89, 97, 98, 102, 104, 115, 117, 127, 128, 130, 133, 139, 141, 158, 164, 169, 195 (n. 98), 197 (n. 3); *cum dignitate otium* (see *Otium cum dignitate*)
Digression. See *Ethica digressio*
*Disciplina*, 108, 109, 115
Disjunctive mode, 55, 82, 139, 149, 154, 161, 166–167, 174 (n. 5), 197 (n. 7), 201 (n. 62)

*Divinatio*, 32, 38
Domitius, Cn., 37
Duties of the orator. See *Officia oratoris*
*Dux togatus*. *See* Cicero, M.: as *dux togatus*
Dyrrhachium, 124

Elatea, 136
*Eloquentia*, 14, 19, 20, 40, 46, 56, 79; of Cicero, 149, 169
Emotions. See *Affectus*
Entechnic proofs, 2, 9
*Epexelenchos* (supplementary refutation), 28
Epicurus, 93
*Epilogos*, 28, 177 (n. 46)
*Epipistōsis* (supplementary proof), 28
Equites, 100, 118
Erucius, 24, 25
*Ethica digressio*, 28–30, 37, 47, 66–68, 74–77, 83–85, 86, 99–104, 105, 134–137, 138, 139, 167; in Greek oratory, 28–29
Ethical narrative, 9, 25, 36, 46, 83, 91, 97, 99, 104, 130, 132, 139, 150, 151, 166
*Ethopoeia*, 3
Ethos (character): in Homer, 1; in Aristotle, 1–6, 9; on equal status with logos and pathos, 2, 4; of the speaker, 2, 4; of the audience, 2–3; dramatic, 3, 115; in Ciceronian oratory, 3–5, 11, 29, 46–48, 59, 60, 78–79, 90, 117, 127, 129, 141, 161–169; in Latin rhetorical treatises, 5; close affinity to pathos, 5, 11, 18, 24, 30, 73, 125, 126, 128, 167, 174 (n. 49); immutability of, 6, 16, 26, 75, 76, 78, 108, 120, 163, 172 (n. 27); Roman attitude toward, 6, 9, 10, 14, 26, 58, 59, 60, 61, 68–69, 74–75, 79, 109, 149, 163, 165–166, 168–169, 180 (n. 187), 185 (n. 42); influenced by social and political milieu of Republican Rome, 6–9, 11, 61, 163, 185 (n. 47); in Roman oratory, 6–11, 29, 31, 46, 59, 60, 78–79, 117, 127, 163, 165–166, 168; in Greek oratory, 10, 31, 166, 173 (n. 42); as chief source of proof in speech, 11, 24, 46, 59, 79, 167, 168, 176 (n. 33); juxtaposition of contrasting characters, 14,